CHANTING THE NAMES OF GOD: AN AWESOME MARVEL

.

CHANTING THE NAMES OF GOD: AN AWESOME MARVEL

Ajaaz Zainul

Copyright © 2019 by Ajaaz Zainul.

ISBN   Softcover   978-1-950580-30-9

All rights reserved. No part of this book may be reproduced or transmitted in any form or by any means, electronic or mechanical, including photocopying, recording, or by any information storage and retrieval system without express written permission from the author, except in the case of brief quotations embodied in critical reviews and certain other non-commercial uses permitted by copyright law.

Printed in the United States of America.

To order additional copies of this book, contact:
Bookwhip
1-855-339-3589
https://www.bookwhip.com

TABLE OF CONTENTS

PREFACE .... **VII**

INTRODUCTION 1

DHIKR **IN THE QUR'AN AND** ***SUNNAH*** 7
    THE MENTIONING OF *DHIKR* 8
    REMEMBRANCE OF ALLAH IN ABUNDANCE 11
    ON GLORIFYING OF ALLAH (S) IN NATURE 18
    DHIKR ON THE DAYS OF *DHUL-HIJJAH* 23
    LOUD *DHIKR* 25
    DHIKR IN AN ASSEMBLY 30

THE BENEFITS OF ***DHIKR*** 47

THE BEAUTIFUL NAMES OF ALLAH 75

FORMULAS OF ***DHIKR*** 95

DHIKR **AND THE EFFECTS OF SOUND** 119
    HEALING WITH SOUND 127
        The process of healing with sound 135
        Disease and healing from an energy perspective 140
        Effect of sound on water 144
        The healing effect of verses of the Qur'an 154
        Sound Therapy 162
    MANTRA AND *DHIKR* 165
        The potency of Mantras and Dhikr 167
        Mantra/Dhikr And Healing 170
        Mantra, Dhikr And Consciousness 187
        Mantra/Dhikr, Ego And Superconsciousness 194
        Dhikr, Sound And Genetics 197
        Examples Of Mantra And Dhikr 203

DHIKR AND MEDITATION 209
BENEFITS OF MEDITATION 215
TM AND *DHIKR* 221
THE EFFECT OF *DHIKR* ON THE FUNCTIONS OF THE BRAIN 224

ON THE EFFECT OF *DHIKR* 231
THE EFFECT OF *DHIKR* ON THE ENVIRONMENT 233
PERSONAL EXPERIENCES 260
THE SUFIS' STATE OF *FANAA'* 265

APPENDIX A 269
QUOTES ON *DHIKR* 271

APPENDIX B 285
GLOSSARY OF ARABIC TERMS 287
GLOSSARY OF TITLES 292

BIBLIOGRAPHY 295
INDEX 311

Preface

The motivation behind producing this work is interesting. It was as a result of a difference of opinion between a relative of mine and myself on whether it was allowable to perform *dhikr* (chanting the Names of Allah (God)) together in an assembly. He believed it was not okay to do so. On the other hand, I knew I had come across a strong *hadith* (the sayings of the Prophet Muhammad (S.A.W)) lauding the practice of doing *dhikr* together.

In order to convince him, however, I felt that I needed to do a thorough research of the topic. This is what started me on an amazing journey of discovery on *dhikr*. The more material I unearthed on *dhikr* the more I became amazed on the greatness of it and the incredible benefits of reciting it. I finally decided that I needed to share this with others. This book is the outcome.

In the current format of the book rather than having separate sections for verses from the Qur'an and from *hadith*, whenever a particular aspect or benefit of *dhikr* is being addressed, all the available knowledge is given. So, for instance, to illustrate the link between doing *dhikr* and experiencing feelings of peace, relevant Qur'anic verses, *hadith*, and statements by scholars are all lumped together.

It is my wish that creating this kind of format would make the book more interesting to read.

I have also included sections in the book addressing available scientific findings on the benefits of practices that may be similar to *dhikr* to some degree. I had to do it this way, unfortunately, due to a dearth of material on research done on *dhikr*. I argue that the benefits proven by research on other meditation techniques are also derived from performance of *dhikr*. For instance, since there appears to be much investigation done on

Transcendental Meditation, I assert that the proven benefits of this practice are also obtained by doing *dhikr* due to the similarities between these two techniques.

In these sections on scientific findings on the benefits of meditation and other practices I realize I have only touched the surface. As I researched articles the vastness of this subject became apparent. Inclusion of some results in this book is thus only to give the reader a glimpse into an area of study of which the potential benefits to the world is mind-boggling.

There is also a small section in the book describing personal experiences from the performance of *dhikr*. For some readers, these experiences may be particularly appealing since they may feel they can relate to them. It is possible that many can attest to experiencing similar kinds of deeply cherishable feelings. Imagine the interest that would be generated for practicing *dhikr* if thousands can speak admiringly about how this practice has affected them. Perhaps a web forum can be created just for that purpose or maybe another edition of this book can contain a chronicle of your experiences.

I would like to state here that in *dhikr* there is much we can offer the world and thus I strongly feel that to do research on *dhikr* is of utmost necessity. It is quite possible that some research have been done that I am not aware of. I would thus very much welcome any feedback or leads that you may have.

While writing this book someone had suggested that a CD be made of *dhikr* chants as a companion so as to allow readers to actually hear what *dhikr* chants sound like. Following up on that suggestion a CD titled "Dhikr – The Music of Paradise" would be available soon *Insha Allah* (God willing).

I am also in the process of setting up a website for further exploration of this topic. The name of the website is "ChantingNamesOfGod.com". If anyone would like to know when the website would be available please send an email to: ChantingTheNamesOfGod@Gmail.com. This email address can also be used for providing feedback to the author.

If you would like to be on the distribution list for notification when the CD on *dhikr* would be available please also indicate thus in your email.

I would like to acknowledge Dr. Zaman Marwat for his useful suggestion in facilitating easy navigation of sections of the book; his help in editing sections of the book; his assistance in the use of footnotes; his explanation of Arabic terms and the meaning of titles; his verification and/or obtaining of the correct references for materials used; his assistance in editing the Names of Allah (S) for correctness in pronunciation; his retrieval from the Qur'an and *hadith* of many additional Names of Allah (S) besides the traditional ninety-nine names; and last but not least his review of the final draft.

My sincere gratitude also goes out to brother Shaheed Khan who thoroughly reviewed the book in amazingly record time and to Khalid Raheem who advised me on how to proof read and willingly offered his services.

Very special thanks go out to my sister Aqeela who spent much time in the initial design of both the front and back covers and the design of title pages for chapters. Although, unfortunately, her cover design could not be used due to issues when uploading the file the design of the title pages of the current book is reflective of her work.

I also would like to acknowledge all others who have given me much moral support in the completion of writing of this book including Sister Shahbano Bilgrami whose comments were quite uplifting, Benjamin Dingel, who made me feel I possessed some ability in writing which I didn't realize I may have had before, and especially my mom, who sacrificed much for allowing us to be educated. My special gratefulness goes out to my wife who patiently allowed me to pursue this task the end of which ever seemed to be unreachable and the outcome of which seem uncertain. I must also mention the positive support of my brothers and sisters for this work.

Above all, however, my greatest gratitude is to Allah Almighty for giving me the ability and time to pursue and complete this task.

Ajaaz Zainul
Fall 2012

Introduction

It appears today that *dhikr* is something little emphasized and viewed poorly. It is looked upon as something trivial, something of no real worth, of no real value. What used to be a regular practice after *Salah* (the Muslim prayer) is not popularly practiced, at least in North America. One evidence of this attitude towards *dhikr* is the fact that hardly anyone is seen with *dhikr* beads doing *dhikr*.

This is indeed a very sad state of affair and is an indication of the spiritual disease that has beset the *ummah* (the Muslim world).

Why is it a sad state of affair?

It is because Allah (S) views *dhikr* as something that is very precious. He has said in the Qur'an that the remembrance of him is the greatest thing in life! Yes, the greatest thing in life. Now, even though the remembrance of Allah (S) can take various forms the specific form of remembrance relating to reciting His Names is of great value as is evident by the Qur'anic verse: "To Allah belong the most beautiful Names, so call Him by them."[1] Here, Allah Himself is beckoning us to call upon Him by His Names.

It is said that there are angels who constantly circumambulate Allah's throne the while doing *dhikr*.[2] It is obvious that glorification of Allah (S) is again meant here. Further, the seedlings of paradise would be *dhikr*.

The exaltedness of this glorification is seen in the following *hadith* (sayings of the Prophet Muhammad (S.A.W)) recorded by

---

[1] Qur'an, 7:180.
[2] Qur'an, 39:75.

Ibn Jarir (R) in the *Tafsir* of Ibn Kathir. He said that Al-Mukl'ariq bin Sulaym (R) said that Abdullah bin Mas'ud (R), said to them:

> If we tell you a *hadith*, we will bring you proof of it from the book of Allah. When the Muslim servant says, "Glory and Praise be to Allah, there is no God worthy of worship except Allah, Allah is Most Great and Blessed be Allah, an angel takes these words and puts them under his wing. Then he ascends with them to the heaven. He does not take them past any group of angels but they seek forgiveness for the one who said them until he brings them before Allah, may he be glorified." Then Abdullah, may Allah be pleased with him, recited, 'To Him ascend the good words and the righteous deeds exalt it.'[3]

It is also found in the *Tafsir* of Ibn Kathir in this *hadith* recorded by Imam Hamad. He said that An-Numan bin Bashir (R), said:

> The Messenger of Allah said, "those who remember Allah by saying Glory be to Allah, Allah is the Most Geat, all Praise is due to Allah, and there is no God worthy of worship except Allah, these words go around the Throne buzzing like bees, mentioning those who said them. Would one of you not like to have something with Allah mentioning him?"[4]

The great benefit of *dhikr* in the next world is evident from the following *hadith*:

---

[3] Sheikh Safiur-Rahman Al-Mubarakpuri et al., *Tafsir Ibn Kathir*, 8:129-130, quoting At-Tabari 20:444.
[4] Ibid., quoting Imam Ahmad 4:268 and Ibn Majah 2:1252.

Mu`adh ibn Jabal (R) said that the Prophet Muhammad (S.A.W) also said: "The People of Paradise will not regret except one thing alone: the hour that passed them by and in which they made no remembrance of Allah."[5]

Dhikr, indeed, then is a blessed thing to perform and, further, it has great rewards.

Today we live in a society that has tremendous lure. Unfortunately our youths are being drawn away from the *deen* (Islamic way of life) by this lure. Our youths, who aught to be the torchbearers of Islam, are indulging in illicit activities such as drugs and alcohol, and you ask yourself how can we pull them to the *deen*? How can we attract them to the beautiful way? And I say one of the most effective means is by *dhikr*.

Regarding doing *dhikr* as a group, my research has unequivocally affirmed the validity of that practice. This collective *dhikr* is not something new being introduced in Islam. Rather, it has existed since the time of the Prophet Muhammad (S.A.W) as will be seen in subsequent sections of this book.

What better way can one's time be spent in the company of others than together reciting the praises of the Being that sustains this universe and all our lives? It would be much worthier than indulging in conversations or activities of this world.

---

[5] Narrated by Bayhaqi in *Shu`ab al-iman,* 1:392 # 512-513 and by Tabarani. Haythami in *Majma` al-zawa'id,* 10:74 said that its narrators are all trustworthy (*thiqat*), while Suyuti declared it *hasan* in his *Jami` al-saghir* (#7701).

Our world today is filled with much suffering, pain, grief, hatred, violence, enmity, and lack of regard for the sacredness of human life. It is not a world we would want our children to be inheritors of.

Can this situation be changed?

I dare to state that perhaps the practice of *dhikr* can be a significant contributor to the creation of a better world, a world where the consciousness of humanity is uplifted and where the striving is for attaining the more refined and loftier goals of life.

Dhikr in the Qur'an and *Sunnah*

"HE IS ALLAH THE CREATOR, THE MAKER, THE FASHIONER; HIS ARE THE MOST EXCELLENT NAMES; WHATEVER IS IN THE HEAVENS AND THE EARTH DECLARES HIS GLORY; AND HE IS THE MIGHTY, THE WISE."
(QUR'AN, 59:24)

The mentioning of *dhikr*

Dhikr is mentioned in many places in the Holy Qur'an. It refers to many ways of the remembrance of Allah (S), dependent on the context. This remembrance includes reflecting on God and His greatness, pondering upon the wonders of nature, avoiding wrong, and studying and reciting of the Qur'an. In many cases it also refers specifically to the glorification (*tasbih*), praising (*tahmid*), and lauding (*takbir*) of Allah (S) and testification (*tahlil*) to His Oneness.

Sheikh Sayyed As Sabiq (R) mentions in the book *Fiqh-us-Sunnah*, "All words of praise and glory to Allah (S), extolling His Perfect Attributes of Power and Majesty, Beauty and Sublimeness, whether one utters them by tongue or says them silently in one's heart, are known as *zikr* (or *dhikr*) or remembrance of Allah (S)."[6]

Allah (S) speaks about His great Names in several places in the Qur'an.

In *Surah* (chapter) *At-Ta-Ha*, He says:

$$\text{اللَّهُ لَا إِلَهَ إِلَّا هُوَ لَهُ الْأَسْمَاءُ الْحُسْنَىٰ}$$

Allah - there is no god but He; *His are the very best names.*[7] (Emphasis mine).

And in *Surah Al-Hashr*, He describes Himself thus:

---

[6] Sayyed As Sabiq, *Fiqh-us-Sunnah*, iv:99.
[7] Qur'an, 20:8.

$$\text{هُوَ اللَّهُ الْخَالِقُ الْبَارِئُ الْمُصَوِّرُ لَهُ الْأَسْمَاءُ الْحُسْنَى يُسَبِّحُ لَهُ مَا فِي السَّمَاوَاتِ وَالْأَرْضِ وَهُوَ الْعَزِيزُ الْحَكِيمُ}$$

> He is Allah the Creator, the Maker, the Fashioner; *His are the most excellent names*; whatever is in the heavens and the earth declares His glory; and He is the Mighty, the Wise.[8] (Emphasis mine).

Of special interest from this verse is the fact that apart from the description of Allah (S)'s grandeur, mention is made of everything in the universe declaring His praise and glory!

In other verses of the Qur'an He beckons us to specifically call upon Him by His beautiful Names.

For example in *Surah Al-A'raf*, He declares:

$$\text{وَلِلَّهِ الْأَسْمَاءُ الْحُسْنَى فَادْعُوهُ بِهَا وَذَرُواْ الَّذِينَ يُلْحِدُونَ فِي أَسْمَآئِهِ سَيُجْزَوْنَ مَا كَانُواْ يَعْمَلُونَ}$$

> And *Allah's are the best names therefore call on Him thereby*, and leave alone those who violate the sanctity of His

---

[8] Qur'an, 59:24.

Names; they shall be recompensed for what they did.⁹ (Emphasis mine).

And in *Surah Al-Isra* He further indicates:

$$\text{قُلِ ادْعُواْ اللّهَ أَوِ ادْعُواْ الرَّحْمَنَ أَيًّا مَّا تَدْعُواْ فَلَهُ الأَسْمَاء الْحُسْنَى وَلاَ تَجْهَرْ بِصَلاَتِكَ وَلاَ تُخَافِتْ بِهَا وَابْتَغِ بَيْنَ ذَلِكَ سَبِيلاً}$$

Say: *Call upon Allah or call upon the Beneficent Allah; whichever you call upon, He has the best names; and do not utter your prayer with a very raised voice nor be silent with regard to it, and seek a way between these.*¹⁰ (Emphasis mine).

---

⁹ Qur'an, 7:180.
¹⁰ Qur'an, 17:110.

Remembrance of Allah in Abundance

Much emphasis is placed by Allah (S) in the Holy Qur'an on the abundant remembrance of Him. This remembrance of Allah (S) includes calling upon Him by His Names as is evident by the two preceding verses. The emphasis on this remembrance is indicated by the following verses:

Allah (S) says in *Surah Al-'Imraan*:

$$\text{قَالَ رَبِّ اجْعَل لِّي آيَةً قَالَ آيَتُكَ أَلاَّ تُكَلِّمَ النَّاسَ ثَلاَثَةَ أَيَّامٍ إِلاَّ رَمْزًا وَاذْكُر رَّبَّكَ كَثِيرًا وَسَبِّحْ بِالْعَشِيِّ وَالإِبْكَارِ}$$

He said: My Lord! Appoint a sign for me. Said He: Your sign is that you should not speak to men for three days except by signs; and *remember your Lord much and glorify Him in the evening and the morning*.[11] (Emphasis mine).

Also in *Surah Al-'Imraan* He states:

$$\text{الَّذِينَ يَذْكُرُونَ اللّهَ قِيَامًا وَقُعُودًا وَعَلَىَ جُنُوبِهِمْ وَيَتَفَكَّرُونَ فِي خَلْقِ السَّمَاوَاتِ وَالأَرْضِ رَبَّنَا مَا خَلَقْتَ هَذا بَاطِلاً سُبْحَانَكَ فَقِنَا عَذَابَ النَّارِ}$$

---

[11] Qur'an, 3:41.

Those who remember Allah standing and sitting and lying on their sides and reflect on the creation of the heavens and the earth: Our Lord! Thou hast not created this in vain! Glory be to Thee; save us then from the chastisement of the fire.[12] (Emphasis mine).

He further says in *Surah An-Nisa*:

فَإِذَا قَضَيْتُمُ الصَّلَاةَ فَاذْكُرُواْ اللّهَ قِيَامًا وَقُعُودًا وَعَلَىٰ جُنُوبِكُمْ فَإِذَا اطْمَأْنَنتُمْ فَأَقِيمُواْ الصَّلَاةَ إِنَّ الصَّلَاةَ كَانَتْ عَلَى الْمُؤْمِنِينَ كِتَابًا مَّوْقُوتًا

Then when you have finished the prayer, remember Allah standing and sitting and reclining; but when you are secure (from danger) keep up prayer; surely prayer is a timed ordinance for the believers.[13] (Emphasis mine).

In *Surah Al-Shu'ara`* Allah (S) mentions:

إِلَّا الَّذِينَ آمَنُوا وَعَمِلُوا الصَّالِحَاتِ وَذَكَرُوا اللَّهَ كَثِيرًا وَانتَصَرُوا مِن بَعْدِ مَا ظُلِمُوا وَسَيَعْلَمُ الَّذِينَ ظَلَمُوا أَيَّ مُنقَلَبٍ يَنقَلِبُونَ

---

[12] Qur'an, 3:191.
[13] Qur'an, 4:103.

Except those who believe and do good and remember Allah much and defend themselves after they are oppressed; and they who act unjustly shall know to what final place of turning they shall turn back.[14] (Emphasis mine).

And in *Al-Ahzab* He declares:

$$\text{لَقَدْ كَانَ لَكُمْ فِي رَسُولِ اللَّهِ أُسْوَةٌ حَسَنَةٌ لِّمَن كَانَ يَرْجُو اللَّهَ وَالْيَوْمَ الْآخِرَ وَذَكَرَ اللَّهَ كَثِيرًا}$$

Certainly you have in the Messenger of Allah an excellent exemplar for him who hopes in Allah and the latter day *and remembers Allah much.*[15] (Emphasis mine).

Also in *Al-Ahzab* He states:

$$\text{وَالذَّاكِرِينَ اللَّهَ كَثِيرًا وَالذَّاكِرَاتِ أَعَدَّ اللَّهُ لَهُم مَّغْفِرَةً وَأَجْرًا عَظِيمًا}$$

... and the men who remember Allah much and the women who remember (Allah much); for [all of] them has God readied forgiveness of sins and a mighty reward...[16] (Emphasis mine).

Likewise in *Surah Al-Ahzab*, Allah (S) says:

---

[14] Qur'an, 26:227
[15] Qur'an, 33:21.
[16] Qur'an, 33:35.

$$\text{يَا أَيُّهَا الَّذِينَ آمَنُوا اذْكُرُوا اللَّهَ ذِكْرًا}$$

> O you who believe! *remember Allah, remembering frequently.*[17] (Emphasis mine).

It is clear that these verses establish the importance of remembering Allah (S) often. Ibn Kathir (R) in his *Tafsir* has narrated the following comments by 'Abdullah bin Abbas (R) pertaining to this subject: "Allah did not enjoin any duty upon His servants without setting known limits and accepting the excuses of those who have a valid excuse apart from *dhikr*, for Allah has not set any limits for it, and no one has any excuse for not remembering Allah unless he is oppressed and forced to neglect it."[18]

He, 'Abdullah bin Abbas (R), continues, "One should make Allah's *dhikr* by night and by day, on land and on sea, when traveling and when staying home, in richness and in poverty, in sickness and in health, in secret and openly, in all situations and circumstances."

"If you do this," he concludes, "He and His angels will send blessings upon you."[19]

Imam Nawawi (R) has the following to say on the importance of *dhikr*:

---

[17] Qur'an, 33:41.
[18] *Tafsir of Ibn Kathir*, 7:707.
[19] Ibid. Also found in *Tafseeraat-e-Ahmedia* by Mullah Jeewan, 207; *Durre Mansoor* by Suyuti, 2:214; *Ihya ul Uloom* by Ghazali, 1:301.

All scholars of Islam agreed on the acceptance and permissibility of *dhikr* by heart and by tongue, for the adult men and women, and for children, for the one who has ablution, and for the one without ablution; even for the lady in her period. Moreover, it is allowed by all scholars that *dhikr* be in the form of *tasbih, tahmid, takbir* and praising and praying on the Prophet Muhammad (S.A.W).[20]

The *Sufis* mention that *dhikr* is "the polishing for the heart, the key for the Divine breeze to revive the dead spirits by directing them to the Blessings of Allah (S) the Exalted and Sublime and decorating them with His Attributes and bringing them from the state of heedlessness to the state of complete wakefulness. If we keep busy with *dhikrullah,* happiness and peace will be granted to us because *dhikr* is the key of happiness and *dhikr* is the key of joy and *dhikr* is the key of Divine Love" (ibid).

In the *hadith* of the Prophet Muhammad (S.A.W) the necessity and exaltedness of abundant remembrance of Allah (S) is clearly expressed. Some of these *hadith* are:

- During the night of Isra' and Mi`raj, the Prophet (S.A.W) was taken up to a point where he heard the screeching of the Pens (writing the divine Decree). He saw a man who had disappeared into the light of the Throne. He said: "Who is this? Is this an angel?" It was said to him, no. He said: "Is it a Prophet?" Again the answer was no. He said: "Who is it then?" The answer was: *"This is a man whose tongue was moist with Allah's remembrance in the world,* and his heart was

---

[20] An-Nawawi, *Futuhaat ar-Rabbani 'ala-al Adhkaar an-Nawawiyya* 1:106-109, quoted in "Dhikr in Islam," by Muhammad Hisham Kabbani, http://www.naqshbandi.org/naqshbandi.net/www/haqqani/Islam/Haqqiqa/Dhikr.html (accessed Oct 11th 2010).

attached to the mosques, and he never incurred the curse of his father and mother."[21] (Emphasis mine).

- A man came to the Prophet (S.A.W) and said, "O Rasulullah, the laws and conditions of Islam have become too many for me. Tell me something that I can always keep (i.e., in particular, as opposed to the many rules and conditions that must be kept in general)." The Prophet (S.A.W) said: "I am advising you in one thing: *Keep your tongue always moist with dhikrullah.*"[22] (Emphasis mine).

- Abu Hurairah (R) reported that when Allah's Messenger (S.A.W) was travelling along the path leading to Mecca he happened to pass by a mountain called Jumdan. He said: "Proceed on, it is Jumdan, *Mufarradun* (the single-hearted) have gone ahead." They (the Companions of the Holy Prophet) asked: "Allah's Messenger, who are *Mufarradun*?" He said: "They are those males and females who remember Allah much."[23]

- He, the Prophet (S.A.W) is also reported to have said, *"Practice dhikr so excessively that people may regard you as a maniac."*[24] (Emphasis mine).

- Ibn Kathir (R) in his *Tafsir* mentions that Imam Ahmad (R) recorded that 'Abdullah bin 'Amr (R) said that the Prophet

---

[21] Muhammad ʿAlawi al-Malaki, "al-Anwar al-bahiyya min isra' wa miʿraj khayr al-bariyya," http://www.scribd.com/doc/15850625/Collated-Hadith-of-Isra-and-Miraj (accessed Oct 11th 2010).
[22] As recorded in Tirmidhi, book 51, chap.4, no. 3386. Also recorded by Ahmad and Ibn Majah. Ibn Hibban declared it fair (*hasan*).
[23] Muslim, book 35, no. 6474.
[24] Narrated by Ahmad in his Musnad, Ibn Hibban in his Sahih, and al-Hakim who declared it *sahih*.

(S.A.W) said, "No people sit together without mentioning Allah but will see that as regret on the Day of Resurrection."[25]

- Anas (R) narrated that Allah's Messenger (S.A.W) said, "As for him who prays the *Fajr Salah* with the congregation and then sits down remembering Allah till the sun has risen then he prays two *rakaat*, there is for him a reward of *Hajj* and *'Umrah*." Anas (R) reported that he said, "Complete, complete, complete!"[26]

---

[25] *Tafsir of Ibn Kathir*, 7:708.
[26] Tirmidhi, book 6, chap. 59, no. 586.

On glorifying of Allah (S) in Nature

Allah (S) says in *Surah Al-Isra*:

$$تُسَبِّحُ لَهُ السَّمَاوَاتُ السَّبْعُ وَالْأَرْضُ وَمَن فِيهِنَّ وَإِن مِّن شَيْءٍ إِلَّا يُسَبِّحُ بِحَمْدِهِ وَلَٰكِن لَّا تَفْقَهُونَ تَسْبِيحَهُمْ إِنَّهُ كَانَ حَلِيمًا غَفُورًا$$

The seven heavens declare His glory and the earth (too), and those who are in them; and there is not a single thing but glorifies Him with His praise, but you do not understand their glorification; surely He is Forbearing, Forgiving.[27] (Emphasis mine).

In *Surah An-Noor* it is mentioned:

$$أَلَمْ تَرَ أَنَّ اللَّهَ يُسَبِّحُ لَهُ مَن فِي السَّمَاوَاتِ وَالْأَرْضِ وَالطَّيْرُ صَافَّاتٍ كُلٌّ قَدْ عَلِمَ صَلَاتَهُ وَتَسْبِيحَهُ وَاللَّهُ عَلِيمٌ بِمَا يَفْعَلُونَ$$

Do you not see that Allah is He Whom do glorify all those who are in the heavens and the earth, and the (very) birds with expanded wings? He knows the prayer of each one and its

---

[27] Qur'an, 17:44.

glorification, and Allah is Cognizant of what they do.²⁸ (Emphasis mine).

Sayyid Qutb (R) comments on this verse as follows:

> Man does not live alone in this universe. All around him, to his right and to his left, above him and underneath him, and in the expanse beyond, whether reached by his imagination or not, there are beings God has created with different natures, forms and shapes. All of them share in their belief in God, turn to Him and extol His praises. He "has full knowledge of all that they do."
>
> The Qur'an directs man to look around him: All is of God's making and all living things everywhere in the heavens and earth are His creatures, glorifying Him and singing His praises. The Qur'an also directs our full attention to something we see every day without stirring any feeling in us because of its familiarity: It is the scene of birds lifting up their legs and spreading out their wings as they fly. They also glorify God. "Each of them knows how to pray to Him and to glorify Him." Only man neglects to glorify his Lord when he is the one who should be most aware of the importance of believing in God and glorifying Him.
>
> In this scene, the whole universe appears full of humility as it turns to its Creator, singing His praises, addressing its prayers to Him. This it does by nature. Its obedience to God is represented in its laws, which operate by God's will. When man refines his senses, he sees this scene as reality, as though he hears the rhythm of God's

---

[28] Qur'an, 24:41.

glorification echoed throughout the universe. He shares with all creatures their prayers and appeals to God. Such was Muhammad, God's messenger, (may peace be upon him). When he walked, he heard the gravel under his feet singing God's praises. Such was David: When he chanted his Psalms, the mountains and the birds chanted with him.[29]

In the book *al-Wujuh al-musfira `an ittisa` al-maghfira* (The Faces Made Radiant By the Vastness of Mercy) it is stated:

> One of Allah's slaves sought to perform the purification using stones after releasing himself. He took one stone and Allah removed the veil from his hearing so that he was now able to hear the stone's praise. Out of shame he left it and took another one but he heard that one praising Allah (S) also. And every time he took another stone he heard it glorifying Allah (S). Seeing this, at last he turned to Allah so that He would veil from him their praise to enable him to purify himself. Allah then veiled him from hearing them. He proceeded to purify himself despite his knowledge that the stones were making *tasbih* because the one who reported about their *tasbih* is the same Law-giver who ordered to use them for purification. Therefore in the concealment of *tasbih* there is a far-reaching wisdom.[30]

Allah (S) says in *Surah Al-Anbiya*:

---

[29] Syed Qutb, *Fi Zhilal Al-Qur'an,* vol. XII, (http://www.kalamullah.com/Books/Fi%20Dhilal/Volume_12_(Surahs_21-25).pdf (accessed Oct 11th 2010).

[30] *al-Wujuh al-musfira `an ittisa` al-maghfira* quoted at http://www.sunnah.org/ibadaat/dhikr.htm (accessed Jan 15th 2010).

$$\text{فَفَهَّمْنَاهَا سُلَيْمَانَ وَكُلًّا آتَيْنَا حُكْمًا وَعِلْمًا وَسَخَّرْنَا مَعَ دَاوُودَ الْجِبَالَ يُسَبِّحْنَ وَالطَّيْرَ وَكُنَّا فَاعِلِينَ}$$

So We made Sulaiman to understand it; and to each one We gave wisdom and knowledge; and We made the mountains, and the birds to celebrate Our praise with Dawud; and We were the doers.[31]

In *Surah As-Saba* it is mentioned:

$$\text{وَلَقَدْ آتَيْنَا دَاوُودَ مِنَّا فَضْلًا يَا جِبَالُ أَوِّبِي مَعَهُ وَالطَّيْرَ وَأَلَنَّا لَهُ الْحَدِيدَ}$$

And certainly We gave to Dawud excellence from Us: O mountains! sing praises with him, and the birds; and We made the iron pliant to him.[32]

Regarding the glorification of Allah (S) by the mountains the author of *al-Wujuh al-musfira* made the following commentary: "It is more likely that they literally glorify, except that this phenomenon is hidden from the people and is not perceived except through the rupture of natural laws. The Companions

---

[31] Qur'an, 21:79.
[32] Qur'an, 34:10.

heard the glorification of food and other objects placed before the Prophet."³³

Specific to the last sentence in the above, it is said that a bowl of food was once brought to the Prophet Muhammad (S.A.W) who mentioned that the food was doing *dhikr*. When it was taken to another person, he also heard the food praising Allah (S). Similarly, a third person also heard the food performing *dhikr*. At that, someone requested that everyone present should hear the food performing *dhikr*. The Prophet Muhammad (S.A.W) replied, however, that if someone failed to hear it, others would think that he is a sinner.³⁴

---

³³ *al-Wujuh al-musfira `an ittisa` al-maghfira* quoted in "Dhikr is the Greatest Obligation and a Perpetual Divine Order,"
http://www.sunnah.org/ibadaat/dhikr.htm (accessed Jan 17th 2010).
³⁴ Muhammad Zakariya, *Faza'il-e-A'maal*, "Virtues of Zikr," 211-212. Bukhari, vol. 4, book 56, no. 779 also records that the companions of the Prophet (S.A.W) heard the meal glorifying Allah (S) when it was being eaten by him.

Dhikr on the days of *Dhul-Hijjah*

Allah (S) says in *Surah Al-Hajj* verse 28, "...and mention the name of Allah on the appointed Days..."

The appointed days has been explained by some scholars to mean the ten days of *Dhul-Hijjah* (the twelfth month of the Islamic calendar in which the Muslim pilgrimage takes place). Scholars thus consider it desirable to increase *dhikr* in these days because of the *hadith* related by Ibn Umar (R) which says, "...so increase in these days the *Tahlil* and *Takbir* and *Tahmid*."[35]

Ishaq (R) narrated from the scholars of the Tabi'in that in the ten days of *Dhul-Hijjah* they used to say:

> *Allahu-Akbar, Allahu-Akbar; Laailaaha illallaah; Wa Allahu-Akbar, Allahu-Akbar; Wa lillaahil-hamd.*
>
> *Allah is Greatest, Allah is Greatest, There is no god but Allah. Allah is Greatest, Allah is Greatest, and to Allah is all praise.*

He stated that it is a beloved act to raise the voice when saying the *takbir* (proclaiming the greatness of Allah) in the markets, the houses, the streets, the masjids and other places, because of the saying of Allah (S) in *Surah Al-Hajj*, "...that you may magnify Allah (S) for His Guidance to you..."[36]

Bukhari (R) records that Umar (R) would be in his tent in Mina and make *takbir* until the people in the mosque heard him and would follow him making *takbir*. Indeed the people in the

---

[35] Ahmad.
[36] Qur'an, 22:37.

markets of Mina also followed them until the whole of Mina would shake with *takbir*.[37]

He also mentions about Ibn Umar (R) and Abu Hurairah (R) that "the two of them used to go out to the market place during the ten days (of *Dhul-Hijjah*) saying 'Allahu Akbar,' causing the people to say it also."[38]

Doing *takbir*, a form of *dhikr*, on the day of *'Eid* is regarded as one of the greatest *sunnahs*. The Holy Prophet Muhammad (S.A.W) is reported to have said that one should beautify the day of *'Eid* by doing *takbir*. It is also reported that he himself used to come out of his home on the day of *'Eid*, reciting the *takbir* and glorifying Allah (S) in a loud voice.

Al-Daraqutni (R) and others reported that when Ibn Umar (R) came out on `Eid Al-Fitr and `Eid Al-Adha, he would strive hard in making *takbir* until he reached the prayer-place, then he would continue making *takbir* until the Imam came.

---

[37] Bukhari, vol. 2, book 15, chap. 12.
[38] Bukhari, vol. 2, book 15, chap. 11.

Loud *dhikr*

Ibn 'Abbas (R) reported, "I used to recognize the completion of the prayer of the Prophet (S.A.W) by hearing *takbir*."[39]

Abu Ma'bad (R), the freed slave of Ibn 'Abbas (R) reported that Ibn 'Abbas (R) told him, "in the lifetime of the Prophet Muhammad (S.A.W), it was the custom to celebrate Allah's praises aloud after the compulsory congregational prayers." Ibn 'Abbas (R) further said, "When I heard the *dhikr*, I would learn that the congregational prayer had ended."[40]

Khallad ibn Saib (R) reported from his father that Allah's Messenger (S.A.W) said, "Jibrail (Angel Gabriel) came to me and instructed me to command my Companions that they should raise their voices on reciting the *talbiyah*." (The narrator was not sure which word the Prophet (S.A.W) used: *ihlal* or *talbiyah*)."[41]

As mentioned before, Ishaq (R) stated that during the ten days of *Dhul-Hijjah* it is a beloved act to raise the voice when saying the *takbir* in the markets, the houses, the streets, the masjids and other places.

It is also appropriate here to again mention the following two *hadith* recorded by Bukhari (R):

"During Umar's stay at Mina, he would say *takbeeraat* in his tent [so loud] that the people in the mosque would hear it and then they would start doing it. Also the people in the market place

---

[39] Bukhari, vol. 1, book 12, no. 803.
[40] Bukhari, vol. 1, book 12, no. 802.
[41] Abu Dawud, book 10, no. 1810; Tirmidhi, book 9, chap. 15, no. 830. Also recorded by Ahmad, Nasa'i and Ibn Majah.

would do the same and all of Mina would resound with the *takbeeraat.*"[42]

About Ibn Umar (R) and Abu Hurairah (R) it is mentioned that they "used to go out to the market saying *takbir* during the first ten days of *Dhul-Hijjah* and the people would say *takbir* after their *takbirs.*"[43]

I will also quote here a Qur'anic verse and a *Hadith Qudsi* (the words of Allah as inspired to the Prophet Muhammad (S.A.W)) in support of loud performance of *dhikr*.

Allah (S) says in the Holy Qur'an: "So when you have accomplished your *Manasik* remember Allâh as you remember your forefathers or with a far more remembrance..."[44]

Commentators of the Holy Qur'an say that in the era of ignorance it was the practice of the unbelievers that when they completed their *Hajj* they would stand in front of the *Ka'bah* and praise their forefathers. In this *Ayah* (verse) Allah (S) says that they should mention Him instead of mentioning their forefathers. Therefore, it is clear that this glorification of Allah (S) has to be loud so that people will be able to listen to it.

The *Hadith Qudsi* is as follows:

> If he (My servant) remembers Me in himself, I, too, remember him in Myself; and if he remembers Me in a group of people, I remember him in a group that is better

---

[42] Bukhari, vol. 2, book 15, chap. 12.
[43] Bukhari, vol. 2, book 15, chap. 11.
[44] Qur'an, 2:200.

than they.[45]

Scholars like Imam Jalalluddin Suyuti (R), Sulaimaan Jumal (R), Khazin (R), and Ibn Kathir (R) argue that this *Hadith Qudsi* endorses the recitation of both loud and soft *dhikr*. In their argument they indicate that Allah (S) did not mention that *dhikr* should only be recited at a certain level of loudness or softness.

In his book *Natijatul-Fikr*, Imam Suyuti (R) states, on the authority of Imam Nawawi (R):

> Just as the traditions of loud and silent *Tilawah* may be combined according to varying circumstances, so too is the case of loud and silent *dhikr*. In case of fear of *riya* (show) or disturbance to *musallis* or sleeping persons, silent *dhikr* will be preferable; but where such situations to do not exist, loud *dhikr* will be more estimable and meritorious as loud *dhikr* arouses others as much as it enlivens the heart of the *Zakir* (the person performing the *dhikr*), focuses his thoughts, drives away sleepiness and reinvigorates him.[46]

Maulana Muhammad Zakariya (R) has this to say on the effect of loud *dhikr*:

> I have observed many times that when some of my religious elders do *dhikr* aloud, the flavor of the sweetness enjoyed by them is so transmitted to the

---

[45] Bukhari, vol. 9, book 93, no. 502; Muslim, book 35, no. 6471; Tirmidhi, book 51, chap. 132B, no. 3614. Also recorded by Ibn Majah.
[46] As-Suyuti, *Natijatul-Fikr* quoted in "Majalis-Zikr," http://www.direct.za.org/Pdfs/Loud_Zikr.pdf (accessed Jan 18th 2010).

> listeners that their mouths also feel the sweetness and they share the ecstasy likewise.[47]

Qari Tayyib narrated that outside the *Khanqah* of Maulana Rashid Ahmad Gangohi (R), a renowned Sheikh from India, there was a large pond. On the opposite side of this pond was a little house where Maulana Yahya (R) (father of Moulana Zakariya) used to live with a few associates. In the latter part of the night, loud *dhikr* used to start-up in the *Khanqah* as well as the *masjid* of Maulana Yahya (R). The entire environs and surroundings of the pond area used to reverberate with the sound of loud *dhikr*. Such was the effect of this *dhikr* that the washer men around the lake also used to join in and it became their lifelong practice to make loud *dhikr* while occupied in their work of washing clothes.[48]

A similar version has been written by Maulana Zakariya (R).

He states:

> Even the most unlettered persons among the disciples of Maulana Gangohi (R) adhered strictly to the *Sunnah*. They were so steadfast on the practice of *Tahajjud* that such firmness I did not encounter even among great men. Even the fifty to sixty washer men around the pond of the *Khanqah* would engage in loud *dhikr* in the latter part of the night instead of making other noises or sounds (ibid).

---

[47] *Faza'il-e-A'maal*, "Virtues of Zikr," 31.
[48] Abd al-Hafiz Makki, "An analysis of the evidence supporting the permissibility of Majalis (gatherings) of zikr in the Masjid" transl. Zubair Bhayat, http://www.yanabi.com/forum/Topic8166-41.aspx (accessed Oct 11th 2010).

Numerous persons relate that, during the time of Maulana Ilyas (R), it was also the standing practice at the Bangla-Wali Masjid in Nizamuddin, New Delhi (the Tabligh Jamaat Headquarters), for the people to awaken in the latter part of the night to offer their *Tahajjud Salah* and then engage in loud *dhikr* in the masjid and the courtyard, right until the time of *Fajr Salah*.

An eyewitness records that, in 1959 and 1960, he personally witnessed many people doing loud *dhikr* before *Fajr Salah* inside and outside the *masjid*. He mentions that, "the entire *masjid* area would reverberate with the sound of their loud *dhikr*" (ibid).

Loud *dhikr* is most noticeable at the most holy of places, in the environs of the Ka'bah. Robert Gass remarks, "In all the world of chant, there is nothing like the collective sound of the sea of chanting that fills the marble-paved courtyard of the great mosque. Abd al-Hayy Moore described *Hajj* to me as "The slow roar of an ocean of human longing, the word of God intoned from ten thousand lips," and in the center of all this sound sits the Ka'aba "in a shaft of silence from the height of heaven.""[49]

Imam Suyuti (R) states that the Sufis have indicated that loud *dhikr* has a very powerful effect in eliminating vile thoughts and evil whisperings from the mind and heart.

---

[49] Robert Gass, *Chanting: Discovering Spirit in Sound*, 92.

Dhikr in an assembly

Because of the importance of this subject and misunderstanding surrounding it, I have also included in this section two relevant Qur'anic verses that were recorded in the first section. These verses are as follows:

In *Surah Al-Anbiya* Allah (S) states:

$$\text{فَفَهَّمْنَاهَا سُلَيْمَانَ وَكُلًّا آتَيْنَا حُكْمًا وَعِلْمًا وَسَخَّرْنَا مَعَ دَاوُودَ الْجِبَالَ يُسَبِّحْنَ وَالطَّيْرَ وَكُنَّا فَاعِلِينَ}$$

> So We made Sulaiman to understand it; and to each one We gave wisdom and knowledge; and We made the mountains, and the birds to celebrate Our praise with Dawud; and We were the doers.[50]

He further declares in *Surah As-Saba*:

$$\text{وَلَقَدْ آتَيْنَا دَاوُودَ مِنَّا فَضْلًا يَا جِبَالُ أَوِّبِي مَعَهُ وَالطَّيْرَ وَأَلَنَّا لَهُ الْحَدِيدَ}$$

> And certainly We gave to Dawud excellence from Us: O mountains! sing praises with him, and the birds; and We

---

[50] Qur'an, 21:79.

made the iron pliant to him.[51]

Ibn Kathir (R), in his commentary on this verse in his *Tafsir*, states, "…And He (Allah) blessed him (Dawud) with a mighty voice such that when he glorified Allah, the firm, solid, high mountains joined him in glorifying Allah, and the free-roaming birds, that go out in the morning and come back in the evening, stopped for him…"[52]

He indicates that the object of glorification in this verse is Allah (S) – this being the view of Ibn 'Abbas (R), Mujahid (R) and others. The root of the word *Ta'wib*, according to Ibn Kathir (R), means to repeat or respond. Thus the mountains and birds were commanded to repeat after Dawud.

What is clear from these verses is that (1) the Prophet David (A) glorified Allah (S) by reciting his praises. (2) The hills and birds repeated Allah (S)'s praise with him. (3) This act of glorification of Allah (S) by David (A) and the hills and birds was something highly commendable to Allah (S).

Now if inanimate objects like the hills celebrated Allah (S)'s praises with David (A) then this clearly indicates that it is not merely okay but also laudable for human beings to celebrate Allah (S)'s praises together. If this is not true we reach the preposterous conclusion that the hills and birds have a greater privilege than man even though man is the noblest of Allah (S)'s creation!

In a *Hadith Qudsi* Abu Hurairah (R) said that the Prophet (S.A.W) said:

---

[51] Qur'an, 34:10.
[52] *Tafsir of Ibn Kathir*, 8:69.

Allah (S) has some angels who look for those who celebrate the Praises of Allah on the roads and paths. And when they find some people celebrating the Praises of Allah, they call each other, saying, "Come to the object of your pursuit." Then the angels encircle them with their wings up to the sky of the world.

(After those people finished celebrating the Praises of Allah, and the angels go back), their Lord asks them (those angels) – though He knows better than them – "What do My slaves say?" The angels reply, "They say: *Subhan Allah, Allahu Akbar*, and *Alham-du-lillah*." Allah then says, "Did they see Me?" The angels reply, "No! By Allah, they didn't see You."

Allah (S) says, "How it would have been if they saw Me?" The angels reply, "If they saw You, they would worship You more devoutly and celebrate Your Glory more deeply, and declare Your freedom from any resemblance to anything more often." Allah (S) says (to the angels), "What do they ask Me for?" The angels reply, "They ask You for Paradise." Allah (S) says (to the angels), "Did they see it?" The angels say, "No! By Allah, O Lord! They did not see it." Allah (S) says, "How it would have been if they saw it?" The angels say, "If they saw it, they would have greater covetousness for it and would seek it with greater zeal and would have greater desire for it."

Allah (S) says, "From what do they seek refuge?" The angels reply, "They seek refuge from the (Hell) Fire." Allah (S) says, "Did they see it?" The angels say, "No! By Allah, O Lord! They did not see it." Allah (S) says, "How it would have been if they saw it?" The angels say, "If they saw it they would flee from it with extreme fleeing and would have extreme fear from it."

Then Allah (S) says, "I make you witnesses that I have forgiven them."

One of the angels would say, "There was so-and-so amongst them, and he was not one of them, but he had just come for some need." Allah (S) would say, "These are those people whose companions will not be reduced to misery."[53]

Muslim (R) has also recorded an almost identical *hadith* to the above. He states, on the authority of Abu Hurairah (R) that the Prophet Muhammad (S.A.W) said:

Allah (S) has mobile (squads) of angels, who have no other work (to attend to but) to follow the assemblies of *dhikr* (of Allah) and when they find such assemblies in which there is *dhikr* they sit in them and some of them surround the others with their wings till the space between them and the sky of the world is fully covered, and when they disperse (after the assembly of *dhikr* is adjourned) they go upward to the heaven.

Allah, the Exalted and Glorious, (then) asks them although He is best informed about them: "Where have you come from?" They say: "We come from Your servants upon the earth who had been glorifying You (reciting *Subḥan Allah*), uttering Your Greatness (saying *Allah o-Akbar*) and uttering Your Oneness (*La ilaha illallah*)

---

[53] Bukhari, vol. 8, book 75, no. 417.

and praising You (uttering Al-ḥamdu Lillah) and begging of You."

He would say: "What do they beg of Me?" They would say: "They beg of You the Paradise of Yours." He would say: "Have they seen My Paradise?" They said: "No, our Lord." He would say: "(What it would be then) if they were to see My Paradise?"

They would then say: "They seek Your protection." He would say: "Against what do they seek protection of Mine?" They would say: "Our Lord, from the Hell-Fire." Allah would say: "Have they seen My Fire?" They would say: "No." He would say: "What it would be if they were to see My Fire?" They would say: "They beg of Your forgiveness." He would say: "I grant pardon to them, and confer upon them what they ask for and grant them protection against which they seek protection."

They (the angels) would again say: "Our Lord, there is one amongst them such and such simple servant who happened to pass by (that assembly) and sat there along with them (who had been participating in that assembly)." He (Allah) would say: "I also grant him pardon, for they are a people the seat-fellows of whom are in no way unfortunate."[54]

The late Imam Ahmad Mashhur al-Haddad (R) said in his book *Miftah al-janna*:

---

[54] Muslim, book 35, no. 6505. An essentially similar *hadith* is also recorded by Tirmidhi. See Tirmidhi, chap.132A, no. 3611. It is also recorded by Ahmad.

This *hadith* indicates what merit lies in gathering for *dhikr*, and in everyone present doing it aloud and in unison, because of the phrases: "They are invoking You" in the plural, and "They are the people who sit," meaning those who assemble for remembrance and do it in unison, something which can only be done aloud, since someone whose *dhikr* is silent has no need to seek out a session in someone else's company.

This is further indicated by the *Hadith Qudsi* that runs:

"Allah says: I am to my servant as he expects of Me, I am with him when he remembers Me. If he remembers Me in his heart, I remember him to Myself, and if he remembers Me in an assembly, I mention him in an assembly better than his…"

Thus, silent *dhikr* is differentiated from *dhikr* said out loud by His saying: "remembers Me within himself," meaning: "silently," and "in an assembly," meaning "aloud."

Dhikr in a gathering can only be done aloud and in unison. The above *hadith* thus constitutes proof that *dhikr* done out loud in a gathering is an exalted kind of *dhikr* which is mentioned at the Highest Assembly *(al-mala' al-a`la)* by our Majestic Lord and the angels who are near to Him, "who extol Him night and day, and never tire."

The affinity is clearly evident between those who do *dhikr* in the transcendent world, who have been created with an inherently obedient and remembering nature, namely the angels, and those who do *dhikr* in the dense world, whose natures contain lassitude and distraction; namely, human beings. The reward of the latter for their *dhikr* is that they be elevated to a rank similar to that of the Highest Assembly, which is sufficient honor and favor for anyone.[55]

The *Hadith Qudsi* quoted by Imam Ahmad Mashhur al-Haddad (R) in the previous passage actually forms part of a longer *hadith*.

The entire *hadith* is quoted below:

> Narrated Abu Hurairah: The Prophet (S.A.W) said, "Allah says: 'I am just as My slave thinks I am, (i.e. I am able to do for him what he thinks I can do for him) and I am with him if He remembers Me. If he remembers Me in himself, I too, remember him in Myself; and if he remembers Me in a group of people, I remember him in a group that is better than they; and if he comes one span nearer to Me, I go one cubit nearer to him; and if he comes one cubit nearer to Me, I go a distance of two outstretched arms nearer to him; and if he comes to Me walking, I go to him running.'"[56]

This *hadith* implies mentioning of Allah (S) whether alone or in a group is a means of drawing closer to Him.

Anas bin Maalik (R) narrates that the Prophet (S.A.W) said, "no group of people gathers to make *dhikr* of Allah (S) with sincerity except that a caller from the skies announces after the *dhikr*:

---

[55] Ahmad Mashhur al-Haddad, *Miftah al-janna*, 107-108.
[56] Bukhari, vol. 9, book 93, no. 502; Muslim, book 35, no. 6471; Tirmidhi, book 51, chap. 132B, no. 3614. Also recorded by Ibn Majah.

'Leave in the condition that you have been forgiven of your sins and your evils being converted to virtue.'"[57]

Agharr Abi Muslim (R) reported: "I bear witness to the fact that both Abu Hurairah and Abu Sa'id Khudri were present when Allah's Messenger (may peace be upon him) said: 'The people do not sit (to remember Allah (S)) but they are surrounded by angels and covered by Mercy, and there descends upon them tranquility as they remember Allah (S), and Allah (S) mentions them to those who are near Him.'"[58]

Abu Hurairah (R) narrates that the Prophet (S.A.W) said, "When you pass the gardens of paradise, pluck the fruits." Rasulullah was asked, "What are the gardens of paradise O Rasulullah." He said, "The *Masaajid*." He was asked about plucking its fruits. He said, "*SubhaanAllah, Alhamdulillah, Laa Ilaaha illa Allaahu* and *Allaahu Akbar*."[59]

Mu`awiya (R) narrates:

> ...The Prophet (S.A.W) went out to a circle of his Companions and asked: "What made you sit here?" They said: "We are sitting here in order to remember/mention Allah and to glorify Him because He guided us to the path of Islam and he conferred favors upon us." Thereupon he adjured them by Allah and asked if that was the only purpose of their sitting there. They said: "By Allah, we are sitting here for this purpose only." At this the Prophet said: "I am not asking you to take an oath

---

[57] Ahmad, Tabarani, and Hakim. Hakim has ruled it *sahih* according to the criteria of Muslim and/or Bukhari.
[58] Muslim, book 35, no. 6520; Tirmidhi, book 51, chap. 7, no. 3389. Also recorded by Ahmad, Ibn Majah, Nasa'i and Bayhaqi.
[59] Tirmidhi, book 51, chap. 87, no. 3520.

because of any misapprehension against you, but only because Gabriel came to me and informed me that Allah, the Exalted and Glorious, was telling the angels that He is proud of you!"[60]

It is mentioned in one *hadith* that a group of *Sahabah*, including Salman Farsi (R) was engaged in *dhikr* of Allah (S), when the Prophet (S.A.W) came to them. They became all silent. In reply to his enquiry as to what they were doing, they submitted that they were practicing *dhikr* of Allah. The Prophet (S.A.W) said, "I saw that the mercy of Allah was descending upon you, and so I desired that I should join your company *Alḥamdulillah* (All Praise is for Allah)." He then continued, "Almighty Allah has raised such people in my *Ummah* that He ordered me to sit in their company."[61]

Shahr ibn Hawshab (R) relates that one day Abu al-Darda' (R) entered the Masjid of Bayt al-Maqdis (Jerusalem) and saw people gathered around their admonisher (*mudhakkir*) who was reminding them, and they were raising their voices, weeping, and making invocations.

Abu al-Darda' (R) said, "My father's life and my mother's be sacrificed for those who moan over their state before the Day of Moaning!"

Then he said:

> O Ibn Hawshab, let us hurry and sit with those people. I heard the Prophet (S.A.W) say: "If you see the groves of

---

[60] Muslim, book 35, no. 6521; Tirmidhi, book 51, chap. 7, no. 3390. Also recorded by Ahmad and Nasa'i.
[61] Al-Hakim, 1:210 with a strong chain of *sahih* narrators.

Paradise, graze in them," and we said: "O Messenger of Allah, what are the groves of Paradise?" He said: "The circles of remembrance, by the One in Whose hand is my soul, no people gather for the remembrance of Allah Almighty except the angels surround them closely, and mercy covers them, and Allah mentions them in His presence, and when they desire to get up and leave, a herald calls them saying: Rise forgiven, your evil deeds have been changed into good deeds!"

Then Abu al-Darda' (R) made towards them and sat with them eagerly.[62]

Anas ibn Maalik (R) reported that Allah's Messenger (S.A.W) said, "When you pass by the gardens of paradise graze (there)." They (the sahabah) asked, "And what are the gardens of paradise?" He said, "Circles of Dhikr." (This means, 'groups (of) people who mention and remember Allah')."[63]

Anas (R) narrated, "The Prophet (S.A.W) offered four *Rakat* of *Zuhr* prayer at Medina and two *Rakat* of the Asr prayer in *Dhul Hulaifa* and I heard them (the companions of the Prophet) reciting *Talbiya* together loudly to the extent of shouting."[64]

Anas bin Malik (R) narrated, "Allah's Prophet offered 4 *Rakat* of *Zuhr* prayer at Medina and we were in his company and two

---

[62] Ibn al-Jawzi, "Mention of those of the elite who used to attend the gatherings of story-tellers" in *al-Qussas wa al-mudhakkirin* (The Story-tellers and the Admonishers), 31. Mentioned in an article "Gatherings of Dhikr" at http://qa.sunnipath.com/issue_view.asp?HD=1&ID=784#gath (accessed Oct 11th 2010).

[63] Tirmidhi, book 51, chap. 87, no. 3521. Tirmidhi declared it as *hasan*. Also recorded by Ahmad.

[64] Bukhari, vol. 2, book 26, no. 620.

Rakat of *Asr* prayer in *Dhul Hulaifa* and then passed the night there until it was dawn; then he rode and when he reached *Al-Baida* he praised and glorified Allah and said *Takbir*. Then he and people along with him recited *Talbiya* and..."[65]

In a narration recorded earlier Bukhari records that (Umar) (R) would proclaim several *takbir*s from his dome in Mina, on hearing which the people in the mosque would also proclaim *takbir* and then all those in the markets would proclaim *takbir* until the whole of Mina would resound with the *takbir*.[66]

In his Hashiya, Ibn `Abidin (R) said about group *dhikr*:

> Imam al-Ghazali (R) compared doing *dhikr* alone and the *dhikr* of a group to the *adhaan* (the call to prayer) of someone alone and the *adhaan* of a group. He said, "As the voices of a group of *mu'adhdhins* (those who give the call to prayer) reach farther than the voice of a single *mu'adhdhin*, so the *dhikr* of a group on one's heart has more effect in lifting dense veils than the *dhikr* of a single person."[67]

Just to clarify, Ghazali (R) is not stating that there is collective *adhaans*. He is probably alluding to when the *adhaan* is given at the same time from various minarets of mosques located close to each other. When this happens, the voices of the *mu'adhdhins* evoke a greater feeling of awe in the heart of the listener. This would most likely happen at the time of *Maghrib Salah* when the prayer commences as soon as sun sets. *Adhaans* from the various

---

[65] Bukhari, vol. 2, book 26, no. 623.
[66] Bukhari, vol. 2, book 15, chap. 12.
[67] Quoted at http://tassavvuf1973.spaces.live.com/blog/cns!3279448D06B9F42A!855.entry and elsewhere.

minarets would occur just about the same time so they would be more or less synchronized.

This is indeed true in many Muslim countries today.

A recent experience testifies to the effect of hearing multiple *adhaans* at the same time. A woman BBC reporter was taken to the top of a building in Jeddah, Saudi Arabia to experience the Muslim call to prayer at the time of *Maghrib Salah*. As soon as she reached the top of the stairs leading to the roof of the building she was subjected to the sound of the *adhaan* simultaneously coming from 36 minarets. The effect of this (and also what she beheld) was so awe-inspiring it brought tears to her eyes. She states, "it's such an incredible sight and sound that I find myself completely overcome."[68]

On the same topic Ibn Taymiyya (R), when asked whether it was acceptable for people to gather in a *masjid* to perform *dhikr* and read Qur'an and to call upon Allah only with the desire to get close to Him, said, "Praise to Allah, it is good and recommended according to Shari`a (*mustahabb*) to come together for reading Qur'an, making *dhikr*, and making *du'a* (supplication)."[69]

Doing *dhikr* in a group is a source of strength. At times one may not have the motivation to do *dhikr*. However, within the group there may be someone who is energized. This energy is transmitted and puts one in the mood.

---

[68] "BBC British Journalist in Saudi Arabia." YouTube video, http://www.youtube.com/watch?v=F_OtXNclB9I (accessed April 4th 2011).
69 Ibn Taymiyya, *Majmu`at fatawa*, King Khalid ibn `Abd al-`Aziz edition. Quoted in "The celebration of Mawlid as understood by the scholars of the "Salafi" movement and those of the four schools of Ahl Al_Sunna," http://www.caribbeanmuslims.com/articles/180/5/Permissibility-of-Mawlid-An-Nabi/Page5.html (accessed April 20th 2011).

This may also be one of the reasons why *Salah* in congregation is so much emphasized for the Prophet (S.A.W) had said that performing prayer in congregation generates 25 to 27 times more reward than praying alone.

Some light on the effect of group *dhikr* may be gleaned by the following statement made by Dr. William Tiller, a material scientist and professor emeritus of Stanford University: "the energetic power of a coherent group is the square of the number of people involved." In other words, the energy generated by a group of people with the same intentions and actions is equal to the square of the energy of each person involved. Thus, when the energy fields of like-minded persons merge (in other words, the fields are coherent) there is tremendous power.[70]

Tiller's statement is based on the physics of electromagnetic waves. The intensity or energy of a wave is directly proportional to the square of its amplitude. Thus, if a wave has an amplitude, A, the energy I of the wave will be given by:

$$I = c A^2 \text{ where c is a constant}$$

If there are two waves that are coherent, the total energy will be:

$$I = c (2A)^2 \text{ or}$$
$$I = c\, 4 A^2$$

And for 4 coherent waves the total energy generated would be:

$$I = c\, 4^2 A^2 \text{ or}$$
$$I = c\, 16 A^2$$

[70.] Walter Weston, *How Prayer Heals: A scientific Approach*, 163.

Thus, if there are n coherent waves, the total energy is proportional to n^2.

Now let us examine how this is applicable to the performance of *dhikr*. When a Name of Allah is chanted, sound waves are generated. An instrument set up to measure the electrical voltage produced by one person performing the chanting may record one volt. Now if two persons are reciting the same Name together at the same time they are producing two coherent waves. The instrument would record four volts. If the number of persons were now four the number of volts outputted would be sixteen!

Application of Dr. Tiller's finding would mean that in the performance of *Salah* in congregation and in doing *dhikr* in a group, if the intention of everyone is the same and there is complete and intense focus on glorifying Allah (S), then the cumulative energy generated would be substantial and the feelings experienced palpable. A group of 100 doing *dhikr* together with deep devotion and sincerity would theoretically generate 10,000 volts of energy!

According to Moulana Zakariya (R) there is a *hadith* indicating that *Salah* and *dhikr* gatherings are the best forms of protection of territory from invasion.

He further states that the accumulation of hearts in the gatherings of *dhikr* has a special effect in drawing the help and mercy of Allah (S) just as *Salah* with *Jama'ah* (congregation) and the gathering of *Hajees* (pilgrims) in *Arafah* does.

Another scholar indicates that the gatherings of *dhikr* increases the keenness for *dhikr*, the *Anwaar* (effulgence) of hearts are reflected upon each other and enthusiasm, punctuality and determination grows; while lethargy is removed and other benefits are achieved.

Being aware of how the world was steeped in materialism and pursuit of carnal desires, it became Moulana Zakariya's (R) heart-felt desire and intense concern during the latter years of his life to establish the gatherings of *dhikr* (*Khanqas*) everywhere around the world.[71]

In a letter to Maulana Abul Hasan Ali Nadwi (R), he writes, "It is my firm conviction that the remedy for all evils is the *dhikr* of Allah (S). For this very aim I am wandering from country to country, because the *Khanqahs* have become extinct all over the world" (ibid).

It is said that these types of letters were written in large numbers to many persons in different countries of the world. Whenever a reply came that a gathering of *dhikr* was established in a certain place, Moulana Zakariya (R) would be immensely happy and would write a letter to the people there letting them know how overjoyed he was. He would also make *du'as* for them. It is believed that there are several hundred such letters (ibid).

Quite recently, I, like thousands of others, were witnesses to an awesome spectacle. On Sunday, January 30th 2011, tens of thousands of Egyptians assembled at Tahrir Square, Cairo in a mass ongoing protest against the regime of Hosni Mubarak. Suddenly two military planes, which looked like F16s, appeared and flew over the heads of the protestors. They circled and came

---

[71] Abd al-Hafiz Makki, "An analysis of the evidence supporting the permissibility of Majalis (gatherings) of zikr in the Masjid" transl. Zubair Bhayat, http://www.yanabi.com/forum/Topic8166-4-1.aspx (accessed Oct 11th 2010).

roaring back but this time lower. The sound of their engines was deafening. The seeming intent was to intimidate the protestors and force them to leave out of fear.

However, when the planes roared over their heads these protestors, in spite of the deafening sounds of the engines, remained rooted in their spots and shouted in unison "Go Away".

The planes circled again and then came roaring back but this time even lower. The deafening roar of their engines was so loud as to cause the body to involuntarily shake. Still no one moved. Again in unison they shouted their chant. The sound of their collective voices appeared to be so powerful that it seemed to drown the sounds of the planes.

When the planes came roaring past them again at even lower altitude no one budged. They remained resolutely in their spots again shouting in unison at the top of their voices.

The planes roared past them a total of six times every time flying closer to their heads. The noise of the engines would have shaken the protestors to the core especially for the last round. Not one of the protestors, however, flinched. They stood their ground resolutely, determined and unperturbed and collectively chanted at the top of their voices when the planes roared overhead.

The planes, after perhaps realizing that the protestors were not intimidated in the least, eventually flew away.

The collective chanting of the protestors seemed to give them a feeling of supreme fearlessness and strength.

This spectacle would go down in the annals of history as one of the most profoundly moving displays of righteous defiance!

The question that comes to mind is that if the collective chanting of the mere words "Go Away" could have such an effect, what if the crowd instead had chanted some specific Names or phrases invoking the power of Allah such as *Allahu Akbar* or *Ya Qawi*?

In that regard an amazing statement has been made regarding the collective chanting of a mantra called the Gayatri. Hindus consider mantras as being the Names of God (more on mantras is given in another section of this book). The Gayatri mantra is considered as one of the most potent of mantras. It is stated by Dr. Pranav Pandya, director of the Brahmavarchas Research Institute in Hardwar, India that *"if millions of people recite the Gayatri mantra at the same time, it can act as an invisible sound wave protection for those people, even in a nuclear holocaust."*[72] (Emphasis mine).

This is quite a remarkable statement. If this is indeed true can the same effect occur if specific *dhikr* formulas are recited together by millions?

---

[72] Quoted in article "Hardwar Institute Tracks Power of Gayatri Yagna" by Archana Dongre. Hinduism Today, Sept 1992.
http://www.hinduismtoday.com/modules/smartsection/item.php?itemid=960 (accessed Jan 25th 2011). This statement by Dr. Pandya appears to be a repeat of a similar statement made by the Hungarian author Arthur Koestler who lived in India in the late 1950s.

The Benefits of *Dhikr*

"CHANTING OF THE LORD'S NAME DOES NOT GO IN VAIN. IT MUST BEAR ITS BENIGN RESULT. IT IS LIKE THE PHILOSOPHER'S STONE CONVERTING ALL BASER METAL INTO GOLD. IT IS LIKE THE MAGIC WAND OF THE MAGICIAN PERFORMING UNBELIEVABLE AND UNTHOUGHT OF MIRACLES; IT TRANSFORMS MAN'S LIFE FOR EVER."
(SWAMI DAYATMANANDA)

The Benefits of *Dhikr*
There are innumerable benefits for performing *dhikr*. Maulana Muhammad Zakariya (R) in fact mentions that Ibn Qayyim al-Jawziyya (R) states more than one hundred virtues for reciting *dhikr*.[73] Below is just a sampling of the many virtues obtained from doing this practice. The list is thus not exhaustive. It does not include, for instance, many other probable physiological, psychological, and sociological benefits. These likely benefits will be discussed in subsequent sections of this document.

1. *Dhikr* keeps away Satan and weakens his strength.

    The Prophet (S.A.W) is reported to have said:

    > ...And, I command you that you remember Allah. The similitude for that is like a man whose enemies pursue him in haste while he comes to a strong fort and protects himself from them. So is the man whom nothing protects from the devil but *dhikr* (remembrance) of Allah...[74]

    According to the Prophet (S.A.W), *Shaitaan* attaches himself to a person's heart. When *dhikr* is recited he moves away. When this is not performed the devil whispers evil thoughts to that person. This is the reason, according to Moulana Zakariya, that the Sufis advise to practice *dhikr* excessively to rid the heart of evil thoughts and to make it strong enough to resist the temptations of the devil.

2. Allah remembers His servant who remembers Him.

    Allah (S) says in *Surah Al-Baqarah*:

---

[73] *Faza'il-e-A'maal*, "Virtues of *Dhikr*," 71.
[74] Tirmidhi, book 47, chap. 3, no. 2872. Also recorded by Ahmad.

$$\text{فَاذْكُرُونِي أَذْكُرْكُمْ وَاشْكُرُواْ لِي وَلاَ تَكْفُرُونِ}$$

> Therefore remember Me, I will remember you, and be thankful to Me, and do not be ungrateful to Me.[75]

In this *Ayah*, Allah (S) indicates He remembers the servant who remembers Him. What an honor to be remembered by the Almighty Creator of all things!

In a *Hadith Qudsi*, He also says:

> And if he (my servant) remembers Me in his heart, I also remember him to Myself, and if he remembers Me in an assembly I remember him in assembly, better than his…[76]

3. It is the cause of earning Allah's pleasure.

4. *Dhikr* of Allah causes one to be mentioned in the Court of Allah.

The rational for (3) and (4) is found in the *Hadith Qudsi* mentioned in (2).

5. It relieves the mind of anxieties, difficulties, and worries.

This is evident from several Qur'anic verses. As an example Allah (S) says in *Surah Ar-R'ad*:

---

[75] Qur'an, 2:152.
[76] Bukhari, vol. 9, book 93, no. 502; Muslim, book 35, no. 6471; Tirmidhi, book 51, chap. 132B, no. 3614. Also recorded by Ibn Majah.

$$\text{الَّذِينَ آمَنُواْ وَتَطْمَئِنُّ قُلُوبُهُم بِذِكْرِ اللّهِ أَلاَ بِذِكْرِ اللّهِ تَطْمَئِنُّ الْقُلُوبُ}$$

Those who believe and whose hearts are set at rest by the remembrance of Allah; now surely by Allah's remembrance are the hearts set at rest.[77]

'Abdul Qadir Jilani indicates that anxiety is caused by the weight of material things such as food, sleep, and idle talk and attachments such as desires, wealth, and family ties that pull the heart downwards. The way to free the heart is by the repetition of Allah's Names. According to him: "With this remembrance and recitation of Allah's Names the heart wakes up from the sleep of heedlessness, is cleansed, and is shined. Then forms and shapes from the hidden unseen realm are reflected in that heart."[78]

Zulfiqar Ahmad states: "Know that *dhikr* will bring *noor*, and *noor* will bring peace.[79]

Moulana Zakariya states that with *dhikr* a person is relieved from "troubles, worries, and fears, and is blessed with peace of mind. His mistakes and sins are forgiven and the devils that are after him are dispersed away."[80]

---

[77] Qur'an, 13:28.
[78] 'Abdul Qadir Jilani, *The Secret of Secrets*, 3rd ed., 41-42.
[79] Zulfiqar Ahmad, "Attaining fina-e-qalbi: Annihilation of the Heart," http://www.islah-e-batin.org/basics.php
[80] *Faza'il-e-A'maal*, "Virtues of *Dhikr*," 76.

He further says that *dhikr* "is a solution to all difficulties, and remedy for all handicaps. It lightens every burden, and relieves every affliction" (ibid., 79).

6. It cleanses the heart of its rust.

Ibn Qayyim al-Jawziyya (R) said in his book *Al-Waabil as-Saib*:

> It is no doubt that the heart oxidizes, as copper and silver oxidize. Its polishing is the *dhikr*, which will make it like a white mirror. The oxidation of the heart is due to heedlessness and sin. Its polishing is through two: repentance and *dhikr*. If someone's heart is oxidized, the reflections of images will be upside-down; he will see falsehood as truth and truth in the image of falsehood (*batil*). Because when there is too much oxidization on the heart, the heart will be darkened, and in the darkness the images of the Truth and Reality never appear. The best way to polish it is through *dhikrullah*.[81]

7. It brings about happiness and success.

Allah (S) says in Chapter *Al-Anfal*:

يَا أَيُّهَا الَّذِينَ آمَنُواْ إِذَا لَقِيتُمْ فِئَةً فَاثْبُتُواْ وَاذْكُرُواْ اللّهَ كَثِيرًا لَّعَلَّكُمْ تُفْلَحُونَ

---

[81] Ibn Qayyim al-Jawziyya, *Al-Waabil as-Saib*, 52 quoted at http://www.naqshbandi.org/naqshbandi.net/www/haqqani/Islam/Haqqiqa/Dhikr.html (accessed Oct 12th 2010).

O you who believe! when you meet a party, then be firm, and remember Allah much, that you may be successful.[82]

Imam Ghazali (R) said in the fortieth book of his *Ihya `al 'Uloom* entitled "The Remembrance of Death and The Afterlife":

It is man's soul and spirit that constitute his real nature... Upon death his state changes in two ways. Firstly he is now deprived of his eyes, ears and tongue, his hand, his feet and all his parts, just as he is deprived of family, children, relatives, and all the people he used to know, and of his horses and other riding-beasts, his servant-boys, his houses and property, and all that he used to own. There is no distinction to be drawn between his being taken from these things and these things being taken from him, for it is the separation itself that causes pain....

If there was anything in the world in which he had found consolation and peace, then he will greatly lament for it after he dies, and feel the greatest sorrow over losing it. His heart will turn to thoughts of everything he owned, of his power and estates, even to a shirt he used to wear, for instance, and in which he took pleasure.

However, had he taken pleasure only in the remembrance of Allah, and consoled himself with Him alone, then his will be great bliss and perfect happiness. For the barriers that lay between him and his Beloved will now be removed, and he will be free of the obstacles and cares of the world, all of which had distracted him

---

[82] Qur'an, 8:45.

from the remembrance of Allah. This is one of the aspects of the difference between the states of life and death.[83]

On the same topic Imam Habib al-Haddad (R) said in *Key to the Garden*:

> Time and days are a man's capital, while his inclinations, desires, and various ambitions are the highway robbers. The way in which one profits on this journey lies in succeeding in coming to Allah and in attaining everlasting happiness, while one loses by being veiled from Allah, and being consigned to the painful torment of the Fire.
>
> For this reason the intelligent believer transforms all his breaths into acts of obedience, and interrupts them only with the *dhikr* of Allah.[84]

8. **The reward of *dhikr* is greater than the reward of *jihad*.**

Abu al-Darda' (R) narrates:

> The Prophet once asked his companions: "Shall I tell you about the best of all deeds, the best act of piety in the eyes of your Lord, which will elevate your status in the Hereafter, and carries more virtue than the spending of gold and silver in the service of Allah or taking part in *jihad* and slaying or being slain in the path of Allah? It is the *dhikr* of Allah."[85]

---

[83] Ghazali, *The Remembrance of Death and The Afterlife*, 124.
[84] Habib al-Haddad, *Key to the Garden*, 104.
[85] Malik's *Al-Muwatta*, chap. 126, no. 485; Tirmidhi, book 51, chap. 6, no. 3388. Also recorded by Ahmad, Ibn Majah and Hakim. Al-Bayhaqi, Hakim and others declared it as *sahih*.

9. The person who does *dhikr* has the highest rank.

Allah mentions in *Surah Al-'Ankabut*:

اتْلُ مَا أُوحِيَ إِلَيْكَ مِنَ الْكِتَابِ وَأَقِمِ الصَّلَاةَ إِنَّ الصَّلَاةَ تَنْهَى عَنِ الْفَحْشَاءِ وَالْمُنكَرِ وَلَذِكْرُ اللَّهِ أَكْبَرُ وَاللَّهُ يَعْلَمُ مَا تَصْنَعُونَ

> Recite that which has been revealed to you of the Book and keep up prayer; surely prayer keeps (one) away from indecency and evil, and certainly the remembrance of Allah is the greatest, and Allah knows what you do.[86]

Abu Sa`id (R) narrates: The Prophet was asked, "Which of the servants of Allah is best in rank before Allah on the Day of resurrection?" He said: "The ones who remember him much..."[87]

10. *Dhikr* is charity.

Abu Dharr (R) reported that the Messenger of Allah (S.A.W) said:

> In the morning charity is due from every bone in the body of every one of you. Every utterance of Allah's glorification (i.e., *Subhan-Allah*) is an act of charity. Every utterance of praise of Him (i.e., *Al-ḥamdu lillah*) is an act

---

[86] Qur'an, 29:45.
[87] Tirmidhi, book 51, chap.5, no. 3387. Also recorded by Ahmad and Bayhaqi.

of charity. Every utterance of profession of His Oneness (i.e., *La ilaha illallah*) is an act of charity and every utterance of profession of His Greatness (i.e., *Allahu Akbar*) is an act of charity; enjoining good is an act of charity, forbidding what is disreputable is an act of charity...[88]

11. *Dhikr* generates multiplicative rewards equivalent to that of good deeds.

    Mus'ab b. Sa'd reported that his father told him that he had been in the company of Allah's Messenger (S.A.W) and narrated the following:

    > The Prophet (S.A.W) asked: "Is one amongst you powerless to get one thousand virtues every day?" Amongst those who had been sitting there, one asked: "How one amongst us can get one thousand virtues every day?" He said: "Recite: 'Hallowed be Allah' one hundred times for (by reciting them) one thousand virtues are recorded (to your credit) and one thousand vices are blotted out." [89]

12. The reward of *Hajj* and *'Umrah* is obtained for performing *dhikr* in the morning.

    Anas bin Malik (R) said, "The Messenger of Allah said: 'Whoever prays the morning prayer in congregation then sits remembering Allah until the sun rises, then prays two units of prayer has the reward like that of Hajj and 'Umrah.'" He

---

[88] Muslim, book 4, no. 1557.
[89] Muslim, book 35, no. 6517.

said, "Allah's Messenger (S.A.W.), said: 'Complete, complete, complete (i.e. reward)'"[90]

13. Doing *dhikr* compared to being alive versus being dead.

   Narrated Abu Musa (R):

   > The Prophet said, "The example of the one who celebrates the Praises of his Lord (Allah) in comparison to the one who does not celebrate the Praises of his Lord, is that of a living creature compared to a dead one."[91]

14. It gives life to the heart.

   Ibn Taimiyyah (R) says that *dhikr* is as necessary for the heart as water is for the fish.

   Sheikh Zulfiqar Ahmad states, "through the abundant *dhikr* of Allah *subḥana wa ta'ala* our dead hearts will Insha'Allah be transformed into living ones. This light of *nisbah* (spiritual connection) is such a blessing that it gives life to an already dead heart that is devoid of all remembrance of Allah.[92]

15. The *dhaakir* (the person engaged in *dhikr*) receives blessings from Allah and His angels.

   'Abdullah bin Abbas (R) states, "if you do this (i.e., engage in constant *dhikr*), He (Allah) and His angels will send blessings

---

[90] Tirmidhi, book 6, chap. 59, no. 586.
[91] Bukhari, vol. 8, book 75, no. 416.
[92] Zulfiqar Ahmad, "Attaining fina-e-qalbi: Annihilation of the Heart," http://www.tasawwuf.org/basics/finae_qalbi.htm (accessed May 4th 2011).

upon you."[93]

Moulana Zakariya mentions, "Nothing is more effective than *dhikr* in attracting Allaha's blessings and in warding off His chastisement."[94]

16. Houses in which *dhikr* is recited radiate light.

Abu Hurairah (R) narrates, "Indeed, those in the heavens see the houses of Allah's rememberers shining as stars shine in the sky for those on earth."[95]

Moulana Zakariya (R) elaborates on this. He states that not only do the inhabitants of heaven see this light. There are also people in this world who have been blessed with spiritual insight by Allah (S) who can see the brightness emanating from houses where *dhikr* is performed."[96]

To further illustrate this he mentions the ability of a Sheikh, Abdul Aziz Dabbaagh, who was able to distinguish between the verses of the Qur'an, *Hadith Qudsi*, and *Hadith Nabawi*. This Sheikh remarked that the words from a person's mouth carry a unique glow. While the words of the Qur'an produce a particular radiance those of the Prophet emit a different kind of radiance. The words of others do not display these types of radiances.

---

[93] *Tafsir of Ibn Kathir*, 7:707. Also found in *Tafseeraat-e-Ahmedia* by Mullah Jeewan, 207; *Durre Mansoor* by Imam Suyuti Ash Shafi'I, 2:214; *Ihya ul Uloom* by Imam Ghazali, 1:301.
[94] *Faza'il-e-A'maal*, "Virtues of *Dhikr*," 78.
[95] As-Suyuti, *Durre Mansoor*, 1:367.
[96] *Faza'il-e-A'maal*, "Virtues of *Dhikr*," 52.

One can deduce from this that the recitation of *dhikr* formulas produce a particular kind of radiance. It is likely that this is the radiance that the dwellers of heaven and those with spiritual insight on earth see emanating from the houses where *dhikr* is performed.

17. The person performing the *dhikr* radiates a certain sweetness and awe that in turn induces the same sweetness and awe in the onlooker (ibid).

    Maulana Muhammad Zakariya mentions:

    > I have observed many times that when some of my religious elders do *dhikr* aloud, the flavor of the sweetness enjoyed by them is so transmitted to the listeners that their mouths also feel the sweetness and they share the ecstasy likewise (ibid., 31).

18. It induces love for Allah.

    It is said that profuse recitation of *dhikr* leads to the love for Allah. This love enables one to achieve the ultimate goal of salvation in the next world (ibid., 71).

19. *Dhikr* enables the practitioner to ultimately reach the stage of *Ihsaan* where a person worships Allah as if he is actually seeing Him (ibid., 71).

20. It opens the door of *ma'rifat* [realization] of Allah.

    The Sufis claim that when *dhikr* is abundantly recited the reciter can attain to a state where "one forgets oneself and all there is, save God..." according to Al-Ghazali in his book

Alchemy of Happiness. This state, named *"fanaa'"* by the Sufis denotes the annihilation of the self or the non-existence of the self.

According to Imam Ghazali this state is when God overwhelms the heart. "When a person has forgotten these worlds which are the existence of creation, they have become his non-existence. And when he has forgotten his own egotism, he, too, has become non-existent with respect to his "self." When nothing else remains with him except God Most High, his existence is God and nothing else."

He continues, "that person sees nothing except God Most High and says "He is everything; except for Him there is no self." At this point the separation between one and God departs and unity is achieved. That is the beginning of the world of Divine Unity and Oneness. That is, when the separateness departs, one is not aware of separation and distance for a person knows separation when he knows two things: himself and God. But this person is, in this state, unaware of his self and knows nothing other that the One..."[97]

21. It is the key to nearness to Allah.

It is said that the greater the performance of *dhikr*, the closer one gets to Allah. On the contrary, the greater the indifference to *dhikr*, the greater is one's distance from Him.

A *Hadith Qudsi*, part of which has been related previously, describes the response of Allah to our seeking Him by his remembrance:

---

[97] Al-Ghazali, *Alchemy of Happiness*, 223.

Abu Hurairah (R), said that the Prophet (S.A.W.) said:

> Allah (S) says: 'I am just as My slave thinks I am, (i.e. I am able to do for him what he thinks I can do for him) and I am with him if He remembers Me. If he remembers Me in himself, I too, remember him in Myself; and if he remembers Me in a group of people, I remember him in a group that is better than they; and if he comes one span nearer to Me, I go one cubit nearer to him; and if he comes one cubit nearer to Me, I go a distance of two outstretched arms nearer to him; and if he comes to Me walking, I go to him running.'[98]

It is written in *Faza'il-e-A'maal* that nothing can be compared to nearness to Allah resulting from *dhikr*. "No words and no writing can describe this nearness. Its taste is known only to those who are blessed with it."[99]

22. The grandeur and greatness of Allah becomes more apparent to the practitioner of *dhikr*. His consciousness of Allah's omnipresence also becomes further strengthened (ibid., 72).

23. The heart and the soul are nourished by *dhikr* (ibid., 72).

24. The body and the mind are strengthened (ibid., 71).

25. It brightens the face and illuminates the heart (ibid., 71).

26. It enables one's sustenance to be provided for (ibid., 71).

---

[98] Bukhari, vol. 9, book 93, no. 502; Muslim, book 35, no. 6471; Tirmidhi, book 51, chap. 132B, no. 3614. It is also recorded by Ibn Majah.
[99] *Faza'il-e-A'maal*, "Virtues of *Dhikr*," 77.

27. It protects one against pitfalls and from committing errors (ibid., 73).

28. Awareness of Allah can be awakened in the heart of a heedless person (ibid., 73).

29. The words of certain *dhikr* travel around the throne of Allah.

    Numan bin Bashir (R) reports:

    > The Messenger of Allah (S.A.W.) said, "those who remember Allah by saying Glory be to Allah, Allah is the Most Great, all praise is due to Allah, and there is none worthy of worship except Allah, these words go around the Throne buzzing like bees, mentioning those who said them. Would one of you not like to have something with Allah mentioning him?"[100]

30. When someone remembers Allah when he is happy Allah remembers him when there is difficulty.[101]

31. *Dhikr* protects one from Allah's punishment (ibid).

32. *Dhikr* causes sins to be forgiven and evil deeds converted to virtues.

    Anas bin Maalik (R) narrates that the Prophet (S.A.W) said, "No group of people gather to make *dhikr* of Allah Ta'ala with sincerity except that a caller from the skies announces after the *dhikr*: 'Leave in the condition that you have been

---

[100] Ahmad, Ibn Majah. Rated as *sahih* by Al-Hakim. Mentioned in *Tafsir Ibn Kathir*.
[101] *Faza'il-e-A'maal*, "Virtues of *Dhikr*," 73.

forgiven of your sins and your evils being converted to virtue.'"[102]

33. It causes Allah's mercy to descend while angels surround the person (s) engaged in *dhikr*.

Shahr ibn Hawshab (R) relates that one day Abu al-Darda' (R) entered the Masjid of Bayt al-Maqdis (Jerusalem) and saw people gathered around their admonisher (*mudhakkir*) who was reminding them, and they were raising their voices, weeping, and making invocations.

Abu al-Darda' (R) said: "My father's life and my mother's be sacrificed for those who moan over their state before the Day of Moaning!"

Then he said:

> O Ibn Hawshab, let us hurry and sit with those people. I heard the Prophet say: "If you see the groves of Paradise, graze in them,' and we said: "O Messenger of Allah, what are the groves of Paradise?" He said: "The circles of remembrance, by the One in Whose hand is my soul, no people gather for the remembrance of Allah Almighty except the angels surround them closely, and mercy covers them, and Allah mentions them in His presence, and when they desire to get up and leave, a herald calls them saying: Rise forgiven, your evil deeds have been changed into good deeds!'"

---

[102] Ahmad, Tabarani, and Hakim. Hakim has ruled it *sahih* according to the criteria of Muslim and/or Bukhari.

Then Abu al-Darda' (R) made towards them and sat with them eagerly.[103]

34. If the *dhaakir* privately cries tears of repentance, he will be fortunate to be in the shadow of the throne of Allah on the Day of Judgement.[104]

35. It prevents one from indulging in backbiting and vain talk and from abusing others (ibid).

36. On the Day of Judgement the *dhaakir* will be free of despair (ibid).

37. The gatherings of *dhikr* are gatherings where angels are present. On the other hand Satan is present in gatherings where there is no *dhikr* (ibid).

38. Because of the virtue of *dhikr*, the person performing the *dhikr* is blessed together with the person sitting by him (ibid).

39. The *dhaakir* have greater reward by Allah than those who remain busy in supplication. This is according to a *hadith* to this effect (ibid., 73-74).

40. It saves one from the punishment of the grave.

This is evident from the following *hadith*:

---

[103] Ibn al-Jawzi, "Mention of those of the elite who used to attend the gatherings of story-tellers" in al-Qussas wa al-mudhakkirin (The Story-tellers and the Admonishers), 31. Mentioned in an article "Gatherings of Dhikr" at http://qa.sunnipath.com/issue_view.asp?HD=1&ID=784#gath.
[104] *Faza'il-e-A'maal*, "Virtues of *Dhikr*," 73.

The Prophet (S.A.W.) said, "A human being cannot do anything that is more effective in saving him from the punishment of the grave than the *dhikr* of Allah."[105]

41. Even though *dhikr* is the easiest form of worship it produces the greatest virtue.

There are many *hadith* to this effect. One example is the following:

Abu Hurairah (R) reported that the Messenger of Allah (S.A.W.) said:

> He who utters a hundred times in a day these words: *La ilaha illallahu, waḥdahu la sharika lahu, lahul-mulku wa lahul-ḥamdu, wa Huwa `ala kulli sha'in Qadeer* (there is no true god except Allah. He is One and He has no partner with Him; His is the sovereignty and His is the praise, and He is Omnipotent), he will have a reward equivalent to that for emancipating ten slaves, a hundred good deeds will be recorded to his credit, hundred of his sins will be blotted out from his scroll, and he will be safeguarded against the devil on that day till the evening; and no one will exceed him in doing more excellent good deeds except someone who has recited these words more often than him.
>
> And he who utters: *Subḥan Allahi wa biḥamdihi* (Hallowed be Allah, and all praise is due to Him) one hundred times

---

[105] Ahmad, Haythami, Tabarani, Tirmidhi, Ibn Majah, al-Hakim and others.

a day, his sins will be obliterated even if they are equal to the extent of the foam of the ocean. [106]

42. *Dhikr* helps the plants of Paradise to grow.

This is evident from the following *hadith*:

Jabir (R) reported: The Prophet (S.A.W.) said, "For him who says: *Subḥan Allahi wa bi ḥamdihi* (Glorified be Allah the Mighty and with His praise), then a tree is planted for him in Paradise."[107]

Ibn Mas`ud (R) reported: Messenger of Allah (S.A.W.) said:

I met Ibrahim (PBUH) on the Night of Ascension (*Al-Asra*), and he said to me: 'O Muhammad, convey my greetings to your Ummah, and tell them that Jannah has a vast plain of pure soil and sweet water. It is a plain, leveled land. The plants grow there by uttering: *Subḥan Allah, Al-ḥamdu lillah, La ilaha illallah* and *Allahu Akbar* (Allah is free from imperfection; praise be to Allah; there is no true god except Allah; and Allah is Greatest).'[108]

43. It increases *Imaan* (faith).

As an example it is said that the greater the devotion in reciting *"La ilaha illallah"* the more firmly will faith be

---

[106] In Bukhari the two sections are recorded as two separate *hadith*. The first *hadith* ends at "more often than him." These *hadith* can be found at Bukhari, vol. 8, book 75, no. 412 and Bukhari, vol. 8, book 75, no. 414, resp. In Muslim both of the two sections form one *hadith*. This is found at Muslim, book 35, no. 6508.
[107] Tirmidhi, book 51, chap. 61, no. 3475.
[108] Tirmidhi, book 51, chap. 60, no. 3473.

entrenched in the heart.[109]

44. It increases purity of intention (*Ikhlaas*).

According to Maulana Zakariya the *Ikhlaas* determines the value of things in the sight of Allah. The greater the purity of intention in performing a deed, the greater is its weight and the lesser the *Ikhlaas* the lesser the weight. Recitation of the *dhikr* "La ilaha illallah" is the most effective in attaining this *Ikhlaas*.

45. *Dhikr* develops spiritual awareness.

Maulana Zakariya relates a story of the Sheikh Ulwan Hamawi who was a great scholar, mufti and teacher in his time. He came to Sayyid Ali bin Maymoon Magrabi to learn *dhikr*. The Sheikh was advised to give up all his routine such as teaching and writing *fatwa* and only spend his time practicing *dhikr*. He was also advised to stop Qur'anic recitation. Needless to say, this caused much commotion among the people who accused the Sayyid of irreligiousness and perversion.

Nevertheless the Sheikh pursued the practice of *dhikr* for some time. He then became aware of the effect of the *dhikr* on his heart. After this, he was then allowed to resume recitation of the Qur'an. It is stated that when he opened the book again, every word and *Ayah* took on new meanings and significance. The Sayyid indicated to him that he had only stopped him from reciting the Qur'an until the spiritual awareness was developed within him by practicing *dhikr* (ibid).

---

[109] *Faza'il-e-A'maal*, "Virtues of *Dhikr*," 108.

46. *Dhikr* promotes spiritual development.

    Nothing compares to *dhikr* in elevating the spiritual status since it can be done at any time and in any situation. By *dhikr* a person's heart is so illuminated that even in sleep he is more awake than the heedless person who is awake the whole night (ibid., 75).

47. *Dhikr* generates *noor* (radiance) that stays with the person in this life as well as in the grave.

    It is said that to obtain this *noor* is a great blessing. The Prophet (S.A.W.) used to pray to Allah to let his flesh, bones, muscles, hair, skin, eyes, ears be filled with *noor* and to let *noor* be above and below him and on all sides (ibid., 76).

48. *Dhikr* is the gateway to Allah's treasures.

    This is because by *dhikr* one gains such closeness to Allah that he gives the *dhaakir* whatever he may desire (ibid).

49. *Dhikr* leads to inner contentment and also to influence over others.

    With *dhikr* the heart feels a contentment which wealth would not produce. The *dhaakir* also gains the respect of people and much influence over them (ibid).

50. *Dhikr* leads to the highest piety.

    It is said that the best of those who are pious are those who constantly remember Allah (ibid., 78).

51. *Dhikr* is a cure for all diseases of the heart.

This includes removal of the feeling of hard-heartedness. Only *dhikr* can replace this with softness (ibid., 78).

52. Allah bestows His grace on those who perform *dhikr* and the angels pray for them (ibid., 78).

53. It enables one to be as if in the gardens of paradise.

    This is evident from the following *hadith*.

    Anas ibn Maalik (R) reported that Allah's Messenger (S.A.W) said, "When you pass by the gardens of paradise graze (there)." They (the sahabah) asked, "And what are the gardens of paradise?" He said, "Circles of Dhikr." (This means, 'groups of people who mention and remember Allah').[110]

54. *Dhikr* increases the worth of good deeds.

    It is mentioned in *Faza'il-e-A'maal* that when *dhikr* is done with a good deed then that deed gains greater worth. An example is that of fasting. If it is done with much *dhikr* then it is of greater value. The same is also true for *Hajj* and *jihad* and other deeds. [111]

55. *Dhikr* produces a love for performing other forms of worship.

    It is said that the recital of abundant *dhikr* results in a love for performing other forms of worship. One now takes delight in

---

[110] Tirmidhi, book 51, chap. 87, no. 3521. Tirmidhi declared it as *hasan*. It is also recorded by Ahmad.
[111] *Faza'il-e-A'maal*, "Virtues of *Dhikr*," 78.

their performance rather than feeling bored or burdened (ibid).

56. *Dhikr* removes fear from the heart.

    A specific effect of *dhikr* is the removal of fear from the heart and creating peace of mind. The greater the amount of *dhikr* the greater is this effect (ibid).

57. It enables divine assistance to be provided.

    This is evident from the following *hadith*:

    > It is reported on the authority of Ali (R) that Fatima (R) had weals on her hand because of working at the hand-mill.
    >
    > There had fallen to the lot of Allah's Apostle (S.A.W.) some prisoners of war. She (Fatima) came to the Holy Prophet (S.A.W.) but she did not find him (in the house).
    >
    > She met A'isha (R) and informed her (about her hardship). When Allah's Apostle (S.A.W.) came, she (A'isha) informed him about the visit of Fatima (R).
    >
    > Allah's Messenger (S.A.W.) came to them (Fatima and her family). They had gone to their beds.
    >
    > 'Ali (R) further (reported): "We tried to stand up (as a mark of respect) but Allah's Messenger (S.A.W.) said: "Keep to your beds," and he sat amongst us and I felt coldness of his feet upon my chest."

He then said: "May I not direct you to something better than what you have asked for?

When you go to your bed, you should recite *Takbir* (*Allahu Akbar*) thirty-four times and *Tasbih* (*Subhan-Allah*) thirty-three times and *Tahmid* (*Alhamdu-lillah*) thirty-three times, and that is better than the servant for you.[112]

58. Those who practice *dhikr* will be ahead of others (i.e., in loftier positions) in the next world.

This can be seen by the following *hadith*:

Abu Hurairah (R) reported that Allah's Messenger (S.A.W) was travelling along the path leading to Mecca when he happened to pass by a mountain called Jumdan. He said: "Proceed on, it is Jumdan, *Mufarradun* have gone ahead." They (the Companions of the Holy Prophet) said: "Allah's Messenger, who are *Mufarradun*?" He said: "They are those males and females who remember Allah much."[113]

59. Houses are built in paradise due to *dhikr*.[114]

60. *Dhikr* protects one against the fire of hell.

If a person deserves hell due to sins the *dhikr* he used to recite will defend him against the fire (ibid).

---

[112] Muslim, book 35, no. 6577. Also found in Bukhari, vol. 8, book 75, no. 330 with the added statement "Ibn Sirin said, '*Subhan Allah*' (is to be said for) thirty-four times."
[113] Muslim, book 35, no. 6474.
[114] *Faza'il-e-A'maal*, "Virtues of *Dhikr*," 80.

61. The land where Allah's name is mentioned rejoices.

The following *hadith* is narrated by Abdullah ibn Masūd (R):

> A mountain calls out to another mountain by its name, 'Oh so and so, has anyone passed you today remembering Allah (S)?' So, when the mountain replies, 'yes', it (the calling mountain) rejoices.[115]

62. Besides *dhikr* the world is worth little.

Abu Hurairah (R) narrates, "I heard the Messenger of Allah (S.A.W) saying, 'the world is accursed, and accursed is whatever it contains except mention of Allah, that which is dear to Him and the scholar or the student.'"[116]

61. *Dhikr* is considered the best wealth.

Thawban (R) narrates:

> We were with the Holy Prophet (S.A.W) on one of his journeys when the verse '...those who gather gold and silver...' was revealed. One of his Companions said, 'this verse has come down regarding gold and silver. Would that we knew what wealth is best so that we might acquire it!' The Holy Prophet (S.A.W) said, 'the best wealth is a tongue which remembers Allah (S), a heart which is grateful and a believing wife who assists him in his faith.'[117]

---

[115] Ibn Kathir, Tabarani, Bayhaqi.
[116] Tirmidhi, book 39, chap. 14, no. 2329. It is also recorded by Ibn Majah, Ahmad and Bayhaqi.
[117] Tirmidhi, book 50, chap. 10, no. 3105. It is also recorded by Ibn Majah, Ahmad and Tabarani.

62. The performer of *dhikr* is protected and supported by Allah (S).

The Sufis state:

> One who regularly and intensively mentions God or recites one or some of His Names is taken under His protection and supported by Him, as if having made a contract with Him. The verse: Remember and mention Me, and I will remember and mention you (2:152) expresses this degree of recitation, by which one's innate destitution becomes the source of wealth, and helplessness the source of power...[118]

63. The performer of *dhikr* obtains help from Allah in overcoming obstacles in both worlds.

It is stated by the Sufis:

> ...One who remembers Him even while going about his or her daily affairs and pre-occupations will find all obstacles removed in both this world and the next. His company will always be felt, and He will befriend one left alone and in need of friendship. If one remembers and mentions Him during times of ease and comfort, His Mercy will reach one during times of trouble and pain. Those who struggle in His way to spread His Name will be saved from humiliation in both this world and the Hereafter. Such sincere endeavors will be rewarded with special favors and ranks that one cannot now imagine (ibid).

---

[118] "Dhikr (recitation of God's Names)," http://www.thewaytotruth.org/heart/zikir.html (accessed April 19th 2011).

The Beautiful Names of Allah

(Asma' al-Husna)

"KNOWLEDGE OF THE MOST BEAUTIFUL NAMES OF ALLAH
IS THE BASIS OF ALL OTHER KINDS OF KNOWLEDGE,
FOR ALL OF THESE OTHER BRANCHES OF KNOWLEDGE
ARE DEVOTED TO EITHER A COMMAND OR A CREATION OF HIS."
(IBN QAYYIM AL-JAWZIYYA)

Asma' al-Husna (Beautiful Names of God)

It is believed that the most noble of sciences is the study of Allah's Names since the most noble of subjects to study is Allah. Because of this, the Prophet Muhammad (S.A.W) gave more attention to explaining it than he did any other matter.

The importance of the knowing and understanding of Allah's Names is indicated by the following statements of Ibn al-Qayyim: "Knowledge of the Most Beautiful Names of Allah" he points out, "is the basis of all other kinds of knowledge, for all of these other branches of knowledge are devoted to either a command or a creation of His."[119]

"The key to the call of the Messengers, the essence of their Message" he declares, "is knowing Allah through His Names, His Attributes, and His Actions, because this is the foundation on which the rest of the Message, from beginning to end, is built."[120]

This is the reason why the greatest verse in the Holy Qur'an is the *Ayat-ul-Qursi*, which specifically describes some of the qualities of Allah. It is also the reason why reciting *Surah Ikhlas*, which captures the essence of *tauhid* (Allah's oneness), is equivalent to reciting one third of the Holy Qur'an.

---

[119] Ibn Qayyim Al-Jawziyya, *Badaa'i' al-Fawaa'id*, 1:163 quoted in "The Importance of Knowing Allah's Names," http://www.islamic-life.com/beautiful-names-allah/article-importance-knowing-allahs-names (accessed Oct 11th 2010).

[120] Ibn al-Qayyim, *Al-Sawaa'iq al-Mursalah `Ala al-Jahmyyah wa'l-Mu`attilah*, 1:150-151 quoted in "The Importance of Knowing Allah's Names," http://www.islamic-life.com/beautiful-names-allah/article-importance-knowing-allahs-names (accessed Oct 11th 2010).

Many Muslims, including the Sufis, believe that the Name "Allah" is the greatest and most beautiful of all the Names of Allah. This Name encompasses all of the divine names and attributes of perfection. The essence of all attributes, descriptions and names are unified in this one Name. Ghazali has this to say about the effect of the exercise of chanting of, and pondering on, this Name:

> Let the worshipper reduce his heart to a state in which the existence of anything and its non-existence are the same to him. Then let him sit alone in some corner, limiting his religious duties to what is absolutely necessary, and not occupying himself either with reciting the Qur'an or considering its meaning or with books of religious traditions or with anything of the sort. And let him see to it that nothing save God Most High enters his mind. Then, as he sits in solitude, let him not cease saying continuously with his tongue, "Allah, Allah," keeping his thoughts on it.
>
> At last he will reach a state when the motion of his tongue will cease, and it will seem as though the word flowed from it. Let him persevere in this until all trace of motion is removed from his tongue, and he finds his heart persevering in the thought. Let him still persevere until the form of the word, its letter and shape, is removed from his heart, and there remains the idea alone, as though clinging to his heart, inseparable from it. So far, all is dependent on his will and choice; but to bring the Mercy of God does not stand in his will or choice. He has now laid himself bare to the breathings of that mercy, and nothing remains but to wait what God will open to him, as God has done after this manner to prophets and saints. If he follows the above course, he

may be sure that the light of the Real will shine out in his heart.[121]

Sheikh Dagestani mentions that if the seeker of God performs *dhikr* with this Name "Allah" silently, from 5,000 to 48,000 times a day, he will "reach a state of perfection in which he becomes impeccable in the *dhikr*. At that time he will find his heart reciting the name Allah, Allah without any need to move the tongue. He will build up his internal power by burning up all the filth within, because the fire of the *dhikr*" will leave "no impurity behind. Nothing will be left, except jewels shining with the power of that spirituality."[122]

He states:

> "As the *dhikr* enters and strengthens in his heart, he will ascend until he reaches the state in which he perceives the *dhikr* of everything in creation. He will hear everything reciting *dhikr* with him in the manner that Allah destined for it. He hears each of Allah's creations, its own tone and melody distinct from any other. His hearing of one does not affect his hearing of another, but he hears them all simultaneously and distinctly and he is able to differentiate between each different kind of *dhikr*" (ibid).

---

[121] Samuel M. Zwemer, *A Moslem Seeker After God*, 92. Ebook available at http://www.archive.org/stream/moslemseekerafte00zwemrich#page/n7/mode/2up (accessed on Jan 12th 2011).

[122] "Grand Sheikh Sharafuddin Ad-Dagestani (KS) – Short Bio." *Sufi Zikr and Meditation*, Mon. 25th Aug. 2008. http://www.sufizikrmeditation.com/2008/08/grand-sheikh-sharafuddin-ad-dagestani.html (accessed June 21st 2011).

It is generally agreed upon that, besides the name "Allah", there are at least 99 Names of Allah. This is based on the following *hadith*:

Abu Hurairah (R) narrated that Allah's Apostle said, "Allah has ninety-nine Names, one-hundred less one; and he who memorized them all by heart will enter Paradise..."[123]

Also narrated by Abu Hurairah (R) that Allah's Apostle said, "Allah has ninety-nine Names, i.e., one hundred minus one, and whoever believes in their meanings and acts accordingly, will enter Paradise; and Allah is *Witr* (one) and loves 'the *Witr*' (i.e., odd numbers)."[124]

These ninety-nine names are listed in the following *hadith* of Tirmidhi: Abu Hurairah (R) reported that Allah's Messenger (S.A.W) said: Surely Allah has ninety-nine Names - a hundred, less one. He who remembers them will enter Paradise. He is Allah besides Whom there is no other God:

> Ar-Rahman, Ar-Rahim, Al-Malik, Al-Quddus, As-Salaam, Al-Mumin, Al-Muhaymin, Al-Aziz, Al-Jabbar, Al-Mutakabbir Al-Khaliq, Al-Ban, Al-Musawwir, Al-Ghaffar, Al-Qahhar, Al-Wahhab, Ar-Razzaq, Al-Fattah, Al-Alim, Al-Qabid, Al-Basil, Al-Khafid, Ar-Rafi, Al-Mu'iz, Al-Mudhill, As-Sami, Al-Basir, Al-Hakam, Al-Adl, Al-Latif, Al-Khabir, Al-Ally, Al-Halim, Al-Azim, Al-Ghafur, Ash-Shakur, Al-Kabir, Al-Hafiz, Al-Muqit, Al-Hasib, Al-Jalil, Al-Karim, Ar-Raqib, Al-Mujib Al-Wasi, Al-Hakim, Al-Wadud, Al-Majid, Al-Ba'ith, Ash-Shahid,

---

[123] Bukhari, vol. 9, book 93, no. 489; Muslim, book 35, no. 6475; Tirmidhi, book 51, chap. 86, no. 3517.
[124] Bukhari, vol. 8, book 75, no. 419; Muslim, book 35, no. 6475.

Al-Haqq, Al-Wakil, Al-Qawiy, Al-Matin, Al-Waliy, Al-Hamid, Al-Muhsiy, Al-Mubdi, Al-Mu'id, Al-Muhyiy, Al-Mumit, Al-Hayyu, Al-Qayyum, Al-Wajid, Al-Majid, Al-Wahid, As-Samad, Al-Qadir, Al-Muqtadir, Al-Muqaddim, Al-Mu'akhkhir, Al-Awwal, Al-Aakhir, Az-Zahir, Al-Batin, Al-Waliy, Al-Muta'aliy, Al-Barr, At-Tawwab, Al-Muntaqim, Al-Afuw, Ar-Ra'uf, Maalik-ul-Mulk, Dhul Jalali Walikram, Al-Muqsit, Al-Jami, Al-Ghaniy, Al-Mughni, Al-Mani, Ad-Darr, An-Nafi, An-Nur, Al-Hadi, Al-Badi, Al-Baqi, Al-Warith, Ar-Rashid, As-Sabur.[125]

Scholars, however, assert that the Names of Allah are not confined to only these ninety-nine. Some posit that the number could be as much as one hundred and fifty. Regardless of the difference of opinion on this there is no disagreement that if an attribute of Allah is found in the Holy Qur'an (or in the *hadith*) then it is an authentic Name of Allah.

Using this criterion, in table 1 I have listed the above ninety-nine Names of Allah (S) along with short meanings and Qur'anic references. This list, compiled by al-Walid ibn Muslim and taken from Wikipedia,[126] has been traditionally used in enumerating the praise of Allah. It should be pointed out that these names refer to specific qualities or attributes of Allah.

There are other Names of Allah (S) that are found in the Qur'an but are not mentioned in this particular list. There are also other

---

[125] Tirmidhi, book 51, chap. 87, no. 3518.
[126] Wikipedia contributors, "Names of God in Islam," *Wikipedia, The Free Encyclopedia*,
http://en.wikipedia.org/wiki/99_names_of_God (accessed Oct 7th 2010).
[Some of the names in Arabic have been slightly modified to enable a more correct pronunciation].

Names of Allah (S) that are found in the *hadith* of the Prophet (S.A.W).

Some of the additional Names of Allah found in the Qur'an are listed in Table 2. Some of these Names are compound words.

Table 3 states some of the Names of Allah found in the *hadith*.

The reader is encouraged (if so desires) to further explore this field.

Table 1: A list of the commonly used Ninety - Nine Names of Allah (S).

Arabic	Transliteration	Translation (can vary based on context)	Qur'anic usage
الرحمن	Ar-Raḥmān	The Compassionate, The Beneficent, The Gracious	Beginning of every chapter except one, and in numerous other places. Name frequently used in *Surah* 55, Ar-Rahman.
الرحيم	Ar-Raḥīm	The Merciful	Beginning of every chapter except one, and in numerous other places
المالك	Al-Maalik	The King, The Master, The Sovereign Lord	59:23, 20:114
القدوس	Al-Quddūs	The Holy, The Pure, The Perfect	59:23, 62:1
السلام	As-Salām	The Peace and Blessing, The Source of Peace and Safety	59:23:00
المؤمن	Al-Mu'min	The Guarantor, The Affirming	59:23:00
المهيمن	Al-Muhaymin	The Guardian, The Protector	59:23:00
العزيز	Al-'Azīz	The Almighty, The Self-Sufficient, The Honorable	3:6, 4:158, 9:40, 48:7, 59:23
الجبار	Al-Jabbār	The Irresistible, The Compeller, The Lofty	59:23:00

المتكبر	Al-Mutakabbir	The Highest, The Greatest	59:23:00
الخالق	Al-Khāliq	The Creator	6:102, 13:16, 39:62, 40:62, 59:24
البارئ	Al-Bāri	The Rightful	59:24:00
المصور	Al-Musawwir	The Evolver, The Fashioner of Forms	59:24:00
الغفار	Al-Ghaffār	The Forgiving	20:82, 38:66, 39:5, 40:42, 71:10
القهار	Al-Qahhār	The Subduer	13:16, 14:48, 38:65, 39:4, 40:16
الوهاب	Al-Wahhāb	The Bestower	3:8, 38:9, 38:35
الرزاق	Ar-Razzāq	The Provider	51:58:00
الفتاح	Al-Fattāḥ	The Opener, The Victory Giver	34:26:00
العليم	Al-'Alīm	The All Knowing, The Omniscient	2:158, 3:92, 4:35, 24:41, 33:40
القابض	Al-Qābid	The Restrainer, The Straightener	2:245
الباسط	Al-Bāsit	The Extender/Expander	2:245
الخافض	Al-Khāfid	The Abaser	95:05:00
الرافع	Ar-Rāfi'	The Exalter	58:11, 6:83
المعز	Al-Mu'izz	The Giver of Honour	3:26
المذل	Al-Mudhell	The Giver of Dishonour	3:26

السميع	As-Samī`	The All Hearing	2:127, 2:256, 8:17, 49:1
البصير	Al-Baṣīr	The All Seeing	4:58, 17:1, 42:11, 42:27
الحكم	Al-Ḥakam	The Judge, The Arbitrator	22:69
العدل	Al-`Adl	The Utterly Just	6:115
اللطيف	Al-Laṭīf	The Gentle, The Subtly Kind	6:103, 22:63, 31:16, 33:34
الخبير	Al-Khabīr	The All Aware	6:18, 17:30, 49:13, 59:18
الحليم	Al-Ḥalīm	The Forbearing, The Indulgent	2:235, 17:44, 22:59, 35:41
العظيم	Al-'Azīm	The Magnificent	2:255, 42:4, 56:96
الغفور	Al-Ghafūr	The All Forgiving	2:173, 8:69, 16:110, 41:32
الشكور	Ash-Shakūr	The Grateful	35:30, 35:34, 42:23, 64:17
العلي	Al-'Aliyy	The Sublime	4:34, 31:30, 42:4, 42:51
الكبير	Al-Kabīr	The Great	13:9, 22:62, 31:30
الحفيظ	Al-Ḥafīz	The Preserver	11:57, 34:21, 42:6
المقيت	Al-Muqīt	The Nourisher	4:85
الحسيب	Al-Ḥasīb	The Bringer of Judgment	4:6, 4:86, 33:39
الجليل	Al-Jalīl	The Majestic	55:27, 39:14, 7:143

الكريم	Al-Karīm	The Bountiful, The Generous	27:40, 82:6
الرقيب	Ar-Raqīb	The Watchful	4:1, 5:117
المجيب	Al-Mujīb	The Responsive, The Answerer	11:61
الواسع	Al-Wāsi'	The Vast, The All-Embracing, The Omni-Present, The Boundless	2:268, 3:73, 5:54
الحكيم	Al-Ḥakīm	The Wise	31:27, 46:2, 57:1, 66:2
الودود	Al-Wadūd	The Loving	11:90, 85:14
المجيد	Al-Majīd	The Glorious	11:73
الباعث	Al-Bā'ith	The Resurrecter	22:07
الشهيد	Ash-Shahīd	The Witness	4:166, 22:17, 41:53, 48:28
الحق	Al-Ḥaqq	The Truth, The Real	6:62, 22:6, 23:116, 24:25
الوكيل	Al-Wakīl	The Trustee, The Dependable	3:173, 4:171, 28:28, 73:9
القوى	Al-Qawwiyy	The Strong	22:40, 22:74, 42:19, 57:25
المتين	Al-Matīn	The Firm, The Steadfast	51:58:00
الولى	Al-Waliyy	The Protecting Friend, Patron and Helper	4:45, 7:196, 42:28, 45:19
الحميد	Al-Ḥamid	The All Praiseworthy	14:8, 31:12, 31:26, 41:42

المحصى	Al-Muḥsi	The Accounter, The Numberer of All	72:28, 78:29, 82:10-12
المبدئ	Al-Mubdi'	The Producer, Originator, The Initiator	10:34, 27:64, 29:19, 85:13
المعيد	Al-Mu'īd	The Restorer, The Reinstater Who Brings Back All	10:34, 27:64, 29:19, 85:13
المحيى	Al-Muḥyi	The Giver of Life	7:158, 15:23, 30:50, 57:2
المميت	Al-Mumīt	The Bringer of Death, The Destroyer	3:156, 7:158, 15:23, 57:2
الحي	Al-Ḥayy	The Living	2:255, 3:2, 25:58, 40:65
القيوم	Al-Qayyūm	The Self-Subsisting	2:255, 3:2, 20:111
الواجد	Al-Wājid	The Perceiver, The Finder, The Unfailing	38:44:00
الماجد	Al-Mājid	The Illustrious, The Magnificent	85:15, 11:73
الواحد	Al-Wāḥid	The One, The Unique	2:163, 5:73, 9:31, 18:110
الاحد	Al-Aḥad	The One, The Indivisible	112:01:00
الصمد	As-Samad	The Eternal, The Absolute, The Self-Sufficient	112:02:00
القادر	Al-Qādir	The Omnipotent, The All Able	6:65, 36:81, 46:33, 75:40
المقتدر	Al-Muqtadir	The All Determiner, The Dominant	18:45, 54:42, 54:55

المقدم	Al-Muqaddim	The Expediter, He Who Brings Forward	16:61, 17:34,
المؤخر	Al-Muakhkhir	The Delayer, He Who Puts Far Away	71:04:00
الأول	Al-Awwal	The First	57:03:00
الآخر	Al-Akhir	The Last	57:03:00
الظاهر	Az-Zāhir	The Manifest, The Evident, The Outer	57:03:00
الباطن	Al-Bātin	The Hidden, The Unmanifest, The Inner	57:03:00
الوالي	Al-Wāli	The Patron	13:11, 22:7
المتعالي	Al-Mutā'ali	The Exalted	13:09
البر	Al-Barr	The Good	52:28:00
التواب	At-Tawwāb	The Ever Returning, Ever Relenting	2:128, 4:64, 49:12, 110:3
المنتقم	Al-Muntaqim	The Avenger	32:22, 43:41, 44:16
العفو	Al-'Afuww	The Pardoner, The Effacer	4:99, 4:149, 22:60
الرؤوف	Ar-Raūf	The Kind, The Pitying	3:30, 9:117, 57:9, 59:10
مالك الملك	Mālik-ul-Mulk	The Owner of All Sovereignty	3:26
ذو الجلال والإكرام	Dhū-l-Jalāli wa-l-ikrām	The Lord of Majesty and Generosity	55:27, 55:78

المقسط	Al-Muqsit	The Equitable, The Requiter	7:29, 3:18
الجامع	Al-Jāmi	The Gatherer, The Unifier	3:09
الغني	Al-Ghaniyy	The Rich, The Independent	3:97, 39:7, 47:38, 57:24
المغني	Al-Mughni	The Enricher, The Emancipator	9:28
المانع	Al-Māni'	The Withholder, The Shielder, the Defender	67:21:00
الضار	Ad-Dārr	The Distressor, The Harmer, The Afflictor	6:17
النافع	An-Nāfi'	The Propitious, The Benefactor, The Source of Good	30:37:00
النور	An-Nūr	The Light	24:35:00
الهادي	Al-Hādi	The Guide, The Way	25:31:00
البديع	Al-Badī'	The Incomparable, The Originator	2:117, 6:101
الباقي	Al-Bāqi	The Immutable, The Infinite, The Everlasting	55:27:00
الوارث	Al-Wārith	The Heir, The Inheritor of All	15:23
الرشيد	Ar-Rashīd	The Guide to the Right Path	2:256
الصبور	As-Sabur	The Patient, The Timeless	2:153, 3:200, 103:3

Table 2: Some additional Names of Allah (S) found in the Qur'an

Arabic	Translation	Some instances of Qur'anic usage
رَبٌّ	Lord, Cherisher	1:1
إِلَهٌ	Worthy of Worship	6:19
الْأَكْرَمُ	The Noblest	96:3
الْعَالِمُ	The Knower	6:73
العَلَّامُ	The Knower in Full	5:109, 9:78
الْقَاهِرُ	The Irresistable	6:18, 6:61
الْقَدِيرُ	The Ever Able, Capable	2:20, 2:148
شَاكِرٌ	Rewarder of Gratitude	2:158
قَرِيبٌ	Ever Close	11:61, 2:186
الْكَافِى	The Sufficient	39:36
الْغَافِرِ	The Forgiver	40:3
الأَعْلَى	The Most Sublime	16:60
مُحِيطٌ	The Ever Encompassing	2:19, 3:120
الرَّازِقِ	The Sustainer	5:114

النَّاصِرُ	The Helper, The Supporter	3:150, 8:40, 4:45, 47:13
الْمَوْلَى	Lord, Supreme Lord, The Protector	3:150, 22:78
الْخَلَّاقُ	The Master-Creator	15:86
الْمُلْتَحِدُ	The One Who gives Shelter	72:22
الْمُسْتَعَانُ	The One Who is sought help from	12:18
سُبْحَانَ	Glorious, Limitless in Glory	21:22
فَالِقُ	The One who causes the dawn to break	6:96
الْمُكْرِمُ	The Bestower of Honor	22:18
الْحَافِظُ	The Protector & Preserver	12:64
الْحَنَّانُ	Compassionate, Merciful, Affectionate, Tender-Hearted	19:13
سُبُّوحٌ	Extremely Glorious	110:3
شَدِيدُ الْعِقَابِ	Giver of Severe Punishment	2:211, 3:11, 5:2
سَرِيعُ الْحِسَابِ	Quick in taking Accounts	2:202, 3:19
فَعَّالٌ لِّمَا يُرِيدُ	The Doer of all that He Intends	11:107
عَالِمُ الْغَيْبِ	The Knower of the Unseen	6:73
عَلَّامُ الْغُيُوبِ	The One Who know in full all that is Hidden	5:109; 9:78

فَاطِرَ السَّمَاوَاتِ وَالأَرْضِ	The Originator of The Heavens and Earth	12:101
غَافِرِ الذَّنبِ	The Forgiver of Sins	40:3
قَابِلِ التَّوْبِ	The Accepter of Repentance	40:3
أَرْحَمُ الرَّاحِمِينَ	The Most Merciful of all the Merciful	12:64
خَيْرُ الرَّازِقِينَ	The Best of Providers	5:114
خَيْرُ الْفَاصِلِينَ	The Best Judge between Truth & Falsehood	6:57
أَحْسَنُ الْخَالِقِينَ	The Best of Creators	23:14; 37:125

Table 3: Examples of Names of Allah (S) found in the *hadith*

Arabic	Translation	Arabic	Translation
اَالْأَكْبَر	The Greatest[127]	الْسَتَار	The Coverer of Faults & Imperfections
رَفِيقٌ	Companion[128]	أَلِيمِ الْعَذَابِ	The Giver of Painful Punishment
الشافِي	The Healer	العَزِيزُ السُّلْطَان	The Mighty in Authority
الْغَالِب	The Ever-Dominant	الأَكْرَمِينِ أَكْرَم	The Most Generous & The Noblest of All
الجَوّاد	The Most Generous	الْمَنَّانُ	The Most Munificient, Benevolent, Bountiful, Generous
فَارِجَ الهَمِّ	The Remover of Anxieties	كَاشِفَ الْغَمِّ	Reliever of Stress and Afflictions
مُبِينٍ	Ever Obvious	مُقَلِّبَ الْقُلُوبِ	Controller/Alteror of the Hearts
أَجْمِيلٌ	The Ever Beautiful		

---

[127] Used in *Salah* (Prayer) and in *Adhaan* (the Call to Prayer). Also highly recommended by Prophet Muhammad (S.A.W) to be recited after the compulsory prayers.
[128] The Prophet (S.A.W) uttered *"Balir-Rafiq al-A'la"* at the time of his death.

Formulas of *Dhikr*

"If the heavens and the earth and all that are in them and everything that is in between were brought and placed in one pan of the Balance, and the witnessing that there is no god but Allah were placed in the other, the latter would outweigh the former."
(Prophet Muhammad (S.A.W))

Subḥan Allah; Alḥamdu-lillah; Allahu Akbar

- Ka'b bin Ujrah (R) reported that Allah's Messenger (S.A.W.) said:

    There are certain ejaculations, the repeaters of which or the performers of which after every prescribed prayer will never be caused disappointment: "Glory be to Allah" (saying *Subḥan Allah*) thirty-three times, "Praise be to Allah" (saying *Alḥamdu-lillah*) thirty-three times, and "Allah is most Great" (saying *Allahu Akbar*) thirty-four times.[129]

- Narrated Abu Hurairah (R):

    Some poor people came to the Prophet (S.A.W.) and said, "The wealthy people will get higher grades and will have permanent enjoyment and they pray like us and fast as we do. They have more money by which they perform the *Hajj*, and *'Umrah*; fight and struggle in Allah's Cause and give in charity."

    The Prophet (S.A.W.) said, "Shall I not tell you a thing upon which if you acted you would catch up with those who have surpassed you? Nobody would overtake you and you would be better than the people amongst whom you live except those who would do the same.

    Say *Subḥan Allah*, *Alḥamdu-lillah* and *Allahu Akbar* thirty-three times each after every (compulsory) prayer."

---

[129] Muslim, book 4, no. 1241.

We differed and some of us said that we should say, *Subḥan Allah* thirty-three times and *Alḥamdu-lillah* thirty-three times and *Allahu Akbar* thirty-four times. I went to the Prophet who said, "Say, *Subḥan Allah* and *Alḥamdu-lillah* and *Allahu Akbar* all together for thirty-three times."[130]

- Abu Malik al-Ash'ari (R) reported that the Messenger of Allah (S.A.W.) said:

  Cleanliness is half of faith and (the expression) *Subḥan Allah* fills the Balance and (the expression) *Alḥamdu-lillah* fills the space between the heavens and the earth.[131]

- Narrated 'Ali bin Abi Talib (R):

  Fatima (R) came to the Prophet (S.A.W) asking for a servant. He said, "May I inform you of something better than that? When you go to bed, recite *Subḥan Allah* thirty three times, *Alḥamdu-lillah* thirty three times, and *Allahu Akbar* thirty four times." 'Ali added, "I have never failed to recite it ever since." Somebody asked, "Even on the night of the battle of Siffin?" He said, "No, even on the night of the battle of Siffin."[132]

- Abu Hurairah (R) reported that Allah's Messenger (S.A.W.) said:

---

[130] Bukhari, vol. 1, book 12, no. 804.
[131] Muslim, book 2, no. 432; In Tirmidhi, book 51, chap. 92, no. 3530 a slightly different version is recorded. In it it is stated: "...*Subḥan Allah* is half of the scale and *Alḥamdu-lillah* fills it up. *Allahu Akbar* fills up that which is between the heaven and the earth..."
[132] Bukhari, vol. 7, book 64, no. 275.

If anyone extols Allah (says *Subḥan-Allah*) after every prayer thirty-three times, and praises Allah (says *Alḥamdu-lillah*) thirty-three times, and declares His Greatness (says *Allahu Akbar*) thirty-three times, ninety-nine times in all, and says to complete a hundred: "There is no god but Allah, having no partner with Him, to Him belongs sovereignty and to Him is praise due, and He is Potent over everything," (*La ilaha illallahu, waḥdahu la sharika lahu, lahul-mulku wa lahul-ḥamdu, wa Huwa `ala kulli shai'in Qadir*) his sins will be forgiven even if these are as abundant as the foam of the sea.[133]

---

[133] Muslim, book 4, no. 1243; Malik, chap. 126, no. 483.

Subḥan Allahi wa biḥamdihi, Subḥan Allahil 'Azim

- Abu Hurairah (R) reported:

    The Messenger of Allah (S.A.W.) said, "There are two statements that are light on the tongue but are vey heavy in the Scales and are very dear to the Compassionate One:

    Subḥan Allahi wa biḥamdihi, Subḥan Allahil 'Azim

    [Hallowed be Allah and Praise is due to Him, (and) Hallowed be Allah, the Great].[134]

---

[134] Bukhari, vol. 8, book 75, no. 415; Muslim, book 35, no. 6511; Tirmidhi, book 51, chap. 61, no. 3478. Also recorded by Ahmad and Ibn Majah.

La ilaha illallahu, waḥdahu la sharika lahu, lahul-mulku wa lahul-ḥamdu, wa huwa `ala kulli sha'in Qadir

- Abu Hurairah (R) reported that Allah's Messenger (S.A.W.) said:

  He who utters a hundred times in a day these words: *La ilaha illallahu, waḥdahu la sharika lahu, lahul-mulku wa lahul-ḥamdu, wa Huwa `ala kulli sha'in Qadir* (there is no true god except Allah. He is One and He has no partner with Him; His is the sovereignty and His is the praise, and He is Omnipotent), he will have a reward equivalent to that for emancipating ten slaves, a hundred good deeds will be written in his account, and one hundred of his sins will be blotted out from his scroll, and it (his saying) will be a shield for him from Satan on that day till night, and nobody will be able to do a better deed except the one who does more than him.[135]

- Abu Ayyub al-Ansari (R) reported: that Allah's Messenger (S.A.W.) said:

  He who utters ten times: *La ilaha illallahu, waḥdahu la sharika lahu, lahul-mulku wa lahul-ḥamdu, wa Huwa `ala kulli sha'in Qadir*, he will have a reward equal to that for freeing four slaves from the progeny of Prophet Isma'il.[136]

- Ya'qub ibn 'Asim (R) reported that two of the Companions of the Prophet (S.A.W) heard the Prophet (S.A.W) say:

  No one at all says *La ilaha illallahu, waḥdahu la sharika lahu,*

---

[135] Bukhari, vol. 8, book 75, no. 412; Muslim, book 35, no. 6508; Malik, chap. 126, no. 481; Tirmidhi, book 51, chap. 61, no. 3479.
[136] Muslim, book 35, no. 6510; Tirmidhi, book 51, chap. 117, no. 3564.

lahul-mulku wa lahul-ḥamdu, wa Huwa `ala kulli sha'in Qadir sincerely with his soul, affirming it with his heart, articulating it with his tongue but that Allah splits open the heaven so that He can look at the one on the earth who says it, and it is a right of the slave at whom Allah looks that He grant him his request.[137]

- Narrated Warrad (the clerk of Al-Mughira bin Shu'ba):

  Muawiya (R) wrote to Al-Mughira (R): "Write to me a narration you have heard from Allah's Apostle." So Al-Mughira (R) wrote to him, "I heard him saying the following after each prayer: '*La ilaha illallahu, waḥdahu la sharika lahu, lahul-mulku wa lahul-ḥamdu, wa Huwa `ala kulli sha'in Qadir.*'"[138]

- Abu Dharr (R) reported that Allah's Messenger (S.A.W) said:

  If anyone says after concluding the *Salah* of *Fajr* while he continues to sit (as he sat in *Salah* during *tashahhud*), before speaking to anyone ten times: *La ilaha illallahu, waḥdahu la sharika lahu, lahul-mulku wa lahul-ḥamdu, Yuḥyii wa Yumitu wa Huwa `ala kulli sha'in Qadir* then ten pious deeds are recorded for him, ten evil deeds are erased from him, ten ranks are elevated for him, and all that day he is protected from every disapproved thing and the devil is not allowed to approach him, and that day no sin will ruin him apart from associating partner with Allah.[139]

---

[137] Nasa'i.
[138] Bukhari, vol. 8, book 76, no. 480.
[139] Tirmidhi, book 51, chap. 64, no. 3485.

- Umarah ibn ash-Shabib (R) reported that Allah's Messenger (S.A.W) said:

    If anyone says: *"La ilaha illallahu, wahdahu la sharika lahu, lahul-mulku wa lahul-hamdu, Yuhyii wa Yumitu wa Huwa `ala kulli sha'in Qadir."*

    ten times after *Maghrib* (*Salah*) then Allah will send to him an angel to protect him from the devil till morning; ten pious deeds will be written down for him and ten destroying evils will be erased from him and reward for emancipating ten believing slaves will be recorded for him.[140]

- Narrated 'Ubada bin As-Samit (R):

    The Prophet (S.A.W) (said) "Whoever gets up at night and says: '*La ilaha illallahu, wahdahu la sharika lahu, lahul-mulku wa lahul-hamdu, wa Huwa `ala kulli sha'in Qadir; Alhamdu-lillahi wa Subhan Allahi wa La ilaha illallah wallahu akbar wa la hawla wala Quwata illa billah.*' (None has the right to be worshipped but Allah. He is the Only One and has no partners. For Him is the Kingdom and all the praises are due for Him. He is Omnipotent. All the praises are for Allah. All the glories are for Allah. And none has the right to be worshipped but Allah, And Allah is Great And there is neither Might nor Power Except with Allah). And then says: 'Allahummaghfirli (O Allah! Forgive me). Or invokes (Allah), he will be responded to and if he performs ablution (and prays), his prayer will be accepted."[141]

---

[140] Tirmidhi, book 51, chap. 102, no. 3545.
[141] Bukhari, vol. 2, book 21, no. 253.

Subḥan Allah

Mus'ab b. Sa'd reported that his father told him that (when) he had been in the company of Allah's Messenger (may peace be upon him) he (the Prophet (S.A.W) said: "Is one amongst you powerless to get one thousand virtues every day?" Amongst those who had been sitting there, one asked: "How one amongst us can get one thousand virtues every day?" He said: "Recite: *Subḥan Allah*' (Hallowed be Allah) one hundred times for (by reciting them) one thousand virtues are recorded (to your credit) and one thousand vices are blotted out."[142]

---

[142] Muslim, book 35, no. 6517.

Subḥan Allahi wa biḥamdihi, ʿadada khalqihi, wa rida nafsihi, wa zinatah ʿarshihi, wa midada kalimatihi

- Juwairiyah bint Al-Harith (R), the Mother of the Believers, reported:

    The Prophet (S.A.W.) came out from my apartment in the morning when I was busy in performing the dawn prayer. He came back in the forenoon and found me sitting there. The Prophet (S.A.W.) said, "Are you still in the same position as I left you." I replied in the affirmative. Thereupon the Prophet said, "I recited four words three times after I had left you. If these are to be weighed against all you have recited since morning, these will be heavier.

    These are: *Subḥan Allahi wa biḥamdihi, ʿadada khalqihi, wa rida nafsihi, wa zinatah ʿarshihi, wa midada kalimatihi* [Hallowed be Allah and praise is due to Him, as many times as the number of His creatures, in accordance with His Good Pleasure, equal to the weight of His Throne and equal to the ink that may be used in recording the words (for His Praise)]."[143]

---

[143] Muslim, book 35, no. 6575; Abu Dawud, book 8, no. 1498; Tirmidhi, book 51, chap. 118, no. 3566.

La ḥawla wa la quwwata illa billah

- Abu Musa (R) reported:

  The Messenger of Allah (S.A.W) said to me, "Shall I not guide you to a treasure from the treasures of Jannah?" I said: "Yes, O Messenger of Allah!" Thereupon he (S.A.W) said, "(Recite) *La ḥawla wa la quwwata illa billah* (There is no change of a condition nor power except by Allah)."[144]

- Abu Saʿid (R) reported:

  The Prophet (S.A.W) said: "Perform the enduring goods deeds more frequently." They asked, "What are these enduring good deeds?" The Prophet (S.A.W.) replied: *"Takbir [Allahu Akbar], Tahlil [la ilaha illallah], Tasbih [Subḥan Allah], al-ḥamdulillah,* and *La ḥawla wa la quwwata illa billah."*[145]

- Qays ibn Uhadah (R) reported that his father placed him at the disposal of the Prophet (S.A.W) that he may serve him. He said, "The Prophet passed by me while I was offering *Salah*. (When I had finished), he struck me with his foot and said, 'Shall I not guide you to a door of the doors of paradise?' I said, 'Certainly!' He said: *'La ḥawla wa la quwwata illa billah.'"*[146]

---

[144] Bukhari, vol. 8, book 75, no. 418; Muslim, book 35, no. 6532; Abu Dawud, book 8, no. 1521.

[145] Nasa'i and Hakim who said its chain is *sahih*. An essentially similar *hadith* is recorded in Malik, chap. 126, no. 484.

[146] Tirmidhi, book 51, chap. 128, no. 3592.

Subḥan Allahi wa bi ḥamdihi

- Jabir (R) reported: The Prophet (S.A.W.) said:

    If anyone says: *Subḥan Allahi wa bi ḥamdihi* (Glorified be Allah the Mighty and unto Him be Praise), a palm tree will be planted in Jannah.[147]

- Narrated by Abu Hurairah (R) that the Prophet Muhammad (S.A.W) said:

    Whoever says, *Subḥan Allahi wa bi ḥamdihi* one hundred times a day, will be forgiven all his sins even if they were as much as the foam of the sea.[148]

- Abu Dharr (R) reported:

    The Messenger of Allah (S.A.W) said: "Shall I tell you the words that Allah loves the most?" I said: "Yes, tell me, O Messenger of Allah." He said: "The words dearest to Allah are: *Subḥan Allahi wa bi ḥamdihi*."[149]

- Abu Hurairah (R) reported that the Prophet (S.A.W) said about one who says in the morning and in the evening a hundred times *Subḥan Allahi wa bi ḥamdihi* that no one will come on the day of Resurrection with a better deed except one who said as he did and one who said it more than him.[150]

---

[147] Tirmidhi, book 51, chap. 61, no. 3475.
[148] Bukhari, vol. 8, book 75, no. 414; Muslim, book 35, no. 6508; Malik, chap. 126, no. 482; Tirmidhi, book 51, chap. 61, no. 3477. Also recorded by Ibn Majah, Ahmad and Nasa'i.
[149] Muslim, book 35, no. 6587; Tirmidhi, book 51, chap. 131, no. 3604.
[150] Muslim, book 35, no. 6509; Tirmidhi, book 51, chap. 62, no. 3840.

Subḥan Allah; Al-ḥamdu lillah; La ilaha illallah; Allahu Akbar

- Ibn Mas'ud (R) reported that Allah's Messenger (S.A.W.) said:

    I met Ibrahim (P.B.U.H) on the Night of Ascension (Al-Asra), and he said to me: 'O Muhammad, convey my greetings to your *Ummah*, and tell them that *Jannah* has a excellent soil and sweet water. It is a plain, leveled land. The plants grow there by uttering: *Subḥan Allah, Al-ḥamdu lillah, La ilaha illallah* and *Allahu Akbar* (Allah is free from imperfection; praise be to Allah; there is no true god except Allah; and Allah is Greatest).'[151]

    Commentary: Trees grow on the plain land of *Jannah* in return for remembrance and glorification of Allah. The more one recites these words of remembrance, the greater is the number of trees that grow.

- Abu Hurairah (R) reported that Allah's Messenger (S.A.W.) said:

    The uttering of the words: *Subḥan Allah, Al-ḥamdu lillah, La ilaha illallah* and *Allahu Akbar* is dearer to me than anything over which the sun rises.[152]

- Samurah ibn Jundab (R) reported that Allah's Messenger (S.A.W.):

---

[151] Tirmidhi, book 51, chap. 60, no. 3473.
[152] Muslim, book 35, no. 6512; Tirmidhi, book 51, chap. 132, no. 3608.

The most beloved words to Allah are four: *Subḥan Allah, Al-ḥamdu lillah, La ilaha illallah* and *Allahu Akbar*. There is no harm for you in which order you begin (reciting them).[153]

- Abu-Hurairah and Abu-Sa'id (R) reported that Allah's Messenger (S.A.W.) said:

    Verily, Allah has chosen four words from all speech: *Subḥan Allah, Al-ḥamdu lillah, La ilaha illallah* and *Allahu Akbar*. Therefore, whoever says: *Subḥan Allah*, twenty good deeds will be recorded for him, and twenty sins will be dropped from him, and whoever says: *Allahu Akbar* will get the same, and whoever says: *La ilaha illallah*, will get the same, and whoever says: *Al-ḥamdu lillah Rab Al-'Alamin* (the Lord of all worlds) spontaneously, thirty good deeds will be recorded for him, and thirty sins will be dropped from him.[154]

- Abu-Hurairah (R) reported that Allah's Messenger (S.A.W) said:

    "Take the means of your protection." We replied: "O Messenger of Allah (S.A.W.), from an arriving enemy?" He said: "No, rather your protection from Hell-fire. Say: *Subḥan Allah*, and *Al-ḥamdu lillah*, and *La ilaha illallah*, and *Allahu Akbar*, for they come on the Day of Resurrection acting as savior and foreparts, and they are the righteous lasting deeds."[155]

---

[153] Muslim, book 25, no. 5329.
[154] Ahmad, Hakim.
[155] Nasa'i, Hakim and others. Hakim said its chain is *sahih*.

- Anas ibn Maalik (R) reported that the Prophet (S.A.W) passed by a tree whose leaves had dried. He struck its branches with his staff so that the leaves fell down. He said, "Indeed, (saying) *Subḥan Allah, Al-ḥamdu lillah, La ilaha illallah, Allahu Akbar* get the sins of a person to drop down just as the leaves of this tree fall down."¹⁵⁶

- Amr ibn Shuayb (R) reported from his father who from his grand father that Allah's Messenger (S.A.W) said:

    > If anyone glorifies Allah (saying *Subḥan Allah*) a hundred times in the morning and a hundred times in the evening then he is like one who performed a hundred *Hajj* (pilgrimages). And he who praises Allah (saying *Al-ḥamdu lillah*) a hundred times in the morning and a hundred times in the evening is like one who gave a hundred warriors horses to ride in the path of Allah (or he said "as though he participated in a hundred battles.") And he who declared Allah's unity (saying *La ilaha illallah*) a hundred times in the morning and a hundred times in the evening is as though he emancipated a hundred slaves who were descendants of Isma'il. And he who extolled Allah (saying *Allahu Akbar*) a hundred times in the morning and a hundred times in the evening (should know that) none would bring that day more than what he brought unless he said as this person said or increased upon it.¹⁵⁷

- Al-Nu`man ibn Bashir (R) that he said: The Messenger of Allah (S.A.W) said:

---

¹⁵⁶ Tirmidhi, book 51, chap. 102, no. 3544.
¹⁵⁷ Tirmidhi, book 51, chap. 63, no. 3482.

Verily, among what (i.e., the words) you say in exalting Allah is *Tasbih (Subḥan Allah)*, *Takbir (Allahu Akbar)*, *Tahlil (La ilaha illallah)*, and *Tahmid (Al-ḥamdu lillah)*, they keep bending around the throne making a buzz like bees, reminding of its owner. Would any of you not like to have something or continues to have something that reminds of them?[158]

---

[158] Ahmad, Ibn Majah, Hakim.

La ilaha illallah

- It is mentioned by Jalaluddin as-Suyuti (R) that 'Ali bin Abi Talib (R) said:

    I asked the Prophet Muhammad (S.A.W.) one time, 'O Messenger of Allah, guide me to the shortest way to Allah's Presence, and the easiest way to worship, and the best way for Allah, Almighty and Exalted.'

    The Prophet Muhammad (S.A.W.) said, 'O 'Ali, you have to be continuously making *dhikrullah*, silently and aloud.' I replied, 'O Prophet Muhammad (S.A.W.), all human beings are making *dhikr*. Give me something special.'

    The Prophet Muhammad (S.A.W.) said, 'O 'Ali, the best of what I, and all Prophets before me, said is, *La ilaha illallah* (there is no god but Allah). If all the heavens and earth were placed on one side of the balance and *La ilaha illallah* were placed in the other, *La ilaha illallah* would be heavier. Judgment Day will never come as long as there are people on this earth saying *La ilaha illallah*.'

    Then I said, 'How should I recite.' The Prophet Muhammad (S.A.W.) said, 'Close your eyes and listen to me reciting *La ilaha illallah* three times. Then you say it three times and I will listen to you.' Then the Prophet Muhammad (peace be upon him) said it and I repeated it in a loud voice.

- In the narration of Imam Ahmad (R) and Tabarani (R) this *hadith* is continued, describing how the Prophet taught his companions the *dhikr*.

Ibada bin Samit (R) said that the Prophet Muhammad (S.A.W.) said, "Is there any stranger among you?" And we said, "No, Ya Rasul-Allah." He said, "Close the door." Then he said, "Raise your hand and repeat after me *la ilaha illallah.*" We raised our hand and said, *La ilaha illallah* for some time.

Then the Prophet Muhammad (S.A.W.) said, "Praise be to Allah that He sent me to this world with this *kalimah,* and He ordered me with it, and He promised me the Paradise with it, and He never changes His Promise." Then the Prophet Muhammad (S.A.W.) said, "Be happy! Allah has forgiven you."[159]

- Abu Hurairah (R) said, "I asked, 'O Allah's Apostle! Who will be the luckiest person who will gain your intercession on the Day of Resurrection?'

    The Prophet said, 'O Abu Hurairah! I have thought that none will ask me about this *hadith* before you, as I know your longing for the (learning of) *hadith*. The luckiest person who will have my intercession on the Day of Resurrection will be the one who says *La ilaha illallah* sincerely from the bottom of his heart.'"[160]

- Abu Hurairah (R) reported that the Prophet (S.A.W.) said:

    If anyone says sincerely *"La ilaha illallah"* then the gates of heaven are opened for him till it is carried over to the

---

[159] Ahmad, Nasa'i, Tabarani, Hakim.
[160] Bukhari, vol. 8, book 76, no. 574.

Throne, provided he has kept away from the major sins.[161]

- Jabir (R) reported that the Prophet (S.A.W.) said, "The best *dhikr* is *La ilaha illallah* and the best supplication is *alhamdulillah*."[162]

- Sa'id ibn al-Musayyib relates: When the death of Abu Talib approached, Allah's Apostle came to him and said: "Say: *La ilaha illallah*, a word with which I will be able to defend you before Allah."[163]

- Abu Hurairah (R) reported that the Messenger of Allah (S.A.W.) said, "Renew your faith." He was asked, "Messenger of Allah (S.A.W.), how do we renew our faith?" He replied, "Say often: *La ilaha illallah*."[164]

- It is narrated on the authority of Sunabihi (R) that he went to Ubada b. Samit (R) when he was about to die. I burst into tears. Upon this he said to me: Allow me some time (so that I may talk with you). Why do you weep? By Allah, if I am asked to bear witness, I would certainly testify for you (that you are a believer). Should I be asked to intercede, I would certainly intercede for you, and if I have the power, I would certainly do good to you, and then observed: By Allah, never did I hear anything from the Messenger of Allah (S.A.W) which could have been a source of benefit to you and then not conveyed it to you except this single *hadith* that I intend to narrate to you today, since I am going to breathe my last. I

---

[161] Tirmidhi, book 51, chap. 130B, no. 3601. Tirmidhi declares it to be *hasan* (fair).
[162] Nasa'i, Ibn Majah.
[163] Bukhari, vol. 8, book 78, no. 672; Muslim, book 1, no. 36.
[164] Ahmad, At-Tabarani.

heard the Messenger of Allah (S.A.W) say: He who testifies that there is no god but Allah and that Muhammad is the messenger of Allah (*La ilaha illallah Muhammadur Rasulullah*), Allah would prohibit the fire of Hell for him.[165]

In a version recorded by Bukhari, 'Utban bin Malik Al-Ansari (R) narrates: Allah's Apostle came to me and said, "If anybody comes on the Day of Resurrection who has said *La ilaha illallah*, sincerely, with the intention to win Allah's Pleasure, Allah will make the Hell-Fire forbidden for him."[166]

- The Companions were talking about Malik ibn Dukhshum, and they wished that the Prophet (S.A.W.) would curse him so that he should die or meet some calamity. The Prophet (S.A.W.) said, "Does Malik ibn Dukhshum not testify to the fact that there is no god but Allah and that I am the Messenger of Allah?"

  They said, "Yes, he no doubt says this but it is not in his heart."

  The Prophet (S.A.W.) replied: "No-one who says: *Ashhadu alla-ilaaha illallah wa annee rasoolullah* (I testify that there is no god but Allah and that I am Allah's Messenger) will ever enter the Fire nor be consumed by it."

  Anas (R) said: "This *hadith* impressed me so much that I ordered my son to write it down (for me) and he did."[167]

---

[165] Muslim, book 1, no. 45.
[166] Bukhari, vol. 8, book 76, no. 431.
[167] Muslim, book 1, no. 52.

- Al-Miqdad (R) said: I asked, "O Messenger of Allah, suppose I and one of the idolaters battled and he cut off my hand, then I was positioned to strike him and he said: *La ilaha illallah*! Do I kill him or spare him?"

  He said: "Spare him."

  I said: "Even if he cut off my hand?"

  He said: "Even so."

  I asked him again two or three times whereupon he said: "If you kill him after he says *La ilaha illallah* then you are like him before he said it, and he is like you before you killed him."[168]

- It is narrated on the authority of Abu Hurairah that the Messenger of Allah (S.A.W) said: "Faith has over seventy branches or over sixty branches, the most excellent of which is the declaration of *La ilaha illallah* and the humblest of which is the removal of what is injurious from the path."[169]

- Usama b. Zaid (R) reported:

  The Messenger of Allah (S.A.W) sent us to Huraqat, a tribe of Juhaina. We attacked that tribe early in the morning and defeated them and I and a man from the Ansar caught hold of a person (of the defeated tribe). When we overcame him, he said: *La ilaha illallah*. At that

---

[168] Ahmad, Nasa'i, Shafi`i and Bayhaqi.
[169] Muslim, book 1, no. 56; Tirmidhi, book 42, chap. 6, no. 2623. Also recorded by Nasa'i, Ibn Majah and Ahmad.

moment the Ansari spared him, but I attacked him with my spear and killed him.

The news had already reached the Apostle (S.A.W), so when we came back he (the Apostle) said to me: Usama, did you kill him after he had made the profession: *La ilaha Ilallah*? I said. Messenger of Allah, he did it only as a shelter. The Holy Prophet observed: Did you kill him after he had made the profession that *La ilaha illallah*? He (the Holy Prophet) went on repeating this to me till I wished I had not embraced Islam before that day.[170]

- `Abd Allah ibn `Amr ibn al-`As (R) reported: On the Day of Resurrection, Allah will pick out a man of my *ummah* in front of all the creatures. Ninety scrolls will be (opened and) presented to him, each scroll the length of the eyesight.

He (Allah) will ask, "Do you deny from it anything? Have My guardian - recorders wronged you?"

He will say, "No, my Lord."

He will ask, "Do you have an excuse?"

He will answer, "No, my Lord."

Allah will say, "Rather! We have with us a pious deed from you, and, indeed, you will not be wronged today."

So a card would be taken out inscribed on it (the words): 'I bear witness that there is on God but Allah and I bear

---

[170] Bukhari, vol. 5, book 59, no. 568; Muslim, book 1, no. 177. Also recorded by Ahmad, Nasa'i, Bayhaqi and others.

witness that Muhammad (SAW) is His slave and His Messenger'. (*Ashhadu alla-ilaaha illallah wa ashadu anna Muḥammadur Rasullulah*).

He (Allah) will say, "Bring your scale."

He will plead, "My Lord, what is this card before these scrolls?"

Allah will say, "You will not be wronged."

So, the scrolls will be placed on one pan and the card on another pan of the balances. The scrolls shall fail and the card shall outweigh them.

The Prophet (S.A.W.) then said: "Nothing is heavier than the Name of Allah."[171]

---

[171] Tirmidhi, book 43, chap. 17, no. 2648. Tirmidhi says it is *hasan*. Also recorded by Ahmad, Hakim and Bayhaqi.

Dhikr and the Effects of Sound

"In the beginning was the Word,
and the Word was with God,
and the Word was God."
(KJV Bible, John 1:1)

Dhikr and the Effects of Sound:
Sound is a primitive and powerful force. It has been used to blast off mountains. In medicine radiologists use it for scanning the body in the form of ultrasound and urologists use it to break kidney and gall bladder stones. Creation of the earth was through a massive sound when Allah said the very powerful word *"Kun,"* and its end, the doomsday, will also be through an extremely powerful sound form called *"Soor"* that will destroy the whole world.

In the Vedanta God is known as Nada Brahma, meaning Sound, the Creator.

The Bible equates "the Word," a form of sound, with God and creation: "In the beginning was the Word, and the Word was with God, and the Word was God."[172]

From this Word, the basic construction of the universe, "the six days were created, being lights emanating from the Word and illuminating the world."[173]

The effect of rhythmic sound
There are many instances recorded in history where rhythmic sound or music has had extraordinary effects. It is said that in the myth of Orpheus his song deflected rocks from falling onto his ship. Wild animals would also listen to him sing and trees would follow him.[174]

---

[172] King James Version of the Bible, John 1:1.
http://theology101.org/bib/kjv/jos006.htm#003 (accessed April 12th 2010).
[173] A.E. Waite, *The Holy Kabbalah*, 230.
[174] The Larouse Encyclopedia of Mythology, *Greek mythology,* 198.

It is recorded in the Bible how the walls of the city of Jericho crumbled when Joshua led the Israeli army around the city shouting and blowing trumpets.[175]

In Indian music, a raga, which is based on a set scale, or a set of scales, is a musical formula on which compositions or improvisations can be based. Ragas evoke specific moods such as joy or wonderment. Certain ragas are only played at certain times of the day such as early morning or late at night. There are also ragas that are played at specific seasons of the year.

There is a belief in India that playing a particular raga at an inopportune time can cause peculiar things to happen. For instance, if the raga called *dipak* is played fire is invoked. Once, a king named Akbar, to test the truth of this, ordered his famous court musician, Tansen, to play this raga for him. It is said that when Tansen began playing the raga, the palace around them began to burst into flames. Just at that moment, a young maiden happened to be walking by and saw what was taking place. She quickly began singing raga *mahlar*, the raga that causes rain to fall, and a great storm appeared in the skies and extinguished the flames.[176]

In the 1730s King Philip V of Spain summoned the Italian castralto Farinelli to sing for him to relieve his symptoms of depression and chronic pain. It is said that Philip was immediately cured of his symptoms after Farinelli sang.[177]

---

[175] King James Version of the Bible, Joshua 6:3-7. http://theology101.org/bib/kjv/jos006.htm#003 (accessed April 12th 2010).
[176] Don Robertson, "Stories about the Effects of the Ragas of India," http://www.dovesong.com/positive_music/India.asp (accessed April 12th 2010).
[177] Don Campbell, *the Mozart Effect*, 149.

Specific to *dhikr*, an interesting story is narrated in the book *Chanting: Discovering Spirit in Sound*.

Allaudin Mathieu, a Sufi teacher, along with thirty others who were attending a summer camp in the French Alps, decided to hike up the mountains early one day. As they hiked, they chanted "Allah, Allah" and *"Ya Hayyu, Ya Qayyumu"* (O Ever-Living, O Self- Sufficent). Along the trail they came upon a large, bowl-shaped area known as a cirque that resonated sound. Allaudin decided for the group to utter "Allah" at the top of their voices and listen to the echo. "The sound was orgasmic," he said, "but the echo was even better. Our chord came back to us like the wake of a boat we had hurled across the glistening ocean of snow and stone. Many choirs ricocheted from the granite galleries. We sang another chord and again the cirque sang back. We thought it was the craziest, juiciest human sound ever to resound from a mountain."

The Sufis became ecstatic upon hearing the echoing effect of their chant. Allaudin continues, "We even imagined we could hear our vibrations coming back to us as a kind of human scream for God." They uttered "Allah" again. But this time the echo came back in French! When they looked across the gorge, lo and behold, they saw the silhouette of six black dots against the white snow nearly a mile from where they were. They realized the black dots were mountain climbers. When they chanted again the sound came back louder but this time it was comprehensible. The mountaineers were shouting in French, "Stop! For the love of God! Stop! Stop!"

"The climbers were yelling at us to stop our mountain music. They were begging for their lives," Allaudin remarks.

The mountaineers understood that the loud chanting could start an avalanche.[178]

Destructive effect of sound
Inayat Khan says that there is no such thing as one saying something and not meaning it – that all words spoken has an effect on life. Sound, therefore, may also produce a destructive effect. There are recorded instances in history where wrong use of sound produced disastrous results. In the Hindu traditions mention is made of the demons destroying themselves when, in a war with the "gods" a mantra was chanted with the incorrect pronunciation. It is also said that a kingdom was destroyed through the mistake of a poet who did not use the proper words in the praise of a king.

In our modern day world we are exposed to many types of sounds some of which can produce negative effects on us. The loud piercing sound of a carbon monoxide detector in alarm mode can immediately result in a splitting headache. Low frequency sounds such as from turbines, tractors and generators can produce muscle aches, stress, and pain.

It is estimated that, of the some sixty million Americans who have hearing loss, more than twenty million are exposed to dangerous levels of sound on a regular basis. Noise-induced hearing loss is the number one contributor to hearing disability. In a study at a public elementary school in New York City, it was found that the students whose classrooms faced the elevated subway were eleven months behind those who were not subjected to the constant sound of moving trains. In California,

---

[178] *Chanting: Discovering Spirit in Sound*, 20–21.

sixty-one percent of freshmen suffered from hearing loss due to high frequency noise. [179]

Noise was found to contribute to increased rate of cardiovascular disease, hypertension, high stress levels and even cancer.[180]

Important contributors to this problem vary widely. They include rock concerts where the sound level could be greater than that of a jet engine on the tarmac; use of headphones while jogging, exercising or working; instruments used in hospitals; power tools; traffic; and industrial machinery.

Don Campbell recalls an interesting incident during a seminar he was conducting at a hotel near Los Angeles airport. While he was teaching a group of students he "felt severe pain" in his back then, after only two hours, he became exhausted – quite an abnormal thing for him. Suspecting that there was some source of sound contributing to his feelings he decided to investigate. What he discovered was that the sound was coming from five industrial-size clothes dryers in operation.[181]

Impression of sound

The Prophet Muhammad (S.A.W.) has indicated according to the following *hadith* that everything that hears the Muslim call to prayer will testify on the Day of Judgment for the person who delivered that call.

'Abdullah ibn 'Abdurahman (R) related from his father that Abu Sa'eed al-Khudri (R) said to him, "I see that you love the sheep

---

[179] *The Mozart Effect*, 36-37.
[180] *Chanting: Discovering Spirit in Sound*, 32.
[181] *The Mozart Effect*, 35.

and the desert. If you are with your sheep or in the desert, then raise your voice while making the call to prayer, for *any jinn, human or any other creature within hearing distance of your voice will be a witness for you on the Day of Resurrection*...I heard the Messenger of Allah say that."[182] (Emphasis mine).

This indicates that even inanimate objects apparently are affected by sound.

Inayat Khan states, "On all objects the impression of sound falls clearly, only it is not always visible..."[183]

In the eighteenth-century the German scientist and musician Ernst Chladni empirically verified that sound affects physical matter. He verified this fact by simple, visual experiments. When he drew a violin bow around the edge of a plate covered with fine sand, he found that the sand formed various geometric patterns. By this he showed that sound vibrations produced a definite rearrangement in the physical properties of the sand.[184]

The Swiss medical doctor and scientist, Dr. Hans Jenny in the 1960s, did extensive exploration on Chladni's results. Using a frequency generator and oscillator he vibrated sand and other materials including iron filings, fine-grained plastic, and mercury on plates.

---

[182] Bukhari, vol. 1, book 11, no. 583; Ahmad, Nisa'i and Ibn Majah.
[183] Inayat Khan, *The Sufi Message of Hazrat Inayat Khan/Music/The Manifestation of Sound on the Physical Sphere,*
http://www.sufimessage.com/music/manifestation-of-sound.html (accessed Oct 12th 2010).
[184] Mitchel L. Gaynor, *Sounds of Healing: A Physician Reveals the Therapeutic Power of Sound, Voice, Music,* 138.

Low frequency sound, he observed, created simple geometrical designs. As the frequency increased more intricate geometrical designs were formed. The designs lasted as long as the vibration continued. When the sound stopped the design collapsed.

The shapes that were created were not only dependent on the frequency but also on the amplitude of the sound and the material used for the plates. There could thus be an infinite variety of shapes created. Some shapes displayed three-dimensional depth and beautiful textures – in some cases similar to natural occurrences such as snowflakes, flowers, and spirals.[185]

Jenny's work had vast implications. He was able to prove that different sounds created different forms. These forms were also maintained by sound. From this it became clear that sound not only could create but could also alter forms.

From Jenny's research the word "cymatics" was created to describe the study of how sound affects matter.

Healing with sound

The awareness that sound could heal is something that has been accepted for centuries by healers who have intuitively used sound's therapeutic powers. In ancient cultures, many examples of the use of sound and vibration as treatment are found. Numerous tools have been used since the beginning of time to create music that aids healing: Chinese meditation gongs, "singing bowls," bells and chanting in Tibet, drums in Africa, and tamboura (a lute-like instrument usually with four strings) in India.

---

[185] Hans Jenny, *Cymatics: A Study of Wave Phenomena and Vibration.*

Gaynor states in his book that Pythagoras was the first person to use music for healing. It is recorded that Pythagoras "would sit in the middle of his disciples who...would sing in unison certain chants...by which they appeared to be delighted...At other times, his disciples also employed music as medicine, with certain melodies composed to cure the passions of the psyche, as well as ones for despondency and mental anguish. In addition to these medical aids there were other melodies for anger and aggression and for psychic disturbances."[186]

Is there empirical evidence to support this assertion on the healing power of sound?

One evidence is the discovery by Jeffrey Levin – a social epidemiologist at the Eastern Virginia School of Medicine – of more than 250 publications of experiments showing the mostly positive health benefits of religious and spiritual practices (ibid., 29). Since sound is a necessary part of many of these practices, its use contributes to obtaining of these benefits.

Researchers have also established more specific evidence of the healing effects of sound.

From his experiments on sound Jenny had speculated that every cell in the human body had its own rate of vibration and that a number of cells with the same vibratory rate could create a new frequency that was in harmony with the original (or, in other words, form a harmonic). Tissues and organs, comprised of many cells together, could simply be vibrating at different harmonics.

---

[186] *Sounds of Healing: A Physician Reveals the Therapeutic Power of Sound, Voice, Music,* 28.

Jenny subsequently became convinced that the body could be healed through sound.

An experiment performed by Fabien Maman, a French composer, acupuncturist and bioenergetician, appeared to verify Jenny's speculation that every cell had its own rate of vibration.

Fabien took a blood sample from a person's finger and then asked the person to sing the seven notes of the major scale to that sample of blood. Using Kirlian photography he noticed that, with each note, the cell's energy field changed its shape and color. When the person sang a 'F', the cells resonated perfectly with the voice, producing a balanced, round shape and vibrant colors of magenta and turquoise.

He remarked from this:

> The cells are completely bathed in light and alive with full resonance, clear evidence that this 'F' is the fundamental sound of the singer...Fundamental sound can be very helpful for the physical body through its harmonizing and regenerating effect at the cellular level.[187]

Other researchers have also remarked on the cells response to sound.

It is reported by the researcher Abduldaem Alkaheel that experiments have shown that:

---

[187] Maman Fabien, *The Role of Music in the Twenty-First Century*, 20.

- When certain words are spoken a cell becomes increasingly active by the appearance of an electromagnetic field around it.
- Sound has been observed to cause changes in the existing electromagnetic field of blood cells.[188]

Researchers have established that sound not only enters the human body through the ears but also through the skin and by bone conduction. Sound passes through the body and in the process the human tissues transduce pressure waves (sound waves) into electrical stimuli primarily by means of the pacinian corpuscles (a special type of mechanoreceptors). The frequency range in which the human tissue can transduce sound waves lie between 50 and 800 cycles per second while the human ear is sensitive to sound waves between 20 and 20,000 cycles per second.

Robert Gass describes an experience where he and his son were listening to Japanese Taiko drummers. He relates, "our bodies were instantly struck by a wall of vibration" from the sound of the massive drums. "We experimented with blocking our ears. Even without any sound entering our ears, we still had a full-body experience of the music, our ribs and sternum pulsing in time with the beats, every inch of our skin tingling rhythmically."[189]

In an experiment done by Jim Oliver to look at how the body responds to sound he reported, "We put the selected sounds exclusively into a pair of headphones and put them on a client's ankles. They responded to the sound even though the ears could

---

[188] Abduldaem Alkaheel, *The Qur'an's Healing Horizon*. http://www.scribd.com/doc/6172917/Healing-by-Quran-Eng, 18-20 (accessed April 12th 2010).
[189] *Chanting: Discovering Spirit in Sound*, 25.

not hear the sound. Once you vibrate a part of the body the blood cells carry this resonance to the whole body very quickly."[190]

In an experiment by Fabien the beneficial effect of this response is quite clearly illustrated. Together with Helene Grimal, a biologist, he experimented with healthy blood cells, hemoglobin, and the 'Hela' cancer cell from the uterus to see how they would respond to the voice and to various instruments.

Maman reports in his book *The Role of Music in the Twenty-First Century* that they were able to capture in their photographs the progressive destabilization of the structure of cancer cells when they were subjected to sounds that progressed up the musical scale.

Fabien recorded:

> The structure disorganized extremely quickly....*It appeared that the cancer cells were not able to support a progressive accumulation of vibratory frequencies.* As soon as I introduced the third frequency in the sequence, the cells began to destabilize.[191] (Emphasis mine).

> While *"the healthy cells appeared supple and able to freely receive, absorb and return the energy,"* he indicated, *"the cancer cells appeared inflexible and immutable in their structure.*[192] (Emphasis mine).

---

[190] From the CD *Harmonic Resonance.*
[191] *The Role of Music in the Twenty-First Century,* 61.
[192] Ibid., 90.

Gaynor states that sound can alter cellular functions, cause biological systems to function more homeostatically, induce calmness to the mind and thus to the body, and regulate the immune system due to its effect on the emotions.[193] Because of these and possibly other effects, application of sound to promote healing now appears to be more and more accepted by mainstream scientists and medical professionals. Sound therapies for treating diseases are also being offered.

Some examples of this are:

- To promote healing with cancer patients Dr. Mitchell Gaynor uses chanting and resonances from the sounds of Tibetan bowls (ibid., 190).
- Dr. David Simon, Medical Director of Neurological Services at Sharp Cabrillo Hospital in San Diego, California declares that music and chants have quantifiable physiologic effects. Chants, according to him, are metabolized in the body and act as healing agents and also as painkillers (ibid., 18).
- Mark Rider, Ph.D., a research psychologist, working in collaboration with Southern Methodist University, have established that music has a strong positive influence on the cells of the immune system thereby enabling greater immunity from disease and enhancing tissue regeneration. This conclusion is based on extensive studies on this effect (ibid).
- Dr. Jeffrey Thompson, a professor at California Institute for Human Science and director of the Center for Neuro-Acoustic Research, pursued pioneering studies on the physical effects of the Tibetan singing bowls and other

---

[193] *Sounds of Healing: A Physician Reveals the Therapeutic Power of Sound, Voice, Music*, 134.

sound frequencies and used his findings to develop treatments for various physical disorders and learning disabilities (ibid).
- Entrainment of brain waves by using specific frequencies by researcher Robert Monroe. According to him the brain "resonated when bombarded with pulsing sound waves." The frequencies used were from .5 Hz to 20 Hz.[194] He was also able to synchronize the left and right hemispheres with sound (ibid., 224).
- Cymatic therapy has been used to treat rheumatism, paralysis, muscle strain, arthritis, and bone fracture among other conditions.[195]

Gaynor notes the results of several experiments indicating the beneficial effect of sound in the form of music on the physical self.

These include (ibid., 80-82):

Reduction in heart and respiratory rates and anxiety level
- Forty patients who had a recent heart attack were treated to "relaxing music." Measurement of these three factors indicated that all three were statistically reduced.

Reduced cardiac complications
- Patients who had heart attacks and then were admitted to coronary care displayed fewer complications when they listened to music than those who didn't.

---

[194] Jonathan Goldman, "Sound entrainment" in *Music Phyician for times to come*, 223.
[195] *Sounds of Healing: A Physician Reveals the Therapeutic Power of Sound, Voice, Music*, 139.

Lower blood pressure
- o The blood pressure of a group of nine subjects who listened to music of a particular frequency range was reduced.

Increased immune cell messenger molecules
- o A 1993 study showed the number of these important molecules increased by 12.5 percent in patients who listened to their preferred types of music.

Reduced levels of stress hormones
- o A German study showed that, during the procedure known as gastroscopy, patients who listened to their types of music displayed significantly lower levels of the stress hormones cortisol and ACTH than others who didn't.

Boost of endorphins
- o In an experiment conducted at the Addiction Research Center in Stanford, California, half of the subjects exposed to music displayed increased levels of endorphins – the brain's natural painkillers.

He also notes the positive effect of music on pregnancy and childbirth and for the terminally ill.

The effect of music is summed up by the following statement by the anesthesiologist, Ralph Spring, M.D., a leading researcher on the use of music in medicine:

> Physiological parameters like heart rate, arterial blood pressure, salivation, skin humidity, blood levels of stress hormones...human growth hormones HGH, cortisol, betaendorphine, show a significant decrease under anxiolytic music, compared with usual pharmacological premedication. EEG studies demonstrated sleep induction through music in the preoperative phase. The

subjective responses of the patients are most positive in about 97 percent (of 59,000). These patients state that music is a real help to them to relax in the preoperative situation and during surgery in regional anesthesia (ibid., 83-84).

Don Campbell states in his book *The Mozart Effect* a quite exhaustive and eye-opening list of additional cases where music has been beneficial. These include: slowing down and equalizing of the brain waves; reduction in muscle tension and improvement in body movement and coordination; optimizing of body temperature; boosting of the immune system; improving perception of space and time; strengthening memory and learning; boosting workplace productivity; stimulating digestion; fostering stamina and endurance; generating a feeling of safety and well-being; treating abuse, acute pain, aggressive and antisocial behavior, AIDS, allergies, Alzheimer's disease, anxiety, arthritis, attention deficit disorder, autism, back pain, asthma, burns, cancer, cerebral palsy, chronic fatigue syndrome, colds, depression, diabetes, down's syndrome, epilepsy, grief, headaches, insomnia, learning disabilities, neuromuscular and skeletal disorders, overweight, Parkinson's disease, premature birth, rehabilitation, schizophrenia, stroke, substance abuse, tinnitus, tooth problems, trauma, and writer's block!![196]

The process of healing with sound
What is the process of healing with sound?

The generally held view is that healing with sound is based on the principles of resonance and sympathetic resonance. One other view is the re-programming of cells due to sound vibrations. This latter view is somewhat connected to the first in

---

[196] *The Mozart Effect*, 64-77, 220-283.

that re-programming of cells is facilitated by the harmony of the sound.

Resonance and sympathetic resonance
The basis of this lies with the understanding that everything in the universe is in a state of vibration. Fritjof Capra, the author of *The Tao of Physics* remarks:

> Rhythmic patterns appear throughout the universe, from the very small to the very large. Atoms are patterns of probability waves, molecules are vibrating structures, and living organisms manifest multiple, interdependent patterns of fluctuations. Plants, animals, and human beings undergo cycles of activity and rest, and all their physiological functions oscillate in rhythms of various periodicities (ibid., 49).

Jenny elaborates to some depth on this in *Cymatics*. He observes that everywhere in nature periodicity and rhythm is evident – in the cosmos, the vegetable kingdom, the biological processes, and even in organic structures. He states: "Since oscillations are omnipresent in Nature, we must expect to find periodic, rhythmic, and cyclic phenomena at virtually every step. We are necessarily surrounded by them every day and hour of our lives."[197]

These vibrations create sound waves of various frequencies. Each celestial body, in fact, each and every atom, produces a particular sound frequency on account of its movement, rhythm or vibration. This is known as its resonant frequency.

---

[197] *Cymatics*, 254.

This resonant frequency is dependent upon the composition of the object.

Now, according to the principle of sympathetic resonance a vibratory body or even an object that is seemingly passive "responds to external vibrations to which it has a harmonic likeness." This can be made clear by the example of two similar tuning forks. If one is mounted on a wooden box and the other one is then struck, placed on the box, and then muted, sound will be heard coming from the un-struck mounted tuning fork.[198]

Another example of this is "the rattling of window panes, light shades and movable panels in the presence of very loud sounds...As these things rattle (or even if they do not audibly rattle) sound energy is being converted into mechanical energy, and so the sound is absorbed...Absorptivity is at its highest at the resonance frequency..." (Ibid).

Sound healers believe that these laws of resonance and sympathetic resonance are also applicable to the human body. Every organ, bone, tissue and other parts of the body has a frequency at which it vibrates when it is in its natural healthy state. This is known as its resonant frequency.[199]

According to Sir Peter Manners, M.D., an English osteopath who developed a therapy called "cymatic therapy" based on Jenny's findings, disease results when there is "an interruption of an

---

[198] Wikipedia contributors, "Sympathetic resonance," *Wikipedia, The Free Encyclopedia*, http://en.wikipedia.org/wiki/Sympathetic_resonance (accessed Oct 7th 2010).
[199] S. G. Asnani Foundation, "Sound Therapy," http://www.sgafsoundtherapy.org/sound/sound_diabetes.html (accessed Oct 12th 2010).

organ's harmonious relationship."[200] In other words, when cells or organs for some reason stop vibrating at their resonant frequencies the body experiences ill health. This state will continue as long as the cells' frequencies are not tuned back to their original harmonious vibration. Sound healers assert that these cells can be brought back to their natural healthy state through the principle of sympathetic resonance if that cell's natural sound is played to it.[201]

Exposing the cells to managed dosages of sound can also make the cells become more able to resist viruses and diseases.[202]

The cymatic therapeutic method that Manners developed employs exposure of targeted parts of the body to managed dosage of sound. He believed that this creates a condition of chemical and homeostatic balance whereby the body heals itself. The cymatic instrument used in the therapy, he states, "adjusts acoustic audible sound frequencies in order to induce beneficial stimulation, activation, and circulation when applied to the body via direct contact with affected areas or by way of acupuncture meridians."[203]

In applying this concept of resonance to explain the explosion of cancerous cells, Fabian felt that the inability of the cancer cells to respond to the sound vibrations was due to the dissonance in

---

[200] *Sounds of Healing: A Physician Reveals the Therapeutic Power of Sound, Voice, Music,* 139.
[201] S. G. Asnani Foundation, "Sound Therapy," http://www.sgafsoundtherapy.org/sound/sound_diabetes.html (accessed Oct 12th 2010).
[202] *The Qur'an's Healing Horizon,* 15.
[203] *Sounds of Healing: A Physician Reveals the Therapeutic Power of Sound, Voice, Music,* 139.

frequencies between the particles within the cancerous cells and the frequency of the sound.

Re-programming of damaged cells
The researcher Abduldaem Alkaheel, who has spent several years investigating the use of Qur'anic verses to cure, argues that all illnesses actually result from one phenomenon. Each cell is programmed with a set of complex information to function in a certain way throughout its lifetime. However, when outside information enters the cell via a virus or other means then the programming of the cell is affected negatively or positively. When the program is damaged the result is illness, sickness or disease.[204]

According to him, when a virus attacks a cell it enters its own program into the cell causing the cell's program to be damaged. This results, in turn, in more of the program of the virus being copied. Subsequently more copies of the virus are made using the cell and its materials. These viruses then enter other healthy cells to repeat the same process (ibid., 27-28).

Alkaheel argues that damage to the cells can be corrected by re-programming them. This can be done by use of certain Qur'anic verses. This re-programming is achieved by (among other factors) (i) the effect of the perfect harmony of reciting the letters and words (ii) the effect of the balanced sound (iii) the power of the information carried inside the Qur'anic verses (ibid., 33-34).

Harmony
What is common among both of the above is the body's attraction to harmony since, by their very nature, according to Jenny, the cells in the body are musical. He states, "every human

---
[204] *The Qur'an's Healing Horizon*, 24.

molecule has a particular corresponding musical frequency. The masses of particles behave...among themselves as if they were musical notes."[205]

When cells vibrate in their natural state the body is in harmony. The contrary is thus also true.

When harmonious sounds are directed to the body it is receptive. This is evident by the feelings of peace experienced when hearing the sounds of nature – the birds chirping, the running brook, the crashing of the waves...

The Rosicrucians recognized this receptivity to harmonious sound. They teach that chants "start certain rates of vibrations in the room which harmonize with other vibrations of the universe and affect a certain condition connected with the aura."[206]

<u>Disease and healing from an energy perspective</u>
Healers explain that healing occurs due to accessing energy that exists in the universe. The terms "Universal Energy Field" and "Universal Energy" are commonly used in explaining how healing is achieved. What do these terms mean and how are they important?

In 1984 physicists John Schwartz and Michael Green introduced the "Superstring Theory" to explain the nature of the universe. This theory postulates that the basic entities of the universe or the most fundamental particles comprising it are one-dimensional objects similar to guitar strings in vibration. These superstrings are very subtle and are much smaller than atomic

---

[205] *Sounds of Healing: A Physician Reveals the Therapeutic Power of Sound, Voice, Music*, 137.
[206] H. Spencer Lewis, *Rosicrucian Manual* (AMORC, 1980), 203.

particles. They are in continuous motion and pervade the entire universe. They also have different frequencies of vibration.

The "Universal Energy Field" refers to the field of superstring particles pervading the universe.[207] Since these particles are in constant vibration, they produce a tremendous amount of energy. This energy is known as "Universal Energy."

Bedri Cetin, the author of *Universal Energy – A Systematic and Scientific Investigation* describes this Universal Energy Field aptly in the following manner:

> All there is, is the Universal Energy Field. There is nothing but the Universal Energy Field. Universal Energy Field is the most fundamental element that constitutes our Universe. All matter – stars, earth, plants, people etc., – are merely intensification of this field. Everything we see around us, including ourselves, is an expression – a manifestation of this One Field. Just as ice is made of water, everything that appears as "solid" around us including our bodies is in essence made of the Universal Energy Field. Different vibrations of this field are perceived by our senses as different forms of matter (ibid., 7).

According to Cetin, "solids", or, in fact, all matter, are produced by superstrings vibrating at a lower frequency. However, superstrings that vibrate at a higher frequency are regarded as very important. It is believed that these superstrings supply what Eastern philosophies and sound healers call "life-force" to

---

[207] Bedri C. Cetin, "Universal Energy – A Systematic and Scientific Investigation," 4, http://sapphirereiki.com/Downloads/universalenergy.pdf. (Accessed March 31st 2011).

human beings. These types of superstrings, Cetin declares, "have the power to cause any physical change and heal any disease" (ibid., 5). He states, in fact, that utilizing the higher vibrations in the Universal Energy Field can be the most efficient way to heal disease since the root cause of the disease is addressed.

As stated earlier, sound healers believe that the cause of disease is due to an organ not vibrating at its resonant frequency. Cetin points out that this is a result of the body's stress response. The tension placed on an organ due to prolonged stress depletes the "vital energy" of the part. When the energy then falls below a critical level, the organ can no longer vibrate at its optimum level resulting in disease (ibid., 19).

According to healers (and others), for the human form, the Universal Energy Field is manifested as the human energy system. Two key components of the human energy system are the "chakra" and the "aura."[208]

Chakras are "energy centers or openings through which the universal life energies" are "drawn into the body and flow through the entire body, including cells and tissues and organs." These centers interact with the glands producing hormones in the body. Each chakra has its own unique form and function, and its frequency of vibration. The frequencies of the different chakras produce different colors and sounds – thus there is a unique color and sound for each chakra. Importantly, "these sounds and colors are associated with different organs and functions of the body…" (Ibid).

---

[208] S. G. Asnani Foundation, "Sound Therapy," http://www.sgafsoundtherapy.org/sound/index.html (accessed Oct 12th 2010).

The aura, also known as the human energy field, "surrounds and interpenetrates the physical body." It "emits its own characteristic radiation." Energy from the Universal Energy Field flows into and out of it by means of the chakras.[209]

There are seven layers of this energy field. Each layer is related to a specific chakra and duplicates either the physical, mental, emotional, or spiritual components of the human being and also interacts with them (ibid., 43).

It is believed that this field is not only a reservoir of information about the entire human being but is also essential for life.

The first layer of the field extending about a quarter of an inch from the skin is known as the physical energy field. *It bears information on every cell and organ of the physical body.* It can be looked at as the blueprint of the physical being. The relationship between an organ and its corresponding imprint in this field is analogous to the behavior of gelatin – just as a gelatin mold shapes hot liquid gelatin, the physical energy field shapes the physical body.[210] In other words, this field exists "prior to" and "not" as "a result of, the physical body."[211]

The second energy field is a storehouse for the emotions. Energy forms reflecting brain activities are stored in the third layer. The fourth, fifth, sixth, and seventh energy fields are related to spirituality, higher consciousness, mature love, and sacredness respectively (ibid., 57).

---

[209] Barbara Brennan, *Hands of Light: A Guide to Healing Through the Human Energy Field*, 41.
[210] *How Prayer Heals*, 58.
[211] *Hands of Light*, 49.

All of the seven layers have their own unique frequency of radiation.

When the chakras are fully functional the universal energy flows freely through them and beneficially affects the physical body, mind, and emotions producing an overall feeling of good health and well-being. The colors in the aura are vibrant and the fields are complete and well defined.

When the channels through which this universal energy flows to the human are not fully functional the passage of this energy becomes constricted or even blocked. This is reflected in missing colors, discoloration, and imbalance in the aura. Disease is a manifestation of this condition in the physical body – thus disease is a result of the inability of the free flow of universal energy into the human body.[212] The restricted flow of universal energy causes specific organs or parts of the body to vibrate below their optimal frequencies.

Many factors can contribute to the chakras not functioning optimally and to defects in the aura. One dominant factor appears to be from stress. However, healers believe that mental issues such as wrong attitudes and beliefs, and spiritual factors such as undeveloped faith can also contribute (ibid).

Sound is one of the ways for remedying this situation. When a particular chakra is corrected, the aura reflects this change.

Effect of sound on water
Masaru Emoto, a Japanese scientist, performed experiments on examining the effects of sound on water by photographing water

---

[212] S. G. Asnani Foundation, "Sound Therapy," http://www.sgafsoundtherapy.org/sound/index.html (accessed Oct 12th 2010).

crystals. His experiments are published in the book series *Messages from Water*. He describes results where playing of classical music, folk songs, and prayer created beautiful geometric crystals in frozen water. Even phrases of thankfulness and love taped onto water containers apparently produced the same beautiful geometric crystals.

In one of his experiments a glass of water was placed on a picture of an elephant. When the water froze to form a crystal the shape of the elephant's trunk was clearly seen in it. A similar thing happened when the experiment was performed with a picture of a Japanese house with a triangularly shaped ceiling.[213]

In another of his experiments, Emoto taped the 99 Names of Allah unto a bottle of water and left the bottle for twenty-four hours and then photographed the crystal formed after the water was frozen. He states that unique and beautiful crystals formed.[214]

Emoto also investigated whether intention (which I would call focused thought) can affect water. In the experiment about 2,000 people located in Tokyo sent positive focused thoughts to water samples located in a room in California that was electromagnetically shielded. At the same time a similar set of water samples were place in a different location as controls. This was not made known to the participants in Tokyo. Crystals from the water samples from both locations were then blindly

---

[213] Lulwa Shalhoub, "Water at the Nano Level," Arab News. April 2008, http://archive.arabnews.com/?page=21&section=0&article=108787&d=15&m=4&y=2008 (accessed Jan 11th 2011).
[214] Masaru Emoto's Website, 29 December 2007, Questions from readers 28, http://www.masaru-emoto.net/english/ediary200712.html#1229 (accessed Jan 11th 2011).

identified and photographed. A group of 100 independent judges then blindly scored the images for aesthetic appeal.

The results showed that the samples that were subjected to intention produced the highest scores. (The statistical metric P was .001, which meant that there was only a .1% likelihood that images with the best appeal had nothing to do with the intentions of the participants in Tokyo).[215]

To confirm or disprove Emoto's findings on how water can be affected, a set of experiments were conducted by Lynne McTaggart, author of two bestselling books and an internationally recognized spokesperson on spirituality and Dr. Konstantin Korotkov of St. Petersburg State Technical University. Dr. Korotkov is the inventor of a technique known as the Gas Discharge Visualization that utilize photography, measurements of light intensity and computerized pattern recognition to capture the electronic glow from the fingertips. Information obtained is then used to determine the state of health of a person.

When used with liquids, this technique is used to examine the changes in the chemical and physical contents of liquids.

In the first experiment, 1,500 participants from many countries across the world were asked to send intentions of love to a sample of distilled water in a lab in St. Petersburg, Russia. The intent of the experiment was to measure the effect of this intention on the signals emitted from the water sample. The result of this experiment seemed to show that during the time

---

[215] Masaru Emoto et al, "Double-Blind Test of the Effects of Distant Intention on Water Crystal Formation," *Explore The Journal Of Science and Healing*, 2, no. 5, 408-411.

intention was sent, there was greater intensity of light emitted from the water and the area where light was emitted increased.[216] This result appeared to be duplicated in the second experiment where the participants were asked to send a more specific intention of "glow and glow" to the water sample.[217]

From these results Korotkov posits an interesting theory – that *charging water* (by intention of love, for example), not only affects the area where this water is located but could also *affect the person who drinks it*.

When we look at the traditions of Islam there is evidence that water, when "treated," can be used for treatment of certain maladies.

Ibn Taimiyya (R) relates in his fatwa the following:

> It is permissible for an ill or troubled person, that certain verses from the Qur'an are written with pure ink, then it is washed and given to the ill to drink. Ibn 'Abbas (Allah be pleased with him) is reported to have mentioned a certain *du'a* that should be written and placed close to the woman who is experiencing hard labor at the time of giving birth.
>
> Sayyidina Ali (R) says: This *du'a* should be written and tied to the arm of the woman. We have experienced that

---

[216] "The First Korotkov Water Experiment – November 30, 2007," http://www.theintentionexperiment.com/korotkov1 (accessed Jan 11th 2011).
[217] "The Second Korotkov Water Experiment, January 18, 2008," http://www.theintentionexperiment.com/the-second-korotkov-water-experiment-january-18-2008 (accessed Jan 11th 2011).

there is nothing more amazing than this. (Fatawa Ibn Taymiyya, 19/65).[218]

It is mentioned that a certain person was so stricken with leprosy that he was embarrassed sitting near anyone due to the offensive smell of his body. One day, however, he met a pious person and after complaining about his situation to him, that person recited a verse from the Qur'an over water and gave it to him to drink. The sick person related that in a few days he was cured of his condition![219]

Recently an interesting story has been recorded regarding the use of this type of water. A lady from Bombay came to visit Moulana Zakariya in Saharanpur. She told him that her husband drank alcohol and asked if he could recite some verses and blow on some water that she could give her husband to drink. Moulana Zakariya complied with her request. After a while he received a letter from her. It said:

> When my husband asked for a glass of water, I gave him the water that you had blown on. He drank the water and then asked, 'Where did you get this water from?' I was afraid to tell him the truth so I kept quiet. He said, 'I am asking because of its delicious taste.' I felt some courage and disclosed the truth. He said, 'from today I shall stop drinking. Just keep giving me this water.' By

---

[218] Quoted at Sunniforum.net. Web address is: http://sunniforum.net/showthread.php?t=103 (accessed Dec 1st 2010).
[219] *Remedies of the Quran*, http://www.scribd.com/doc/17621/Remedies-From-the-Holy-QurAn (accessed April 13th 2010).

the grace of Allah our home is now a peaceful, enjoyable house.[220]

Walter Weston also records in his book *How Prayer Heals* several cases of healing with "treated" water. One case dealt with an eighty-six year old woman, Gertrude, who suffered from calcium deposits (spurs) on her spine. This condition could not be treated by conventional medicine. Because of the great degree of pain Gertrude experienced when trying to walk, she was confined to a wheelchair.

Gertrude was given a prescription of drinking four times a day two ounces of water that had been charged with healing energy by Weston. According to Weston, this water was charged by him holding the glass pitcher in his hand for twenty minutes.

Four days after the treatment began, Weston received a phone call from her requesting that he come over to her house. He states: "She greeted me at the door in her finest dress. She had awakened that morning pain-free, gotten up, taken a shower, dressed, and fixed the family breakfast." [221]

In another case, Wanda, a thirteen-year old girl suffered daily for three years from Crohn's disease, which produced nausea, vomiting, dizziness, and abdominal pain. Weston had several sessions of healing with her. In addition he gave her to drink, on a daily basis, water that he had charged with healing energy. Marked improvement in her condition was observed. Each session gave her relief for about a week. This routine, says Weston, can keep her "system-free." On the effect of the

---

[220] Faraz Rabbani, "Effective Ta`wizes," SunniPath, July 05, 2005. http://qa.sunnipath.com/issue_view.asp?HD=1&ID=647&CATE=115 (accessed Dec 9th 2010).
[221] Walter Weston, *How Prayer Heals*, 146.

"treated" water he remarks: "The symptoms of Wanda's illness are alleviated by healer-charged water, just as insulin relieves the symptoms of diabetes" (ibid).

Some idea about the unique nature of "treated" water can perhaps be gained from a 1986 study by the Mobius Society. The infra-red absorption spectra of sealed vials of water that were "treated" by fourteen healers were compared to that of controls. The "treated" water displayed statistically significant different absorption spectra. This was attributed to the change in the chemical bonding between hydrogen and oxygen atoms in the water for the "treated" water (ibid., 67). The energy generated by the healers would have had to be the reason for this.

From the above it appears that the quality of water seems to be affected by reciting of Qur'anic verses, by focused intent, by being prayed on, among other factors. In administering to the ill person this special type of water healing is achieved or, in the case of a person with a bad habit, the ability to break free of that habit. If this is so, then it is a strong likelihood that the chanting of *dhikr* beneficially affects the water that resides in our bodies whether it is in the blood stream or in tissues. The frequencies of sound produced in chanting the *dhikr* charge the water and thus provide it with healing qualities. This healing reaches to the cells.

Weston posits that this healing occurs because of the frequency of the "treated" water. He indicates that the frequencies of charged water range from 7.8 to 8.0 Hz. This is the same as the frequency range emitted by healers (ibid., 128).

The healing affect of charged water would also be further enhanced if the water used is Zam Zam for in the Islamic tradition the water from the Zam Zam well is thought to be blessed. It possesses healing qualities.

Ibn Qayyim (R) is reported to have said:

> Myself and others tried seeking healing with Zam Zam water and saw wondrous things. I sought healing with it from a number of illnesses, and I was healed by the permission of Allah. I saw someone who nourished himself with it for a number of days, half a month or more, and he did not feel hunger; he performed *Tawaaf* along with the other people just as they did. And he told me that he consumed nothing but Zam Zam water for forty days and he had the strength to sleep with his wife, to fast and to perform *Tawaaf* numerous times.[222]

It is mentioned that Ibn Qutaibah (R) once asked a person how he became completely cured of paralysis. The person indicated he had read verses 22-24 of *Surah Al-Hashr* and verse 82 of *Surah Al-Isra* and then blew into Zam Zam water and then drank it.[223]

Recently, Dr. Knut Pfeiffer, a medical doctor and manager of the largest private medical center in Munich, Germany, was interviewed regarding experiments he performed investigating the effects of several factors on the energy field surrounding the fingertips. His experiments included examining the effect of

---

[222] Shawana A. Aziz, "The Blessings of Al-Masjid Al-Haram in Makkah" Islamic Subjects, January 2004,
http://www.aljazeerah.info/Islam/Islamic%20subjects/2004%20subjects/January/The%20Blessings%20of%20Al-Masjid%20Al-Haram%20in%20Makkah%20By%20Shawana%20A.%20Aziz.htm (accessed Dec 3rd 2010).
[223] *Remedies of the Quran,* http://www.scribd.com/doc/17621/Remedies-From-the-Holy-QurAn (accessed April 13th 2010).

cigarette smoking, drinking coffee, meditation, drinking water from Munich (this water is thought to be compositionally very pure), and drinking Zam Zam water.[224]

His results showed that cigarette smoking, drinking coffee and even drinking water from Munich, produced a breaking-down of the field. On the other hand, practicing meditation and drinking Zam Zam water produced a vibrant, complete energy field.

These results are of significance in several respects. *Dhikr* is considered to be meditation, as the next section of this book would describe. Hence, the results show that performing *dhikr* actually enhances the energy field. Secondly, the Zam Zam water used for the tests was brought all the way from Mecca to Munich, two geographical distinct regions. It was also more than 14 days old. However, regardless of the age of the water and the climatic differences between Mecca and Munich, it produced consistently the same results on all of 60 persons tested. This testifies to the true inherent universal curative power of the Zam Zam water.

In an experiment by Emoto using Zam Zam water, .1 cc of Zam Zam water was diluted with 100 cc of regular water. When the word *"Bismillah"* (in the Name of Allah) was recited to it in Arabic the drops of water formed into the shape of a beautiful double crystal.[225]

---

[224] Knut Pfeiffer, "Islam's Zamzam water positive effect on human cells," YouTube video, http://internalmedicinebooks.net/dr-knut-pfeiffer-islams-zamzam-water-positive-effect-on-human-cells.html (accessed Dec 9th 2010).
[225] Masaru Emoto's Website, 29 December 2007, Questions from readers 28, http://www.masaru- emoto.net/english/ediary200712.html#1229 (accessed Jan 11th 2011).

Is this effect somehow related to the advice of the Prophet (S.A.W) to recite the word *"Bismillah"* before eating and drinking? In other words does reciting this word make the food or drink wholesome and a means of healing for the body?

The healing effect of verses of the Qur'an

Is there any basis from the Qur'an and *hadith* that use of Qur'anic verses would create healing?

What actual evidence, if any, exists to support this?

The healing power of the Qur'an is mentioned in several verses of the Qur'an. These include:

Surah Yunus, verse 57, which reads:

يَا أَيُّهَا النَّاسُ قَدْ جَاءَتْكُم مَّوْعِظَةٌ مِّن رَّبِّكُمْ وَشِفَاءٌ لِّمَا فِي الصُّدُورِ وَهُدًى وَرَحْمَةٌ لِّلْمُؤْمِنِينَ

> O men! *There has come to you indeed an admonition from your Lord and a healing for what is in the breasts* and a guidance and a mercy for the believers.[226] (Emphasis mine).

Surah Isra, verse 82, which states:

وَنُنَزِّلُ مِنَ الْقُرْآنِ مَا هُوَ شِفَاءٌ وَرَحْمَةٌ لِّلْمُؤْمِنِينَ وَلاَ يَزِيدُ الظَّالِمِينَ إِلاَّ خَسَارًا

> And *We reveal of the Qur'an that which is a healing and a mercy to the believers* and it adds only to the perdition of

---

[226] Qur'an, 10:57.

the unjust.²²⁷ (Emphasis mine).

And *Surah Fussilat*, verse 44, which reads:

$$\text{وَلَوْ جَعَلْنَاهُ قُرْآنًا أَعْجَمِيًّا لَّقَالُوا لَوْلَا فُصِّلَتْ آيَاتُهُ أَأَعْجَمِيٌّ وَعَرَبِيٌّ هُوَ لِلَّذِينَ آمَنُوا هُدًى وَشِفَاءٌ وَالَّذِينَ لَا يُؤْمِنُونَ فِي آذَانِهِمْ وَقْرٌ وَهُوَ عَلَيْهِمْ عَمًى أُولَٰئِكَ يُنَادَوْنَ مِن مَّكَانٍ بَعِيدٍ}$$

> And if We had made it a Qur'an in a foreign tongue, they would certainly have said: Why have not its communications been made clear? What! A foreign (tongue) and an Arabian! Say: *It is to those who believe a guidance and a healing*; and (as for) those who do not believe, there is a heaviness in their ears and it is obscure to them; these shall be called to from a far-off place.²²⁸ (Emphasis mine).

Is the healing that is mentioned referring only to the effect on the soul and mind from understanding the meaning of the verses? Or does it also imply that there are curative powers in these verses for maladies that affect the physiological and psychological selves?

---

²²⁷ Qur'an, 17:82.
²²⁸ Qur'an, 41:44.

One evidence that there are curative powers within Qur'anic verses for maladies comes directly from this *hadith* of the Prophet (S.A.W).

Abu Said Al-Khudri (R) narrated:

> A group of the companions of Allah's Apostle proceeded on a journey till they dismounted near one of the Arab tribes and requested them to entertain them as their guests, but they (the tribe people) refused to entertain them. Then the chief of that tribe was bitten by a snake (or stung by a scorpion) and he was given all sorts of treatment, but all in vain.
>
> Some of them said, "Will you go to the group (those travelers) who have dismounted near you and see if one of them has something useful?"
>
> They came to them and said, "O the group! Our leader has been bitten by a snake (or stung by a scorpion) and we have treated him with everything but nothing has benefited him. Has anyone of you anything useful?"
>
> One of them replied, "Yes, by Allah, I know how to treat with a *Ruqya*. But, by Allah, we wanted you to receive us as your guests but you refused. I will not treat your patient with a *Ruqya* till you fix for us something as wages."
>
> Consequently they agreed to give those travelers a flock of sheep.
>
> The man went with them (the people of the tribe) and started spitting (on the bite) and reciting *Surat-al-Fatiha*

till the patient was healed and started walking as if he had not been sick.

When the tribe people paid them their wages they had agreed upon, some of them (the Prophet's companions) said, "Distribute (the sheep)." But the one who treated with the *Ruqya* said, "Do not do that till we go to Allah's Apostle and mention to him what has happened, and see what he will order us."

So they came to Allah's Apostle and mentioned the story to him and he said, "How do you know that *Surat-al-Fatiha* is a *Ruqya*? You have done the right thing. Divide (what you have got) and assign for me a share with you."[229]

From this it is apparent that the sound of the recitation of *Surah Fatiha* did something to the saliva so that it became a medium for counteracting the effect of the snakebite.

Exactly what happened to the saliva can be gleaned from the following statement of Inayat Khan. He asserts, "every syllable has a certain effect" and "therefore every sound made, or word spoken before an object, has charged that object with a certain magnetism." "By the power of sound," healers charge an object. "When that object is given, as water or as food, that object brings about a desired result."[230]

---

[229] Bukhari, vol. 7, book 71, no. 645.
[230] Inayat Khan, *The Sufi Message of Hazrat Inayat Khan/Music/The Manifestation of Sound on the Physical Sphere*, http://www.sufimessage.com/music/manifestation-of-sound.html (accessed Oct 12th 2010).

I would like to add to his statement by mentioning that all Qur'anic verses came directly from Allah, the Divine power that governs the whole universe. Hence, these verses should be pregnant with Divine power, reflective of their origin.

Ibrahim Syed, in his article "Spiritual Medicine in the History of Islamic Medicine" mentions that the book *Khawass al-Quran* (Miraculous Properties of the Qur'an) discusses the "miraculous powers" of virtually all verses of the Qur'an. This includes their ability to cure diseases.[231]

Mention is made about *Surah Saad* (Chapter 38). If someone is experiencing a problem in breathing it cures him of it if it is recited on him when he is sleeping. A sick patient is cured of his/her illness if this *Surah* is written down and read when the person is awake. Continuous recital of this chapter ensures that a person will have a trouble-free night (ibid).

Abduldaem Alkaheel, the Syrian researcher, states unequivocally that it is one hundred percent true that the Qur'anic verses heal. He states that Qur'anic verses cure all types of maladies including physical, psychological, effects of evil, envy, magic, and worry.[232]

Sheikh Muhammad Yaqoubi of Syria attests that in his lifetime he has witnessed hundreds of cases of people being cured by verses of the Qur'an. In his words he has seen "miracles

---

[231] Ibrahim Syed, "Spiritual Medicine in the History of Islamic Medicine," http://www.scribd.com/doc/3321827/islamic-medicine (accessed Feb 16th 2010).
[232] *The Qur'an's Healing Horizon*, 6.

happen." "We don't know the impact of the words of the Qur'an," he states.[233]

An e-book titled *Remedies of the Quran* lists many curative benefits of verses of the Qur'an. These include treatment of: paralysis, epilepsy, leprosy; bone fracture, disease of the spleen, kidney pain, headaches, migraine, poor eyesight, and inflammation of the eyes...[234]

The stories of a leper and a paralyzed man who were cured of their conditions by drinking water over which Qur'anic verses were recited have already been mentioned.

Recently I came across the website of an organization called "Hope To Heal." This organization offers free healing sessions for physical, psychological, and spiritual maladies to all persons irrespective of their religion, race, or national origin. Its methodology is based on the traditions of the Prophet Muhammad (S.A.W) and the Qur'an.

It claims to have successfully treated many types of illnesses including: "Cancer, Tumors, Hodgkin's disease, Diabetes, Blood Pressure, Migraine, Speech Problems, Infertility; social ills such as addiction to Crack, Cocaine, Marijuana, Alcohol or other substance abuses; Mental conditions such as Phobias, Schizophrenia, Bipolar Disorder, Severe Depression, and spiritually-linked conditions."

---

[233] Muhammad Al-Yaqoubi, *Remembering Allah* track 6. UK: Sacred Knowledge, 2009. CD-ROM.
[234] *Remedies of the Quran*, http://www.scribd.com/doc/17621/Remedies-From-the-Holy-QurAn (accessed April 13th 2010).

The healing sessions are available in Freemont and Sacramento, California and Surrey, Vancouver.[235]

It is quite likely that there is more of this type of organization appearing in North America.

In the documented cases of persons who were successfully healed there is one of a patient suffering from Hodgkin's Disease. This is a malignant growth of cells in the lymph node system. The report reads[236]:

> The patient was suffering from nausea and vomiting, a sore throat, stomach pain, sore mouth, and bone pain. Some of this nausea and vomiting may have been due to chemotherapy or radiation. The patient had some success with chemotherapy and radiation, and still continued the treatment during the course of *Ruqya* treatment. The patient had tumors in his underarm area.
>
> He received a continuous forty-one day treatment during which Qur'anic verses were recited and blown on the patient's underarms.
>
> The patient reported feeling energized after receiving these treatments. After approximately 10 days of *Ruqya* treatment the tumors had disappeared. When the patient appeared before the medical doctors, they were surprised at the disappearance of the tumors and had not expected the chemotherapy to be able to act so quickly.

---

[235] "Hope to Heal Counseling and Healing." Hopetoheal.Org. http://hopetoheal.org/ (accessed Jan 18th 2011).
[236] "Spiritual Healing in Islam," 14. Islamic Educational and Cultural Research Center. http://www.iecrcna.org/publications/Spiritual_Healing_Single.pdf (accessed Jan 18th 2011).

Currently the patient is fully cured.

Curing Of Black Magic, Envy And Cancer
Muhammad Abdullah Al-Ayed is well known in Saudi Arabia and the Gulf states for healing with the Qur'an. It is said that he has cured thousands of people over the past seven years who claim to be ill from black magic, envy or cancer.

His clientele comprise mostly of women who, due to sorcery or envy, are unable to find a spouse or suffer from cancer, miscarriage and infertility.

His clients also include people of various nationalities. Of these there was one person, an American, who was diagnosed with cancer. He, too, was healed. Al-Ayed says, "An American, who had been diagnosed with cancer, came to me to be healed and while unable to understand the words of the Qur'an, he responded to the reading and was healed. This is evidence that the Qur'an can heal Muslims and non-Muslims alike."[237]

Tranquility
Research on volunteers in the USA who were subjected to recitation from the Qur'an indicated that 97% of them displayed a reduction in tension from listening to the Qur'an. EEG recordings revealed that during the recitation the subjects were also experiencing a state of deep calmness. This was true even with subjects who did not know Arabic – the majority of subjects.[238]

---

[237] Jamal Abdul Khaliq, "Al-Ayed Explains Quran's Healing Powers," *arab news* http://archive.arabnews.com/?page=1&section=0&article=32939&d=3&m=10&y=2003 (accessed Oct 12th 2010).
[238] Sharif Kaf Al Ghazal, "Reflections on the Medical Miracles of the Holy Quran," *Islamic Medicine On Line*,

Sound Therapy

Today companies and organizations are developing and offering sound therapy for a variety of ailments. For example, one company, S.G. Asnani Foundation, offers sound for treatment of major diseases like diabetes, cancer, and AIDS.[239] Another company uses Cymatics, or Bioresonance, therapy that was developed by Manners to use sound to transform diseased tissue back to its healthy state.[240] Snoezelen is a sound therapy targeted for patients suffering from Alzheimer's.[241]

Music is also another therapy that has now become popularly adapted. A new branch of sound therapy, called Music Thanatology, has evolved that seeks to ease the emotional and physical suffering of terminally-ill patients through soothing sounds at specific frequencies.

The acceptance of music as a therapy is as a result of studies in recent times showing music can reduce pain and ease anxiety during surgical procedures. These studies include: (i) Doctors in the Bethesda Naval Medical Center in Maryland, USA, discovering that men who listened to music during sigmoidoscopies feeling more relaxed during this uncomfortable procedure[242] (ii) Results of a Meta analysis showing music

---

http://www.islamicmedicine.org/medmiraclesofquran/medmiracleseng.htm (accessed Oct 12th 2010).

[239] S. G. Asnani Foundation, "Sound Therapy," http://www.sgafsoundtherapy.org/sound/index.html (accessed Oct 12th 2010).

[240] See the website: http://www.jilaensherwood.com/cymatics.html for some details (accessed Oct 12th 2010).

[241] See the weblink: http://www.altmd.com/Articles/Sound-Therapy--Encyclopedia-of-Alternative-Medicine for details (accessed April 13th 2010).

[242] Kerry C. Palakanis et al., "Effect of music therapy on state anxiety in patients undergoing flexible sigmoidoscopy," *Diseases of the Colon & Rectum* 37, no. 5: 478-481,

beneficially affected patients' experience with colonoscopy[243] (iii) Music producing a more satisfactory experience in elderly patients undergoing cataract surgery.[244]

I would like to mention here an interesting observation. Music Thanatology calls to mind the Muslims' practice of reading the *Surah Yasin* for those who are very ill. It has been witnessed on at least ten occasions (by this writer and others) that the recitation of this *Surah* eases the pain of death and facilitates a quicker transition into the next world. Some patients have passed away within a few hours of the recitation of this *Surah*. Others have passed away within several days. Can this practice be of benefit to terminally-ill non-Muslims also? Can this be an area where greater humanity can be benefitted? This needs further research.

One example of the efficaciousness of reading *Surah Yasin* is with a Muslim cancer patient who was the maternal aunt of this writer. Before the reading was performed, she had displayed no signs of consciousness for several weeks. There was great concern that if she continued to remain unconscious there would be further complications such as collapsing of the ribs. Family

---

http://www.springerlink.com/content/g2ru65w235t4v230/ (accessed May 4th 2011).

[243] Matthew L. Bechtold et al., "Effect of Music on Patients Undergoing Colonoscopy: A Meta-Analysis of Randomized Controlled Trials," *Digestive Diseases and Sciences* 54, no. 1: 19-24, http://www.springerlink.com/content/m678364870x0q108/ (accessed May 4th 2011).

[244] Charles J. Cruise et al., "Music increases satisfaction in elderly outpatients undergoing cataract surgery," *Canadian Journal of Anesthesia* 44, no. 1: 43-48, http://www.springerlink.com/content/lx6226654587m221/ (accessed May 4th 2011).

members recited the *Surah* around the hospital bed on a Friday. She died the very next day.

This *Surah* is also believed to quicken recovery from illness. Two cases of this occurring have been relayed to this writer. In one case a patient became paralyzed on the whole one side of the body from the head to the feet. *Surah Yasin* was recited to this person three times a week. After about two months the patient was able to ride public transportation – displaying a remarkable recovery!

Mantra and *dhikr*

The previous section mentions the treatment of disease by using specific sound frequencies.

What role does *dhikr* play, if any, in healing? Can the healing frequencies that scientists are seeking be found in the various *dhikr*? What really occurs when *dhikr* is recited?

To explore these questions we first have to look at what yogis and researchers have said about mantras and examine the relationship between mantras and *dhikr*.

What is a mantra?

Mantra is a Sanskrit word that literally means, "to save the mind from suffering and illness."[245] This can also be understood to mean, "that which protects the mind" or "that which protects the mind from negativity."[246]

It is, essentially, pure sound energy.

A point of interest here is that the yogis regard mantras as the repetition of the Names of God.[247] In the yogic tradition these mantras were believed to have been revealed from God to minds that were in an attuned state of higher consciousness.

---

[245] International Academy for Traditional Tibetan Medicine – Faculty of Mantra Healing, http://www.iattm.net/uk/faculties/mh-welcome.htm (accessed Oct 12th 2010).
[246] Sogyal Rinpoche, *The Tibetan book of living and dying*, 71.
[247] H. H. Krishnanandaji Maharaj, "Mantra Shakti," *Fruits From the Garden of Wisdom* chapter 7, http://www.swami-krishnananda.org/fruit/fruit_07.html. Ebook.

It is evident from the above that dhikr, which in the Islamic tradition is the chanting of the Names of God, is also defined as being mantra by other traditions.

The Names of God in Islam are found in the Qu'ran that was revealed to the Prophet Muhammad (S.A.W) from God via the angel Gabriel. Muslims are urged by God to invoke Him by those names.

This fact that *dhikr* and mantra appear to be similar has been acknowledged by Sogyal Rinpoche, a representative of Tibetan Buddhism, and Inayat Khan, a representative of the Islamic spiritual practice known as Sufism, among others.[248]

This similarity of *dhikr* and mantra is mentioned so that the reader can gain a greater appreciation of the value of *dhikr* by deductive reasoning. Essentially what this is saying is that if repeating mantra produces certain benefits and effects, chanting of *dhikr* should also produce similar or even greater beneficial results. The reader would also gain from research undertaken on mantra. Ultimately the intent is to convey as much useful information as possible to help the reader gain greater insight and awareness on the value of *dhikr*.

Dhikr is like a precious gem hidden in a heap of mud, undervalued and under appreciated. May the great value of reciting it be brought to light.

---

[248] *The Tibetan Book of Living and Dying,* 71; also see Inayat Khan, in *The Sufi Message of Hazrat Inayat Khan/Music/The Manifestation of Sound on the Physical Sphere,*
http://www.sufimessage.com/music/manifestation-of-sound.html (accessed Oct 12th 2010).

The potency of Mantras and *Dhikr*
In his book *The Tibetan book of living and dying*, Sogyal Rinpoche describes mantra as "the essence of sound" and that it is an "embodiment of truth in the form of sound." According to him, *"Each syllable is impregnated with spiritual power"* and *"condenses spiritual truth."*[249]

It is said that in ancient India mantras, if recited in a certain manner, would produce extraordinary results such as changing the weather and even materializing palaces. They also have been used to produce weapons, like the brahmashtra, which is thought to be equivalent to today's nuclear bombs. Certain mantras, when recited on arrows, would cause powerful explosions when the arrows reached their targets. Mantras have also been used to raise consciousness to a higher level or to attain spiritual enlightenment.

Recitation of one mantra in particular, namely the Gayatri, is said to have very potent effects. Arthur Koestler, the Hungarian author who visited and lived in India in the 1950s is reported to have said, "the Gayatri mantra is like an antidote to the nuclear holocaust… this powerful mantra can act as a great shelter to India. If millions of people recite the mantra at the same time, the collective consciousness can act as a septic guard for them."[250]

Swami Krishnanandaji Maharaj, speaking of the potency of mantras in the ebook *Fruits From the Garden of Wisdom*, compares the effect of a mantra to that of chemical reaction on the body.

---

[249] *The Tibetan book of living and dying*, 71.
[250] Quoted in article "Hardwar Institute Tracks Power of Gayatri Yagna" by Archana Dongre. *Hinduism Today*, Sept 1992. http://www.hinduismtoday.com/modules/smartsection/item.php?itemid=960 (accessed Jan 25th 2011).

"Sometimes the chemical reaction is such that it can produce a tremendous effect. Mantras produce such effect, similar to the reaction of chemical elements, because of the peculiar combination of letters," the Swami states.[251]

The Swami further explains that "sounds are really energy manifest" and thus "every letter of the alphabet is a condensed form of energy." When a packet of energy in the form of a letter of the alphabet comes in contact with another letter which is another packet of energy, "they collide with each other, act upon each other, or fuse into each other." Thus the utterance of a group of letters, or mantra, "produces by the process of permutation and combination of these letters, a new form of energy which gets infused into our system." Hence "because it has arisen from our own mind, thought and the recesses of our being, *we get charged with that force, as if we have touched a live electric wire*" (ibid).

This effect, says the Swami, occurs even without one contemplating the actual meaning hidden behind a mantra.

He indicates that because words are forces and not merely empty sounds "they are powers by themselves." This is the reason, he observes, that "the words of saints take immediate effect" and that these words *"are forces that are released like atom bombs"* which *"can manifest themselves in the physical world, and events can take place"* (ibid).

The Swami further says that one will be able to clearly see how reciting of mantra transforms one into a different person. In addition to this transformation of oneself, the Swami asserts, the chanting of mantra also produces a profound effect on the

---

[251] *Fruits From the Garden of Wisdom*, chap. 7.

society. He states, *"it would not be an exaggeration if I say that you will be doing the greatest service to mankind"* with that practice. With intense devotion to it *"you will see wonders, miracles manifesting themselves"* (ibid).

According to him, *an aura is produced around the sincere practitioner of mantra that causes the surrounding atmosphere to become purified.* "Things will take shape without your knowing what happens. The atmosphere will slowly change," says the Swami.

This effect, according to him, is not due to the individual's personal strength or thought but rather by that which the mantra is able to "rouse into activity and which is omniscient."

"God's name is a wonder. It is a miracle by itself" the Swami declares, and so the invocations made *"are converted into an impersonal force, which is the power of God, and the miracle is worked by God Himself"* so that the action appears not to be done by oneself but rather by God himself (ibid).

In the Islamic tradition the Sufis incorporate *dhikr* into a practice called *"wazifa." Wazifa* is commonly used to describe an exercise of focusing the attention, by means of recitation of, and/or meditation on, a particular Divine Name or Attribute in order to enable more powerful expression of that quality in one's day-to-day life.

Wazifa, the Sufis claim, has "the powerful capability to *transform one's self, circumstances, or even the chemistry of things.*" According to them "each single sound which is uttered from the mouth has shape, form, and magnetic field." The magnetic field is controlled by intention of the mind. The words of *dhikr* however, are also very important for they "have their own divine forces" most of which are unknown to mankind.[252]

When chanted to a prescribed number of times, these *wazifas* "create specific fields which are stronger than the object's or person's own magnetic field…" When some *wazifas* are chanted, the fields created are "so intense" the "required goal is achieved almost instantly." For other *wazifas*, the effects may take some time to be manifested (ibid).

Since intention plays such a crucial role in the effect of *wazifas*, the Sufis believe that the purer and stronger the intention, the quicker and greater is the effect achieved. Thus someone who has achieved some level of spiritual maturity (a saint in Sufi terminology) can produce an effect a million times stronger than that of a layperson. However, a person in desperate circumstances such as being close to the point of death who performs the *wazifa* can also produce a stronger effect (ibid).

The Sufis warn that the effect of some *wazifas* are so extremely powerful that one needs to be properly grounded and have permission before performance of these particular *wazifas* – otherwise, they pronounce, "the results could be catastrophic" (ibid).

Mantra/*Dhikr* And Healing
Chants, currently, are being employed to facilitate healing. Gaynor uses them to help cancer patients' recovery. They are also used as painkillers among other applications.[253]

---

[252] "Scientific Definition of Wazifa (Sacred Spells)." YouTube video. http://www.youtube.com/watch?v=5Ee-SYjq5Do (accessed Jan 18th 2011).
[253] *Sounds of Healing: A Physician Reveals the Therapeutic Power of Sound, Voice, Music*, 18 & 190.

What role does chanting (and thus *dhikr*) play in the healing process?

The following statement by Robert Gass captures a glimpse into why chants are being used for this purpose:

> Our breathing is fundamental to the way we feel in our body and the repetitive nature of chanting induces us to breathe deeper, slower, and more rhythmically. The sound vibrations caused by making vocal sounds resonate throughout our bodies – as though we were being massaged from the inside out. Our brain-wave patterns are measurably altered, evoking states of relaxation, or heightened creative energy. Our muscle tension relaxes and skin temperature changes; our blood pressure and heart rate go down. A regular practice of chanting can elicit the relaxation response. Reduce stress, sharpen mental clarity, open and expand all of our senses and help support our overall health and wellness.[254]

According to an article in the Washington Times, Sister Ruth Stanley, the head of the complementary medicine program at the Central Minnesota Heart Center at St. Cloud Hospital, has had great success using chants to help with pain and other ailments. She is convinced particularly about the health benefits of one kind of chant known as the Gregorian. "The body can move into a deeper level of its own inherent, innate healing ability when you play chant," she says. "About 85 percent of the time, the body goes into very deep healing modes. It's quite remarkable."[255]

---

[254] *Chanting: Discovering Spirit in Sound*, 12.
[255] "Chant: A healing art?" *The Washington Times* June 25, 2008, http://www.washingtontimes.com/news/2008/jun/25/chant-a-healing-art/ (accessed Oct 12th 2010).

It is believed that mantras, which are specific types of chants, enable freedom from suffering by breaking through the barriers of the mind thus liberating the self from the bondage of the phenomenal world. This is the spiritual benefit of mantra.

The yogis believe that in addition to the spiritual benefit, the energy contained in the syllables of mantra can be a means of healing also to the physical and psychological bodies. This is because the different mantras vibrate at different wavelengths. Thus a specific mantra affects a specific part of one's being – the cells, body, or mind by accessing and manipulation of very specific subtle energies.

Utilizing these effects of sound is similar to what the Rosicrucians advocate. In their teachings vowel intonations are used to stimulate psychic centers in the human being. This serves two purposes – one, health is maintained and secondly, "the consciousness of the cells," which is associated with spiritual growth, is raised.[256]

Physical healing
In regards to the physical it is thought that one of the reasons for ill-health or disease is due to an imbalance in the cell's vibration rate or frequency of vibration. This is similar to the reason stated by sound healers. The yogis believe that recitation of a mantra can return cells to a healthy state of balance thus facilitating healing.

Tibetan medicine considers the presence of disease as an indicator that there is a disturbance in the underlying subtle

---

[256] Melanie Braun, "Exploring the Efficacy of Vowel Intonations" *The Rose+Croix Journal* 2, 2005.
http://www.rosecroixjournal.org/issues/2005/articles/vol2_11_21_braun.pdf (accessed Oct 12th 2010).

energy flowing through the body. In healing with mantra sound energy is used to correct this underlying disturbance. It is believed that this method of disease treatment is more holistic than that of western medicine since the root cause of the disease as well as perpetuating factors are addressed rather than simple treatment of the symptoms.[257]

In Tibetan medicine there are hundreds of mantras that are used for healing. Some are used for specific problems such as: Diarrhea, Vomiting, Constipation, Viruses, Influenza, Infection, Pimples, Broken Bones, Childbirth, and Bleeding from an open wound.

Others are used for treating more general conditions such as disorders of Solid Organs such as the Heart, Lungs, Liver, Spleen, and Kidneys; disorders of Hollow Organs such as the Gall Bladder, Stomach or Colon; disorders of the Senses such as Sight and Hearing; or to alleviate pain.

The three humors, Wind, Bile and Phlegm, are considered the three vital energies of the human body, according to the Tibetan medicinal teachings. Disease occurs when these humors are imbalanced. Certain mantras are employed to re-balance these humors.

There are also mantras in the Tibetan tradition that are used for treatment of all sorts of diseases including complex illnesses or even for illnesses the causes of which are unknown (ibid).

Now, specific to *dhikr*, is there information on its health benefits?

---

[257] International Academy for Traditional Tibetan Medicine – Faculty of Mantra Healing, http://www.iattm.net/uk/faculties/mh-welcome.htm (accessed Oct 13th 2010).

Firstly, one can logically conclude that since *dhikr* and mantra appear to be similar, chanting of *dhikr* should also produce the same therapeutic benefits as that for mantra.

However, **there appears to be a dearth of clinical experiments exploring the beneficial health benefits of** *dhikr*. Much research is therefore needed in this area. It is this author's belief that there is great potential value to humanity in undertaking this research.

Much of the information that is available on the benefits of *dhikr* appears to be only attainable from the Sufis. They state that the four elements: fire, air, earth, and water pervade the human body. However, the nature and character of these elements are different from their literal meanings. For instance 'water' implies liquidity, and 'fire' refers to glow or heat, dryness, radiance, or all that is living.[258]

When these elements are in balance, the body is healthy. Importantly, *all diseases and disabilities, physical or spiritual, result when there is an excess or deficiency of any one of these elements.*

These elements are related to certain organs of the body as follows:

Air – associated with the liver. It is also regarded as a hot and moist element.

Fire – associated with the spleen. It is regarded as the hot and dry element.

---

[258] Inayat Khan, *The Sufi Message of Hazrat Inayat Khan/Music/The Mystery of Color and Sound*, http://www.sufimessage.com/music/mystery-of-color-sound01.html (accessed May 25th 2011).

Earth – associated with the gall bladder. It is regarded as the cold and dry element.

Water – associated with the lungs and brain. It is regarded as the cold and moist element.

Earth and water are regarded as heavy elements that are strong, negative, passive, and female.

Fire and air are regarded as light elements that are weak, positive, active, and male.[259]

The Sufis state that each of the Names of Allah also corresponds to one of these elements thus chanting of a specific name would have a beneficial effect on associated parts of the body.

The Sufis also subscribe to the belief of the existence of cosmic energy that pervades the universe. According to them it is this spiritual energy that "is behind the life of every drop of blood in animate beings, the motion behind every living cell, and the driving force of constellations and galaxies." Without its influence "nothing can grow or live in the entire universe." It is this energy that sustains the growth of grass, trees, and vegetation and also the force that nourishes the soul and the spirit.

Now, as relates to the human body, it is also this energy that is the driving force behind all the body's activities and processes. It maintains the effective functioning of all organs, blood vessels

---

[259] Muhammad Sajad Ali, "Sufi Introduction to the 99 attributes of Names of Allah and especially that of Ya Latif," 9, http://www.docstoc.com/docs/22976421/Beautiful-Names-of-Allah-as-mentioned-the- Qur%60an-and-Hadith (accessed Oct 13th 2010).

and other body parts. When there is depletion of this energy "the anatomic relations of the body's organs are altered and disrupted, which leads to pain, organ dysfunction and an overall deterioration of health."[260]

In the human body there are certain points that obtain the maximum of this cosmic energy. These are known in Sufi terminology as *"lata'if."* These points also maintain the proper balance of the energies within the body.

Similar to the belief of healers, the Sufis indicate that, normally, when the human body is healthy, the *lata'if* operate in harmony harnessing the cosmic energy and distributing it to the various parts of the body. When the body is diseased, however, this harmony is broken and the flow of energy is affected.

In Sufism, spiritual healing is viewed as being similar to harnessing the energy generated from a waterfall. The cosmic spiritual energy is harnessed and channeled to produce healing effects to the human body. This process is described as having three phases. In the first phase the cosmic energy is harnessed and channeled to the cerebral cortex of the brain. Focusing of this energy then stimulates the vagus nerve that transmits this energy to the heart thereby strengthening it and relieving it of cardiac-related diseases. In the third phase this energy is then pumped out of the heart and distributed to the entire body via the blood. In this way every cell receives the healing spiritual energy.

---

[260] Hisham Muhammad Kabbani, "Spiritual Healing in the Sufi Tradition," http://www.nurmuhammad.com/Meditation/EnergyHealing/harvardhealinglecture.htm (accessed Oct 13th 2010).

In the Sufi healing technique, dependent on the type of disease, a certain *dhikr* is employed by the healer to activate a particular *lateefa* (singular of *lata'if*). This activation, in turn, enables cosmic energy of the same frequency to be accessed. This results in the healer becoming the recipient of huge amounts of this cosmic energy. (According to the Sufis, recitation of the holy Names of Allah in this way is like generating "energy sparks which ignite more flow from the universal energy source.") (Ibid).

In a way similar to the use of a laser to send focused beams of light, the healer then directs this energy onto the patient. The patient, in turn, is asked to repeat certain *dhikr* formulas several thousand times during the day while in a relaxed state of mind.

Repetition of the above process for several days or even for weeks facilitates recovery of the patient from the disease.

The Sufis also indicate that when a heart is spiritually dead this manifests in physical, psychological, and spiritual diseases. The key to awakening the heart is *dhikr*.

There is some mention of the effects of the frequencies generated when *dhikr* is performed in an article titled "The Cosmic Code Of Man: The Genetic Vibrations of Allah." found on the website Moors Gate.

In the article the beneficial effect of *dhikr* on the immune system is acknowledged by the following statement, "...this science of intoning the divine Names of Allah...increases the production of infection-fighting cells by generating frequencies that directly destroy invading bacteria."[261]

---

[261] Zothyrius Ali El, "The Cosmic Code Of Man: The Genetic Vibrations of Allah," *Moors Gate,*

Mantra, Dhikr And Mental Healing
In a global study of the burden of disease done by the World Health Organization for the years 2000 – 2002 it was found that mental disorders such as depression, bipolar disorder, schizophrenia, and alcohol use disorder were among the 20 leading causes of disability. Mental disorders contributing to disability were found to be more common to age groups spanning across a wide band (from 0 – 59 years).[262] For adults 15 years and older, neuropsychiatric conditions accounted for one third of the Years Lost due to Disability (YLD). (Ibid., 36).

Of particular worry is the prevalence of unipolar depressive disorders. For high-income countries, this contributed to 14.6% of YLD. For low and medium countries 10.4% of YLD was a result of these disorders (ibid., 37). Ominously, the WHO predicts that by year 2030, unipolar depressive disorders would be the number one contributor to the number of healthy years lost due to being in a state of poor health or disability (ibid., 51).

Using *dhikr* (including Qur'anic verses), patients with different types of mental illnesses including schizophrenia, bi-polar disorder, and depression and also drug abusers have been treated. Those following their prescribed regime have been completely cured within a year.[263]

A research for curing mental diseases was conducted in the Psychiatry Hospital, Shahar Taif, Saudi Arabia by a group of

---

http://www.moorsgate.com/2007/06/24/ (accessed Oct 14th 2010).
[262] World Health Organization, "The Global Burden of Disease 2004 Update," http://www.who.int/healthinfo/global_burden_disease/GBD_report_2004updat e_full.pdf (accessed Jan 4th 2011).
[263] MujahidAbdullah, thread "Re:Mental Illness in Islam" posted on 15-10-2009 01:49 AM. http://www.sunniforum.com/forum/showthread.php?50973-Mental-illness-in-Islam

investigators headed by Dr. Mubarik Gilani. Gilani had developed a healing methodology called El Gilani Methodology (EGM) that was gaining increasing recognition in Pakistan.

All experiments were performed in the presence of other psychiatrists from other countries, tests were done under controlled conditions, and results were carefully analyzed.

The results showed that *thirty-nine patients suffering from various types of mental diseases were cured. These included: epilepsy, schizophrenia, psychosis, neurosis, depressive states, insomnia, night terrors, and chronic joint pain with edema.*[264]

One case was of Mohammad Ashram, 48 years old who suffered from schizophrenia since the age of ten. Mohammad's brother states that he, Mohammad, "got frightened at the age of ten when going to his farm from his house at midnight, developed high fever the following day and afterwards became insane. He started preaching to people, considering himself a person to fulfill a divine mission. He carried tree branches and said these were his flags."

After two months of treatment, Mohammad was completely cured of all his symptoms. No relapses have occurred even after five months.[265]

Another case dealt with a 55 year-old Princess of Saudi Arabia who suffered from chronic depression, rheumatic pains,

---

[264] Jemille Wasi, "Dr. Jemille's Introduction to Qur'anic Psychiatry : The El Gilani Methodology," *The Islamic Post*, Aug 18th 2008, http://islamicpost.wordpress.com/tag/quranic-psychiatry (accessed Oct 12th 2010).
[265] Mubarak Ali Gilani, "Pillar of Lies" http://www.iqou-moa.org/sheikh_jilani/pillar_of_lies1.htm (accessed Jan 4th 2011).

sleeplessness, tightness of the chest, and fatigue. She had been previously treated using drug therapy in Europe unsuccessfully.

Mubarak Ali Gilani, the person treating her relates: "I treated the patient for one hour upon her admittance, and again the following day. After her first treatment the pains lessened, sleep was improved and she admitted that there was a general feeling of relief and lightness. The patient was treated for three days, consecutively, and after the third sitting her complaints, which had been persisting for the last five years, vanished" (ibid).

The third case stated here is that of Ahmad Salmee, a 27-year-old soldier. Dr. Munir Jaber, of the Institute of Qur'anic Psychiatry at the Psychiatric Hospital at Taif, Saudi Arabia records in his scientific report that Ahmad "suffered from a peculiar problem; from the moment he closed his eyes, he would see a horrifying snake. He would try to run away from it, but was frightened. Due to this, he did not sleep and was going crazy."

Mubarak Ali Gilani, who was assigned to treat Ahmad, remarks that the only remedy that had been offered, was that, since the snake represented the reproductive organs according to Freudian thinking, the patient was encouraged to indulge in adultery.

The patient had also undergone electric shock treatment and had been on tranquilizers for two years.

Gilani states that Ahmad was made to recite *dhikr* and also to visualize the name "Allah" for one month. When "Allah" could clearly be visualized, Ahmad was then told to close his eyes and project that Name onto the image of the snake. When this was done, it is stated, "the snake virtually exploded, and he was healed." Ahmad was also asked to seek Allah's forgiveness.[266]

Dhikr has also been employed in the correctional facilities in New York for rehabilitating inmates suffering from mental health illnesses and also substance abuse issues. It is believed that the healing therapy of *dhikr* was partly responsible for the successful recovery of possibly thousands of inmates in the 1990's.[267]

It is believed that mental illnesses can also be cured by use of mantra. Specific mantras have been stipulated for curing various diseases including restlessness and fear, anxiety, depression, insomnia, nightmares, addiction, thoughts of harming oneself and others, and schizophrenia.[268]

A randomized controlled study was performed on the effect of repeating mantra by HIV patients. Results were published in the Journal of Behavioral Medicine and also online in July 2006.

The study measured the effect of mantra on psychological distress such as stress, anxiety, anger, and depression, quality of life enjoyment and satisfaction, and spiritual well being. In the test 46 patients were randomly selected to practice mantra. There were also 47 patients in a control group.

---

[266] Lorna Swaine-Abdallah, "Aids is curable," *The Islamic Post*. Jan 2, 2009. http://islamicpost.wordpress.com/2009/01/02/aids-is-curable/ (accessed Jan 4th 2011).
[267] Wikipedia contributors, "Dhikr," *Wikipedia, The Free Encyclopedia*, http://en.wikipedia.org/wiki/Dhikr (accessed Jan 3rd 2011).
[268] "Vedic mantra for all type of diseases-Cure life long diseases with Vedic mantra-Use Mantra for protection of oneself" *India Scanner*. Posted June 19th 2010, http://indiascanner.com/vedic-mantra-for-all-type-of-diseases-cure-life-long-diseases-with-vedic-mantra-use-mantra-for-protection-of-oneself-3528 (accessed Jan 4th 2011).

The results showed that, over time, the group practicing mantra displayed greater control over anger than the control group and displayed increased faith and spiritual connectedness. Practice of mantra appeared to positively benefit quality of life, spiritual well being, and psychological distress.[269]

How does *dhikr* or mantra help to cure mental illnesses?

Robert Gass asserts that chanting helps in releasing stress, creates peace within ourselves and in the outside world and also connects us with God.

These effects are not unrelated to each other. The Qur'an has mentioned, "Those who believe and whose hearts are set at rest by the remembrance of Allah; now surely by Allah's remembrance are the hearts set at rest."[270] This means that when *dhikr* is performed a connection is made with Allah. This connection produces tranquility to the heart and thereby reduces feelings of stress. A reduction of stress subsequently relieves one of several psychological maladies such as anxiety, fear, depression, and worry.

Moulana Zakariya aptly refers to this when he says that with the performance of *dhikr* a person is relieved from "troubles, worries, and fears, and is blessed with peace of mind."[271]

---

[269] Jill E. Borman et al., "Effects of Spiritual Mantram Repetition on HIV Outcomes: A Randomized Controlled Trial," *Journal of Behavioral Medicine* 29, no. 4, http://www.springerlink.com/content/e1pn576111862603/ (accessed Oct 12th 2010).
[270] Qur'an, 13:28.
[271] *Faza'il-e-A'maal*, "Virtues of Zikr," 76.

Ian Prattis, Professor of Anthropology at Carleton University in Ottawa, Canada, seems to imply that both the mind and spirit are benefitted when mantra is chanted by the fact that this produces greater integration and interconnection among the different levels of our beings and enhances the free flow of energy.[272] It also activates the various chakras and optimizes the energy within them.

He states that the "resonance of the sound of mantra operates as a total energy system that engages with all levels of an individual's being. Each syllable in a mantra is a set of tonal frequencies that resonate with, and activate, energy centers (chakras) in the body, connecting and unifying them into a single integrated system...The variation in pitch, tone and resonance adjusts the effect of the mantra's tonal set of frequencies to the energy center's capacity to receive activation." With repetition of the mantra the resonance of the syllables of the mantra with the chakra is deepened" (ibid., 1).

Sogyal Rinpoche explains that the mind utilizes what he terms the subtle energy of the breath. This energy travels through the subtle channels of the body and purifies it. When a mantra is recited the breath and energy are charged by the energy generated by the mantra. This in turn benefits the mind and subtle body.

He mentions that when one is "nervous, disoriented, or emotionally fragile, chanting a mantra inspiringly can change the state of your mind completely, by transforming its energy."[273]

---

[272] "Mantra and Consciousness Expansion in India" 3, http://www.ianprattis.com/pdf/mantraandconsciousness.pdf (accessed Jan 5th 2011).
[273] *The Tibetan book of living and dying*, 71.

Rusill Paul posits that mantras can be regarded as "spiritual pharmaceuticals" where, because of the unique combination of sounds they possess, they are able to break through the barriers of the analytical mind and affect the nervous system very directly. This enables the mind to rise above its conditionings and to view life from a different perspective that is beneficial for healing.[274]

The Sufis claim that for many cases of mental illnesses the source of the problem is spiritual. Vices such as immorality, polytheism, greed, jealousy, lewdness, and hatred blacken the heart; hence the solution cannot be found using medication. The cure lies in the purification of the heart. The way to remove this condition is by using the Divine Words of God and his Divine Names. The patient is also required to change his/her wrong habits and behaviors.[275]

Mubarak Gilani elaborates that it is the impact of a person's intentions, thoughts, and actions that can contribute to mental illnesses. Interestingly, he also suggests that the intervention of "certain non-human intelligent beings" can also be the reason for some cases of this condition.

He states:

> A person's intentions, faith, and deeds leave an indelible mark upon our physical and esoteric face – the heart (*qalb*). Esoterically with one's intentions, thoughts, and deeds, esoteric forms are created within the esoteric self.

---

[274] Russill Paul, "Why Sanskrit for Mantra? Why not English?" http://www.russillpaul.com/articles/article/1162814/14980.htm.
[275] Lorna Swaine-Abdallah, "Aids is curable," *The Islamic Post*. Jan 2, 2009. http://islamicpost.wordpress.com/2009/01/02/aids-is-curable/ (accessed Jan 4th 2011).

> If the intentions are pure, the thought-forms made within the esoteric self will, in turn, give life to identical mental beings whose creator shall be the person himself. These mental beings, as forms, derive their nourishment from pious deeds and the inflow of divine light from the heart (*qalb*)...Fortunate individuals shall see beautiful mental forms in dreams and visions in the initial stages, whilst individuals with evil intentions and dark deeds shall create horrible thought-forms and mental images. These will derive their nourishment from the darkest pole of his psyche – the baser self.[276]

He continues:

> I have treated many clients who complained that their houses were haunted by some weird and horrible looking beings. I told them that these were of their own creations. I have also observed that mental forms do grow, and if unchecked, these very images cause the so-called poltergeist and other spirit haunting phenomena, and also cause mental diseases like paranoid schizophrenia, psychosis, etc. At the same time, I do not rule out the possibility of intervention of certain non-human intelligent beings, which are always willing to take advantage of certain situations. It must be emphasized that, at no cost, should the mental patient be subjected either to electric shock therapy or sedation (ibid).

Gilani believes that not only Muslim patients can be cured of mental illnesses. He feels, rather, that any non-Muslim infant or

---

[276] Mubarak Ali Gilani, "Pillar of Lies" http://www.iqou-moa.org/sheikh_jilani/pillar_of_lies1.htm (accessed Jan 4th 2011).

child and even adults who believe in one God and the Ten Commandments can be healed.

Mental illnesses such as depression, anxiety, dissociation and derealization all appear to be associated with activity from the right prefrontal cortex of the brain. Activity from the left prefrontal cortex appears to be associated with positive emotions such as happiness.[277]

The question is, is there a way of reducing the activities of the right prefrontal cortex and stimulating activities on the left side?

A research was done on meditating Buddhist monks who were experts in performing "compassion meditation". Using MRI, the researchers observed that the activity "in the left prefrontal cortex…swamped activity in the right prefrontal…something never before seen from purely mental activity. A sprawling circuit that switches on at the sight of suffering also showed greater activity in the monks. So did regions responsible for planned movement, as if the monks' brains were itching to go to the aid of those in distress."[278]

The author of "Neuroplasticity, *Dhikr* and Recovery" argues then that *dhikr* "can train the brain to switch out of 'anxiety' mode by increasing activity in the left pre-frontal cortex." He cautions,

---

[277] "Neuroplasticity, *Dhikr* and Recovery," http://jamilalighthouse.wordpress.com/2007/06/28/neuroplasticity-*dhikr*-and-recovery/ (article no longer available on Oct 14th 2010).

[278] Sharon Begley, "Scans of Monks' Brains Show Meditation Alters Structure, Functioning," *The Wall Street Journal*, Nov 5th 2004, http://psyphz.psych.wisc.edu/web/News/Meditation_Alters_Brain_WSJ_11-04.htm (accessed April 19th 2010).

however, that the process is not a quick one and other factors related to depression should also be considered.[279]

Mantra, Dhikr And Consciousness

It is stated that Jenny, in his research, had also stumbled upon another interesting discovery. He noticed that *spoken vocals from ancient languages like Hebrew or Sanskrit produced the same shape as the written vowels*. In other words, the vowels are preserved in the shapes that are produced by sound. Modern languages like English, on the other hand, did not produce the same effect.[280]

Jenny questioned how this was possible. What qualities do these "sacred languages" possess? He also wondered if this could be the reason for the healing power of sacred languages.

Now if we study ancient Egyptian culture we come upon an interesting finding.

In the Corpus Hermeticum in a letter from Asklepios to King Amman he states: "As for us, we do not use simple words but sounds all filled with power."

In another passage of the *Corpus Hermeticum* it is mentioned:

> Sacred…language is not to be understood as a succession of terms with definite meanings…the excitation of certain nervous centers [cause] physiological effects [which] are

---

[279] "Neuroplasticity, *Dhikr* and Recovery."
[280] This writer has not seen this particular discovery mentioned in Jenny's Cymatics published in 2001. It is possible, however, that this has been mentioned in the previous edition published by Basilius Presse. This discovery by Jenny has been mentioned in numerous articles.

evoked by the utterance of certain letters or words which make no sense in themselves.[281]

Elsewhere we read that the Hermetic writings state, "...*Egyptian words contain in themselves the energy of the objects being spoken about,* that is, each symbol contained in itself a vibrational complexity. A word was "the sound of spirit striking the air and declaring a person's whole wish...a sound full of action.""[282] (Emphasis mine).

This relationship between language and reality is also found with the Sanskrit language. Swami Akandanda of the SYDA Yoga Foundation in New York states, "there is an inherent connection between the sound of Sanskrit and the actual reality that it represents."[283]

What the above seems to imply is *that the reality contained in the words of sacred scriptures appears to be preserved when these words are vocalized or conveyed.*

Let us explore this some more.

Sheikh Yaqoubi speaks about curing of maladies by using verses of the Qur'an.[284] In one example he states that if a baby is crying the following verse from *Surah Ta-Ha* should be recited over it:

---

[281] R.A. Schwaller de Lubicz, *Sacred Science* quoted on the website: http://www.cymascope.com/cyma_research/egyptology.html (accessed Oct 14th 2010).
[282] Melanie Braun, "Exploring the Efficacy of Vowel Intonations" *The Rose+Croix Journal* 2, 2005. http://www.rosecroixjournal.org/issues/2005/articles/vol2_11_21_braun.pdf (accessed Oct 12th 2010).
[283] *Chanting:Discovering Spirit in Sound,* 70.
[284] Muhammad Al-Yaqoubi, *Remembering Allah.* UK: Sacred Knowledge, 2009. CD-ROM.

$$\text{يَوْمَئِذٍ يَتَّبِعُونَ الدَّاعِيَ لَا عِوَجَ لَهُ وَخَشَعَتِ الْأَصْوَاتُ لِلرَّحْمَنِ فَلَا تَسْمَعُ إِلَّا هَمْسًا}$$

> All voices are calm for the Most Merciful so that you don't hear anything except murmuring.[285]

What is evident in this verse is that Allah speaks about calmness. Upon recitation of this verse this reality of calmness is conveyed!

For treatment of sleeplessness Sheikh Yaqoubi mentions two verses. One of these is verse 18 from *Surah Kahf*, which reads:

$$\text{وَتَحْسَبُهُمْ أَيْقَاظًا وَهُمْ رُقُودٌ}$$

> You think they are awake but they are sleeping.[286]

The second is verse 11 of *Surah Anfal*:

$$\text{إِذْ يُغَشِّيكُمُ النُّعَاسَ أَمَنَةً}$$

> When He reveals on you sleep out of security from Him.[287]

In both of these two verses sleep is mentioned and again when these verses are recited they cause someone who couldn't sleep

---

[285] Qur'an, 20:108.
[286] Qur'an, 18:18.
[287] Qur'an, 8:11.

to fall asleep!

So in both of these two examples it appears that the words contain within themselves the reality of the object spoken about and this reality is then transferred to the listener.

One can find other examples of verses of the Qur'an that, when uttered, convey to the listener the feeling that is contained in the meaning of the words. One example can be seen in *Surah Dukhan* (chapter 44) verse 16 which is stated as follows:

$$يَوْمَ نَبْطِشُ الْبَطْشَةَ الْكُبْرَى إِنَّا مُنتَقِمُونَ$$

On the day when We will seize (them) with the most violent seizing; surely We will inflict retribution.

The recitor of this verse will *feel the turbulence and shaking* that the first part of this verse conveys.

The same feeling would be experienced from verse 14 of *Surah Muzzamil* (chapter 73) that reads as follows:

$$يَوْمَ تَرْجُفُ الْأَرْضُ وَالْجِبَالُ وَكَانَتِ الْجِبَالُ كَثِيبًا مَّهِيلًا$$

On the day when the earth and the mountains shall quake and the mountains shall become (as) heaps of sand let loose.

What's the significance of this?

It is apparent that the verses were specifically designed by Allah to convey the effect that is expressed in the understanding of the verses. The sound structure, the particular combination of letters and the rhythm all were uniquely chosen to convey the reality that Allah is talking about.

It also appears to imply that in the recitation of *dhikr the reality that is contained in the words of the dhikr is unveiled in the recitor* leading to a gradual transformation of the person's being.

So, for instance, if one regularly recites *Ya Noor*, which means light, the light that is contained in this *dhikr* is unveiled!

The same can be said for *Ya Rahman* which means, for brevity, merciful. In the recital of this *dhikr* the mercy that is contained within it is unveiled within the recitor making him or her more merciful!

Can this be the reason why *La illaha illalah* is the greatest *dhikr*?

The Prophet Muhammad (S.A.W) had mentioned that all the previous Prophets used to recite this *dhikr*.

The Sufis claim it to be the quickest way to God.

If the above hypothesis that the reciting of *dhikr* provokes the unveiling of the reality contained in the word is indeed true, then what would happen when this *dhikr* is recited?

The reality that this *dhikr* refers to is that, in actuality, there is nothing in the universe but God. He is the reality. Everything else is just temporal or delusion.

The unveiling of this reality within the recitor would produce the effect of loosening of the grip of attachments to this world in the heart and replacing it with the true reality of the eternal being!

The Sufis assert that *practice of dhikr unlocks the angelic power contained in the Names of Allah and releases the power, grace, and virtues of these Names into the consciousness, heart and soul.* Not only is the practitioner benefited but also the surrounding area is protected from troubles and afflictions.

They state that since we were brought into being with the beautiful Names of Allah, when the Names of Allah are constantly repeated in the mind, the brain is enabled to reveal better the meanings corresponding to these names and the capabilities such names indicate. *Qualities and potentialities bestowed by Allah and lying dormant are awakened and expressed.*

Dhikr, they claim, is a system of practice to increase the activity of cellular groups in the brain. Hence, *the qualities of the names that, according to one source, exist dormant and "holographically" in one's being are manifested through increase of the brain capacity with the degree of manifestation dependent on the strength of activation.*[288]

To illustrate this, if a loud-mouthed, rowdy and quick-tempered person repeats *Ya-Halimu* (briefly translated as the Forbearing or the Indulgent) he/she would display tolerance shortly after repeating the name (ibid).

---

[288] Aulia-e-hind, http://aulia-e-hind.com/Zikr.htm (accessed April 1st 2010).

By this means, the Sufis claim, repetition of specific *dhikr* formulas over a period of months would cause someone to quit smoking, drinking or drug addiction without any exertion (ibid).

For the advanced practitioner who becomes deeply engrossed with a particular name, the resonance of that name within him eventually makes him become at one with that name. In other words he "becomes that divine name."

Thus, if such a person recites, for example, *Ya-Latifu* (briefly translated as the Subtle) he becomes the manifestation of that quality. His heart opens up enabling him to see with the inner eye of the heart. He gains the power of insight and "is able to see or read the reality of all things."[289]

This phenomenon of how sound can be used to transform the mind appears to have been known to the yogis.

Although detailed explanations can be found elsewhere a brief, simple and well-put explanation of how this occurs has been stated in the article "The Effect of Mantra." It goes as follows:[290]

In their tradition, the yogis indicate that there is a type of mantra known as the "Bij" that embodies "a certain kind of consciousness." When one achieves a certain mastery in chanting it paying regard to the right rhythm and pronunciation among other things, then one "will begin to embody that state of consciousness that the mantra teaches."

---

[289] "Sufi Introduction to the 99 attributes of Names of Allah and especially that of Ya Latif."
[290] "The Effect of Mantra," http://www.tracysvision.com/effect_of_mantra.htm (accessed April 13th 2010).

It is said that this "Bij" mantra acts like the planting of a seed in the consciousness. "The seed gets planted in your consciousness by the chanting of it and then the continued use of it begins to "grow" it in your awareness...working from the inside out, everyday and in everyway, redirecting your mind, your thoughts, your emotions, towards the Infinite nature, bringing you more and more into alignment with the embodied consciousness of that mantra."

A good analogy of this effect is given of the Grand Canyon. Over millions of years water carved away and eroded rock leaving behind a spectacle that is breadth-taking. Similarly, the "Bij" mantra, like water, carves away the rock formations of the mind (or shapes it) creating what can be termed a "beautiful mind" or a mind aligned "with the beauty and grace of" one's inner being, of one's true nature (ibid).

Mantra/*Dhikr*, Ego And Superconsciousness
It is said that repetitive harmonious sounds like chants are an effective means of loosening the grip of the ego on the self.

Robert Gass expresses this aptly:

> The repetitive sounds of chants vibrate in our brains, again and again, washing our minds, our wavelengths gradually into resonance with the tone and feeling of the musical prayer. Our bodies and energy start to beat with the rhythm of the chant, the repeating pulses start to shift our sense of being into a more aligned, more harmonious state. As we continue, we move in and out of more or less immersion in the chant. Sometimes it is clearly "me" sitting here...other times, we touch moments where the separation between chanter and the chant, the sense of

"me" doing something fades away. There is only "chanting" and I am a part of it.[291]

Elsewhere he states, "As we give ourselves to the chant...if we are so graced, there are moments seemingly out of time when something happens – when the boundaries that separate "me" from "you" disappear. There may seem to be one breath through us all, voices so attuned that it seems but one voice is singing, and a joining of hearts in communion" (ibid).

The yogis believe that this loosening of the grip of the ego can potentially usher in a state of superconsciousness where one experiences a feeling of "oneness" with the universe.

A glimpse of this state can probably be obtained from the following description of the Sanskrit scholar Dr. Vyaas Houston of his teacher chanting the Sanskrit text: "When he chanted, it was as though every molecule of his body was vibrating. It felt as if the entire universe dissolved into a state of vibration" (ibid., 70).

The yogic method for arriving at this state is described by the following (obtained mainly from the website yogaworld.org):

In mantric meditation the mantra is first chanted loudly. This produces a calming of the mind and body. The surrounding atmosphere becomes peaceful. The chanting then gradually drops to a whisper. In the process the life force of the human body called *"prana"* becomes withdrawn from being externally directed. It becomes harmonized and balanced allowing for deeper feelings of peace. The mind and the emotions also become balanced.

---

[291] *Chanting: Discovering Spirit in Sound*, 16.

Continued repetition of the mantra produces an evolution from the whispering of it to the chanting of it in the mind. The life force simultaneously moves deeper within. The mental chanting continues as long as thoughts occur in the mind. When thoughts occur, the mental chanting performed in the same area of the mind where they occur brings one back to the stillness and helps one in not being drawn into the thought process.

[The yogis claim that the continued chanting of the mantra always eventually manages to remove the mind from thoughts. This is because, "the energy encased in the vibrational structure of mantra works on multidimensional levels within the mind and body"].[292]

As the mantra continues to be recited, with the mind now free of thoughts, the mind of the performer now reaches a state close to superconsciousness. At this point, it is said that the chanting of the mantra becomes effortless and pleasurable. One experiences feelings of peace and joy.

Two things then occur:

    A. The mantra can dissolve into superconsciousness or

    B. The mantra can help to relieve the subconscious of the burden of old thoughts, feelings, and memories that were negatively affecting it. It "may create an opportunity for old thoughts and feelings, old fears and guilts, to be released or healed or let go."

If the latter occurs then when the mind is freed from residual clingings the chanting moves one into the realm of the

---

[292] *Mantra and Consciousness Expansion in India*, 3.

superconscious. There the words of the mantra dissolve leaving only "the energy surge of the mantram." This leaves one's awareness full of bliss and light. There is a sense that one has returned home. One experiences a feeling that this is where one truly belongs.

After about 15-20 minutes in this state the mantra wants to move outwards again and one experiences a desire to touch everything external with the feelings acquired. The mantra becomes a whisper mantra and then it becomes loud again, the entire process having been reversed.[293]

Dhikr, Sound And Genetics
The subject of DNA being affected by sound is an exciting new area of research.

Susan Alexjander who teaches in Sacramento, California and has an MA in music pursued an investigation to determine if the vibrations of the atoms and molecules that make up the DNA could be recorded and heard and, if that were achievable, what kinds of sounds would be produced.

With the help of University of California biologist Dr. David Deamer, the molecular vibrations were easily determined using infrared spectrophotometry. These were then converted into sound frequencies.

The resulting effect, according to a BBC article, was "strange, beautiful music." "Some of the combinations of frequencies,"

---

[293] "Mantra Yoga," *YogaWorld*, http://www.yogaworld.org/mantra2.htm (accessed Dec 6th 2010).

Alexjander said, "are just stunning. I find it very arresting. It sounds alive to me."[294]

She also discovered that most of the frequencies in the DNA were microtonal – i.e. between the half-tone steps.

The following statement by Donald Hatch Andrews aptly captures this vibratory and musical nature of the atoms that comprise our existence:

> Our very bones, blood vessels, and nerves are singing the song of the universe: From the deepest interior of the atom there are shrill tones dozens of octaves above the highest tones of a violin. This is the music of the atomic nucleus ... this is the symphony of life, this unimaginably complex tapestry of music that is sounding within us every moment of our life.[295]

This observation is echoed by Fabian Maman who states:

> We are musical beings because the very substance of our universe is music...all vibration in our aura, in the energy field around us, is full of musical notes in suspension. Sound and music are such a vital part of our lives because we ourselves are composed of musical vibration. We are music deeply, to the smallest particle of our being. We are music in the nucleus of our DNA, in

---

[294] David Whitehouse, "Listen to your DNA" BBC News, Sci/Tech, Nov 26, 1998, Thursday, http://news.bbc.co.uk/2/hi/science/nature/222591.stm (accessed Oct 13th 2010).
[295] Donald Hatch Andrews, *The Symphony of Life* 55, 58 quoted at http://www.rosecroixjournal.org/issues/2005/articles/vol2_11_21_braun.pdf (accessed Oct 13th 2010).

our molecular structure. In our melodic consciousness rests the essence of our origin. This resonance reflects the divine pattern, the archetype, which enables us to become more than our personality and our biology.[296]

If atoms and molecules have vibrational frequencies then they should also be susceptible to sound frequencies targeted at them.

Sir Peter Guy Manners writes about an interesting research done in this regard. He states:

> Recently, in Germany, researchers took the DNA of a 17-year-old boy, recorded its sound frequencies, and saved them. The boy was accidentally killed, but the scientists still had his DNA frequency patterns. Later, the DNA frequencies of the 17-year-old were transmitted into the body of a man in his late thirties. And the man almost became the young boy. His skin became youthful, he became slim, his hair went back to its natural color. Today he's in his forties and he still looks like a much younger man.[297]

In the article authored by Zothyrius Ali El, it said that the purpose of the Names of Allah is to empower and uplift mankind to function at a higher evolutionary level. This is achieved by the effect of *dhikr* on the DNA and RNA. By this effect practice of *dhikr* enables development of greater levels of understanding and psycho-spiritual growth.

The author says:

---

[296] *The Role of Music in the Twenty-First Century*, 14.
[297] Quoted in "Cymatics and The New Age of Miracles," http://www.spiritofmaat.com/archive/mar1/cymatics.htm (accessed Oct 14th 2010).

The ancient science of *Dhikr*, the intoning of the divine Names of Allah, was utilized to linguistically compose for the activation of higher states of creativity and genetic transformation. More specifically, the ancient science of *Dhikr* utilized the cosmic forces that yield reactions that come from intoning the divine Names of Allah as a mantra. The ancient practice can increase the energy flow in the asiatic's individual's garment of light and calibrate the individual's DNA and RNA within the nuclei of the cells to release or unfold greater levels of understanding and psycho-spiritual development. Hence, this science of intoning the divine Names of Allah not only musically resonates a calibrating source for the asiatic's emotional body, but also increases the production of infection-fighting cells by generating frequencies that directly destroy invading bacteria.[298]

What evidence, if any, exists to supports these contentions?

An article by Grazyna Fosar and Franz Bludorf titled "The Biological Chip in our Cells Revolutionary results of modern genetics"[299] describes some startling discoveries about DNA.

In the article, based on experiments by the German bio physicist Fritz Albert Popp and others, they state the following:

- DNA, in addition to being deeply involved in biophotons (a radiation of light emitted from all living organisms), is

---

[298] Zothyrius Ali El, "The Cosmic Code Of Man: The Genetic Vibrations of Allah," *Moors Gate*, http://www.moorsgate.com/2007/06/24/ (accessed Oct 18th 2010).
[299] Grazyna Fosar and Franz Bludorf, "The Biological Chip in our Cells Revolutionary results of modern genetic," http://www.fosar-bludorf.com/archiv/biochip_eng.htm (accessed Jan 10th 2011).

also affected by light and other electromagnetic frequencies.
- DNA acts as a storage device for storing light energy, effectively acting like a high-speed microchip with 3 Gb storage capacity. This implies that the human body is nourished not only by food, but also by light to a small degree.
- When electromagnetic energy impinges on the DNA, the DNA oscillates with very little loss. It thus behaves as an organic superconductor but with operation at room temperature! (An artificial superconductor requires extremely low temperatures between -253 and -272°C to function). The frequency of oscillation is 150 MHz, which is within the frequency range used by humans for telecommunications and microwave engineering.

A group of Russian scientists headed by Pjotr Garjajev also has made the following discoveries:

- Genetic code follows the same rules as human language – i.e., the syntax (how words are put together to create phrases and sentences) and semantics (the study of meaning) are similar. [300]
- The arrangement of the elementary bases in the DNA follows grammar and has set rules just like human languages (ibid).
- Ninety percent of the DNA that was thought to be useless is in fact used for communication, more exactly - for hypercommunication (or data exchange on DNA level using genetic code). (Ibid).

---

[300] Baerbel, "Russian DNA Discoveries Explain Human 'Paranormal' Events," Rense.com. Extracted from book *Vernetzte Intelligenz* by Grazyna Fosar and Franz Bludorf (accessed Jan 10th 2011).

- The similarity between human language and DNA is found in this ninety percent portion of the molecule that is not used for protein synthesis (ibid).
- *If one modulates a laser beam by a certain frequency then one may affect with this the information of the DNA waves and so the genetic information itself.*
  The Russians were able to prove this by transmitting the DNA information patterns that transformed frog embryos to salamander embryos (ibid).
- Since the DNA-alkaline pairs and human language have the same structure no DNA decoding is necessary (ibid).
- *DNA substance in vivo (in living tissues) reacts to language-modulated laser light and even to radio waves, if one keeps the correct resonant frequencies* (ibid).

The authors argue that these findings have vast implications. They explain why hypnotism works – because the DNA responds directly to language. Genetic defects can be repaired without the risks and side effects of current medical procedures by targeting the cells using modulated sound or light waves. New medical therapies can be developed for major diseases such as AIDS and cancer.

The benefits of these discoveries also extend to the plant kingdom. Seeds that are apparently "dead" can be brought to life. Plants can be made to display phenomenal growth.

An experiment was performed to examine the effect of irradiating seeds taken from the site of the Chernobyl nuclear blast in 1987. Garjajev and his team obtained normal living seeds of the Arabidopsis thaliana plant (a small plant belonging to the mustard family) and also seeds from this same type of plant that came from Chernobyl. They then shone a laser beam unto the normal seeds. This same laser beam was then directed to the seeds that came from Chernonyl that were in all likelihood dead. What they saw was nothing short of a miracle. The seeds from Chernobyl sprouted within a few days and appeared normal.[301]

In another experiment potatoes were exposed to a high dose of DNA radiation. This produced an amazing 1-cm/day growth of the potatoes (ibid).

These results of experiments on DNA indicate that what Zothyrius Ali El asserts is not far fetched. They appear to scientifically establish the fact, claimed by some for ages – that the body is programmable by language, words, and thought. Since DNA directly responds to sound frequencies it is affected by the frequencies of *dhikr*. It is most likely then that recitation of *dhikr* can affect genetic information and produce genetic transformation. The therapeutic and transformational benefit of this would be enormous and needs serious investigation. The important thing would be in determining what particular *dhikr* to use.

Examples Of Mantra And *Dhikr*
Examples of mantras are:

- *Aum* – it is said to be the name of God, the vibration of the Supreme, a reflection of the absolute reality, without beginning or end and embracing all that exists;[302] It is considered as the all-connecting sound of the universe – one

---

[301] Lynne McTaggart, "DNA double helix: Our body's recording studio and radio station," *The Healing Universe*, http://www.thehealinguniverse.com/library.html (accessed Jan 17th 2011).
[302] Wikipedia contributors, "Aum," *Wikipedia, The Free Encyclopedia*, http://en.wikipedia.org/wiki/Aum (accessed Oct 7th 2010).

word interpreted as having three sounds representing creation, preservation, and destruction.

- *Aum Mani Padme Hum* – the literal meaning of which is, 'The Jewel is in the Heart of the Lotus'. It is, however, said to possess many meanings among them being purification of the six realms of existence from suffering;[303]

- The Gayatri mantram:
  Om Bhur Buvaha Suvaha   Thath Savithur Varenyam
  Bhargo Devasya Dheemahi   Dhiyo Yonaha Prachodayath

  Which, according to Swami Vivekanand, means, "We meditate on the glory of that Being who has produced this universe; may He enlighten our minds."[304]

  Repetition of this mantra is believed to produce very powerful effects. Dr. Pranav Pandya, director of the Brahmavarchas Research Institute in Hardwar, India asserts "if millions of people recite the Gayatri mantra at the same time, it can act as an invisible sound wave protection for those people, even in a nuclear holocaust."[305]

Dhikr are comprised of syllables, words, or phrases. One example of the various *dhikr* is *La ilaha illallah*, which literally

---

[303] Indopedia contributors, "Om Mane Padme Hum," *Indopedia*, http://www.indopedia.org/Om_mani_padme_hum.html (accessed Oct 18th 2010).

[304] Wikipedia contributors, " Gayatri Mantra," *Wikipedia, The Free Encyclopedia*, http://en.wikipedia.org/wiki/Gayatri_Mantra (accessed Oct 7th 2010).

[305] Quoted in article "Hardwar Institute Tracks Power of Gayatri Yagna" by Archana Dongre. *Hinduism Today*, Sept 1992. http://www.hinduismtoday.com/modules/smartsection/item.php?itemid=960 (accessed Jan 25th 2011).

means, "There is no God but Allah" but implies that the only permanent reality in the universe is God.

This *dhikr* is regarded as the greatest of all *dhikr*. It is regarded as being of greater value than everything in the world. The following statement of the Prophet Muhammad (S.A.W.) indicates the power of it, "...the best of what I, and all Prophets before me, said is, *La ilaha illallah*. If all the heavens and earth were placed on one side of the balance and *La ilaha illallah* was placed in the other, *La ilaha illallah* would be heavier..."[306]

The Sufis explain that *La ilaha illallah* is a "statement of Divine Truth, and a lesson on how to know it." It means that only Allah truly exists and the quickest way to directly experience this reality is by denying all else.[307]

The first two words *"La ilaha" is* a negation of the illusory world that exists in our mind. *"La"* means no or nothing. *"Ilaha"* refers to all the things the mind is attached to, cares about, respects, deifies, worships, or believes exists. Taken together these two words thus mean, "nothing exists." In other words nothing is worthy of consideration except that which remains when the mind is free of its attachments.

What remains is what is affirmed by the next two words *"illa"* and *"llah"*. *"Illa"* means only, but, or except. *"llah"* means Allah. Thus *"illallah"* means except a reality that, in a true sense, is ungraspable by the mind. This reality is Beyond Comprehension, Self Aware, All Comprehending, All Seeing, All Knowing, All

---

[306] Tabarani, Suyuti in *Durr al-manthur*.
[307] Extracted from http://www.surrenderworks.com/library/esoterics/kalimah.html (accessed Jan 25th 2011).

Hearing, All Perfect, Incomparable, and Who remains when everything else is gone.

That which remains is the Permanent Reality of God Alone.

The Sufis, remarking about the greatness of *La ilaha illallah*, proclaim, "In the mystic accounts spoken from the lips of the Prophet of Allah, it is related that in the realm of pre-eternity, Divine Reality is a hidden treasure. There is no form, no light, no heavens, no earth, nothing of creation is there. Sublime Reality speaks of this, "I was a hidden treasure, unknown and unknowable. Desiring to be known, I brought forth from my essence the light of humanity.""

"As the Light bursts forth from the Hiddenness, it proclaims *La ilaha illallah* ceaselessly. Divine Sublimity responds, *Muḥammadur Rasulullah* – 'Humanity is My hidden treasure, My representative in creation, the mirror in which I gaze. By humanity am I known and praised and loved. Humanity manifests *La ilaha illallah*, expressing My own secret.'"

"This mystery of original manifestation" they declare, "is not located in a historical past – it is an ever-unfolding splendor in the eternal *Now*."[308]

The exaltedness of this *dhikr* formula is expressed by the following:

---

[308] Nur Ashki Jerrahi Community, "Tasbih: Personal Dhikr," 2008, http://www.nurashkijerrahi.org/teachings/union_012.htm (accessed Oct 18th 2010).

La ilaha illallah is the resonance of Allah's Existence.

La ilaha illallah is the sheer beauty of Allah, beyond conception and literal meaning.

La ilaha illallah is Allah's delight, Allah's own praise and *dhikr*.

La ilaha illallah is the song of Allah's Love, Muhammad Rasul-ullah is the form beloved.

La ilaha illallah is the mustard seed of faith, the sword of light, the key of the heart.

La ilaha illallah is the great news brought by all Prophets, the essence of all holy books, the medicine for all ills, the balm for all hearts.

La ilaha illallah is the cry of New Humanity. Humanity will know itself when it gazes at its essence and origin. *La ilaha illallah* is the eye of this gaze (ibid).

Someone practicing this *dhikr* relates the following experience:

> One day, after midday Friday prayer, I was sitting... (in) the mosque and was practicing my invocation saying the pure words *La ilaha illallah* with (a) group of worshipers of God and among them were well traveled Sufis. I was following the rhythm as advised by Muhammad Mustafa to his spiritual heir Ali ibn Abu Talib, peace and blessings and pleasure of Allah be with them...
>
> While performing the *dhikr* a vision opened up.

...While saying the kalima (*La ilaha illallah*), my awareness was becoming more and more subtle and in that moment the truth was engulfing my being (and) my consciousness more and more that there is no other reality in the entire manifestation but Allah and consciousness associated with the *nafs* was disappearing in the ecstasy of the *dhikr* and (I) was given a ...glimpse of the entire cosmos as far as the human eye can see as a panoramic view. The entire cosmos with all its galaxies, stars, innumerable cosmic bodies – all were shown in that vision in a single utterance of *La ilaha illallah*.[309]

---

[309] "Invocation of La ilaha illa'llah." *Technology of the Heart*, http://www.mysticsaint.info/2011/01/invocation-of-la-ilaha-illallah.html (accessed Jan 25th 2011).

Dhikr and Meditation

"Verily, it is in the remembrance of Allah that hearts find rest."
(Qur'an 23:28)

Dhikr & Meditation:
A physician in China 4,600 years ago stated the following: "But the present world is a different one. Grief, calamity, and evil cause inner bitterness...there is disobedience and rebellion...Evil influences strike from early morning until late at night...they injure the mind and reduce its intelligence and they also injure the muscles and the flesh."[310]

One wonders what he would have written had he lived in our current time. The world's problems, far from being solved, have gotten progressively worse. This has taken its toll on the stress level of human existence.

More than 20 years ago concern was voiced on the effect of stress of modern day society on physical and mental well-being. In fact the cover story of the June 6, 1983 edition of Time magazine's named stress "The Epidemic of the Eighties" and referred to it as the leading health problem. An overload of information, domestic issues, job insecurity, crime, wars and world tensions were some of the factors that contributed to increased stress. Inability to manage that stress level produced negative consequences on one's overall well-being.

The situation since that time has not improved. Rather the opposite can be said to be true. With the creation of the Internet and the availability of numerous TV channels, for instance, we have become bombarded with information. This places increased stress on us in filtering information and in responding to it. The economic upheaval in 2009 had a severe impact on many of us. There is also a significant increase in natural disasters. Wars continue to devastate lives and bring on unimaginable miseries.

---

[310] Quoted in Herbert Benson, *The Relaxation Response*, 11.

One can arguably say that since the beginning of human history the stress level of our current day existence is the highest ever.

Today stress is still the number one reason for ill health and contributes to about 70% of visits to primary care physicians.[311]

Stress in the workplace, according to the American Psychological Association (APA), costs businesses $300 billion per year. This cost is due to loss of productivity, absenteeism, turnover, and increased medical costs. A poll conducted by the APA indicates that three-quarters of American employees say their stress level is significantly impacted by work.[312]

Several types of chronic health problems including cardiovascular disease, musculoskeletal disorders, psychological disorders and disorders of the endocrine, respiratory and immune systems are directly related to stress.[313]

The question is how can this stress level be reduced?

It is said that one method that has been used to reduce stress for a long time is the practice of meditation.

So what is meditation?

---

[311] David B. Posen, "Stress Management for Patient and Physician," Internet Mental Health,
http://www.mentalhealth.com/mag1/p51-str.html (accessed Oct 19th 2010).
[312] American Psychological Association, "Overwhelmed by workplace stress? You're not alone."
http, ://www.apa.org/helpcenter/work-stress.aspx (accessed Oct 19th 2010).
[313] "Physical Effects of Stress," *Stress mnt for Health*, 2009,
http://www.stress-management-for-health.com/physical-effects-of-stress.html (accessed Oct 19th 2010).

Definition of meditation

Roger Walsh of the University of California at Irvine Medical School refers to meditation as "...a family of practices that treats attention in order to heighten awareness and bring mental processes under greater control."[314]

John C. Gowan of California State University, Northridge, refers to meditation in his book *Trance, Art and Creativity* as "...a conscious effort to open the doors to the preconscious through clearing and tranquilizing the conscious mind."[315]

V. V. Nalimov of Moscow State University states in his book *Realms of the Unconscious* that the objective of meditation is "...to achieve a state which could be called a controlled waking dream... It is also possible to say that the aim of meditation is dehypnotization, the liberation of consciousness from the induced rubbish of thoughts, images, and fantasies."[316]

Meditation, according to Deanne H. Shapiro of California College of Medicine at the University of California at Urvine, "refers to a family of techniques which have in common a conscious attempt to focus attention in a nonanalytical way and an attempt not to dwell on discursive, ruminating thought."[317]

Forms of meditation

Some of the major meditative techniques that fulfill these definitions, according to Daniel Goleman in his book *Varieties of the Meditative Experience*,[318] include:

---

[314] R. Walsh, *Meditation practice and research*.
[315] J. C. Gowan, *Trance, art and creativity*, 332-333.
[316] V. V. Nalimov, *Realms of the unconscious: the enchanted frontier*, 108.
[317] D. H. Shapiro, *Overview: clinical and physiological comparison of meditation and other self-centered strategies*.
[318] D. Goleman, *The varieties of the meditative experience*.

- Vipassana meditation of Buddhism where, with training, the mind focuses on observing one's thoughts, emotions, and feelings;

- Zen Buddhism meditation where the mind is made to contemplate a riddle that cannot be solved through rational thought;

- Yogic techniques including physical exercises, breath control, Mantra (chanting), and practicing of kundalini yoga. (Kundalini yoga is an attempt to unlock latent spiritual energy located at the base of the spine);

- *The Dhikr chanting of the Sufis belonging to the Muslim faith. According to Goleman, this remembrance of God through chanting his Names will lead the practitioner to a total purity of heart and mind and will open the way to God;*

- Transcendental Meditation or TM. According to Goleman, this is a form of mantric meditation that has been tailored for Westerners.

Besides these, other meditative practices have been mentioned including, in the Judaic tradition, meditation on the Name of God from the teachings of the Kabbalah[319] and the religious meditative technique of the Quakers where worshippers sit together in silent contemplation.[320]

---

[319] G. G. Scholem, *Major trends in Jewish mysticism.*
[320] M. H. Bacon, *The quiet rebels.*

Benefits of meditation

It has been claimed that meditation produces benefits that are wide ranging. These include a reduction in stress and anxiety, improved mental health, increased creativity, and regulation of the nervous, vascular, and immune systems. It appears to be beneficial to persons suffering from high blood pressure, heart disease, arthritis, cancer, loss of sleep, and depression among many other afflictions.

As an example, in one systematic review on evidence supporting the medical benefits of meditational practices, results from 20 randomized studies showed that meditation was of benefit for treating certain types of mental illnesses particularly nonpsychotic mood and anxiety disorders. They were also beneficial for treating auto-immune illness and emotional disturbance in neoplastic disease. They appeared to be most efficacious in treating epilepsy, symptoms of premenstrual syndrome, and menopausal symptoms.[321]

In another example studies employing various types of meditation techniques have shown oxygen consumption reduced by as much as 55%, carbon dioxide elimination reduced by up to 50%, and respiration rate lessened to one breath per minute.[322]

Deeper feelings of relaxation

In a physiologic research done in 1970 by Robert Keith Wallace, Benson and Arhie F. Wilson, 36 TM meditators of ages 17 to 41

---

[321] Albert J. Arias et al., "Systematic Review of the Efficacy of Meditation Techniques as Treatments for Medical Illness," *Journal of Alternative and Complementary Medicine* 2006.
[322] S. Donovan, M. Murphy and E. Taylor, *The Physical and Psychological Effects of Meditation*, 70.

were studied. When the readings of physiologic functions before and after meditation sessions were compared they found that after meditation the subjects all displayed a reduction in heart and respiratory rates and in oxygen consumption and carbon dioxide elimination. Blood lactate level was also reduced resulting in increased blood flow thereby contributing to an increased feeling of relaxation.[323]

They also observed that the galvanic skin response (GSR), which is the response of the skin to mild electrical stimuli, increased during meditation. This increased skin response is another indicator of a greater state of relaxation (ibid).

Significant amounts of alpha waves were also observed being generated from the brain. This was a third indicator of a state of relaxation.

Results of other research on TM
Stress reduction
Since much research has been done on TM a summary of the results of these research is presented here. This summary is taken largely from the website "tm.org." Detailed results can, however, be found in other places. For those interested, the book *The Physical and Psychological Effects of Meditation* is a valuable resource.

This website states that research has shown that practicing of TM not only produces decreased stress by the physiological changes mentioned previously, but also by related psychological changes. These include "decreased anxiety

---

[323] R. K. Wallace, H. Benson and A. F. Wilson, *A wakeful hypometabolic physiologic state*.

and depression, decreased post-traumatic stress syndrome, and increased self-actualization."

It further states that "Stress reduction is also demonstrated by the sociological changes, such as decreased hostility, increased family harmony, and reduced criminal behavior in incarcerated felons."

Decreased Risk of Cardiovascular Disease and Improved General Health
In a most recent study, the results of which has been summarized by the Telegraph in the United Kingdom in Nov 2009, it has been discovered that patients with heart disease who practice TM have the risk of heart attack, strokes, or death reduced by half.

The study, which lasted over 9 years, involved 201 African Americans with an average age of 59 who had been diagnosed with heart disease. One group was randomly assigned the practice of TM while the other had health education classes about diet and exercise.

The researchers from the Medical College of Wisconsin in Milwaukee working in collaboration with the Institute for Natural Medicine and Prevention at Maharishi University of Management in Fairfield, Iowa found that in addition to a 47 % reduction in the risk of heart attack, strokes, or death, those who practiced TM had lower blood pressure and significant reductions in their stress levels.

Dr Robert Schneider, lead author and director of the Center for Natural Medicine and Prevention, sums up the importance of these findings. He states ".... this is the first controlled clinical trial to show that long-term practice of this particular stress reduction program reduces the incidence of clinical cardiovascular events, that is heart attacks, strokes and mortality."[324]

The trial, in his opinion, revealed the effect of Transcendental Meditation to be like a newly discovered medicine for the prevention of heart disease. The only difference, he points out, is that "in this case, the new medications are derived from the body's own internal pharmacy stimulated by the Transcendental Meditation practice" (ibid).

The above results on the effect of practicing TM support what TM researchers have claimed for a while. The website "tm.org" states:

> Medical researchers have found a reduction of important cardiovascular risk factors such as high blood pressure and serum cholesterol. Large health insurance studies have found that people practicing the Transcendental Meditation and TM-Sidhi programs, in all age groups combined, display a 50 percent reduction in both inpatient and outpatient medical care utilization compared to controls. Hospitalization is 87 percent lower for heart disease and 55 percent lower for cancer. And what is most remarkable, meditators over 40 years old have approximately 70 percent fewer medical problems than others in their age group.

---

[324] Rebecca Smith, "Meditation 'cuts risk of heart attack by half,'" *Telegraph.co.uk*. Nov 17, 2009.
http://www.telegraph.co.uk/health/healthnews/6581495/Meditation-cuts-risk-of-heart-attack-by- half.html (accessed Oct 19th 2010).

Decreased Biological Age and Increased Life Expectancy
On biological age and life expectancy the website indicates that the biological age of TM practitioners in their mid-50s have been found to be "twelve years younger than their chronological age," and that "people beginning the practice even at 80 years of age live longer and are healthier and happier than controls of the same age."

Greater feeling of stability
The website further states that the benefits of TM extends to the holistic way in how one perceives the world and in the experiencing of a greater feeling of anchor and stability.

Increased Concentration, Creativity and Intelligence
Practicing of TM is also said to increase the ability to concentrate and understand, increase creativity, and improve perception and memory. "TM.org" mentions, "School children who practice the Transcendental Meditation technique significantly improve in their basic skills in mathematics, reading, language, and study skills within a semester." The IQs of all level of students who practice TM also have displayed "significant increase."

Improved Moral Reasoning, Emotions, Maturity, and Self Development
TM practitioners displayed greater comparative self-development, more spontaneity, more productivity, and more self-sufficiency and were better able to meet challenges.

Sociological Benefits
Regarding sociological benefits practicing TM has been found to be effective in preventing and treating drug and alcohol abuse; treating post-traumatic stress from fighting wars; decreased smoking; decreased insomnia; and creating

positive changes in overall health of prisoners and decreased rate of their returning to prison.

Ecological Benefits
The website asserts that practicing TM also benefits the surrounding environment. It points out that extensive scientific research has been carried out on the city, state, national, and international levels to measure the effect on society when groups practice TM. "A study of 160 US cities found a significant reduction in crime trend from 1974 to 1978 in proportion to the number of people in the city who had learned the technique by 1973" the website states.

It further says, "Research has further demonstrated that when groups practicing the Transcendental Meditation and TM-Sidhi programs are introduced into a city, state, or country anywhere in the world, then crime decreases, there are fewer traffic accidents, and the quality of life improves in that area."

World Peace
Finally, "tm.org" argues that dependent on the size of the group practicing TM, "international relations improve and regional conflicts decrease worldwide."

TM and *Dhikr*

The question to be answered is: Are the above health benefits also achievable from the chanting of *dhikr*?

The effects mentioned above are not unique to practitioners of TM as other studies show. Benson had noted that the physiologic changes observed with practice of TM also occur using most forms of meditation.[325] A study of the book *The Physical and Psychological Effects of Meditation* would bring one to the same conclusion.

Some examples of this include:

- Reduction in heart rate has been noticed using other quiet meditative practices such as in Zen Buddhism sitting, yoga, and in Herbert Benson's "relaxation response."[326] In one striking illustration of this a yogi was hooked up to an EKG and then placed in a small underground pit for eight days. It was observed that from the second to the eight day the EKG activity was below the recording level indicating that the yogi's heart had either stopped beating or its electrical activity had been considerably reduced.[327]
- A lowering in blood pressure has been observed by employing a yoga relaxation technique.[328]
- A lowering in blood pressure has also been recorded by employing Buddhist meditation.[329]

---

[325] H. Benson, *The relaxation response*.
[326] *The Physical and Psychological Effects of Meditation*, 45.
[327] L.K. Kothari et al., "The Yogic Claim of Voluntary Control over the Heart Beat: An Unusual Demonstration," *American Heart Journal* 1973.
[328] C. H. Patel and W. R. North, "Randomized Controlled Trial of Yoga and Biofeedback in Management of Hypertension," *Lancelot Journal* 1975.

- Improved cardiorespiratory performance and psychologic profile and increase in secretion of melatonin (which might be responsible for improved sense of well-being) have been achieved from practice of Hatha Yoga and Omkar meditation.[330]
- Marked improvement in cardiovascular rhythms have been noticed when prayer and mantra were recited.[331]
- Quiet meditation is being used to combat cancer. In an article in AARP Bulletin April 2010 on Battling Cancer one cancer patient at Memorial Sloan-Kettering Cancer Center in New York is recorded as saying "I don't know how I would have survived without it."[332]

Since the medical benefits of meditation are found in many meditation techniques then this implies that *the chanting of dhikr also generates these health benefits*. Unfortunately, there is a lack of scientific experiments done on the therapeutic benefits of *dhikr* that can support this. This is, therefore, an area that needs extensive research. Researchers are hereby challenged to take this up. Positive results from these investigations may be of enormous benefit to the world.

One other indicator that *dhikr* may yield the same health benefits is the similarity between the technique of TM and that of *dhikr*.

---

[329] R. Stone and J. DeLeo, "Psychotherapeutic Control of Hypertension," *New England Journal of Medicine* 1976.
[330] K. Harinath et al., "Effects of Hatha yoga and Omkar meditation on cardiorespiratory performance, psychologic profile and melatonin secretion," *Journal of Alternative and Complementary Medicine* 2004.
[331] Luciano Bernardi et al., "Effect of rosary prayer and yoga mantras on autonomic cardiovascular rhythms: Comparative study," *British Medical Journal* 2001.
[332] Peter Jaret, "Battling Cancer with Complementary Therapies and Treatments," *AARP Bulletin* April 1, 2010.

According to Maharishi Mahesh Yogi, the person who introduced TM to the west, the mind is similar to the ocean. Thoughts arise from the depths of the ocean, rise to the surface and then become translated into action. The aim of TM is be able to access deeper levels of the mind. It is believed that when a person functions from a deeper level of the mind, a transformation occurs in all aspects of the practitioner's life. All spheres of life are impacted beneficially – physiologically, psychologically, sociologically, and ecologically.

In TM by sitting quietly and silently repeating a mantra one achieves the access to these deeper layers. The repetition of the mantra gradually turns the mind inwards upon itself. In other words, the consciousness switches from external orientation towards the inner self.

Regarding the chanting of *dhikr*, the practitioner of *dhikr* may begin the *dhikr* recitation audibly. Then as the chanting continues the consciousness gradually turns inwards. As it focuses on the word (s) of the *dhikr* subtler layers of the mind opens up. Eventually the practitioner becomes aware of an inner vastness akin to an ocean. He/she perceives the *dhikr* arising from the unfathomable depths of that ocean. In the process, the consciousness experiences deeper and deeper layers of the mind.

It is therefore apparent that the objectives of *dhikr* and TM techniques are quite similar although the approaches may be different. Recitation of *dhikr* should therefore produce the same benefits as the practicing of TM.

The Qur'an mentions in verse 23:28, *"Verily, it is in the remembrance of Allah that hearts find rest."*

This can be interpreted to mean that in the recitation of *dhikr* one experiences a feeling of relaxation. This is well in agreement with the results mentioned above on the effect of meditation on physiologic functions.

The effect of *Dhikr* on the functions of the brain

Theta, Alpha, Beta and Gamma waves and brain synchronization
Generation of theta, alpha, beta and gamma waves from the brain all appear to be indicative of positive well-being.

Theta waves have a frequency of 4 to 7 cycles per second and are believed to be related not only to drowsiness[333] but also to serenity and creativity;[334] Alpha waves have a frequency of 8 to 12 cycles per second and are generally associated with a state of relaxation;[335] Beta waves vibrate between 12-30 Hz and are thought to be indicative of active, busy or anxious thinking and active concentration;[336] The release of gamma waves, vibrating between 30 and 100 Hz, is believed to be indicative of an integrated functioning of neural activities via neural networks (ibid) and is associated with higher mental activities such as consciousness.[337]

---

[333] Wikipedia contributors, "Electroencephalography," *Wikipedia, The Free Encyclopedia*, http://en.wikipedia.org/wiki/Electroencephalography (accessed April 19th 2010).
[334] H. H. Blommfield, M. P. Cain & D. T. Jaffe, *TM: discovering inner energy and overcoming stress*, 58.
[335] Wikipedia contributors, "Electroencephalography," (accessed April 19th 2010).
[336] Ibid.
[337] Sharon Begley, "Scans of Monks' Brains Show Meditation Alters Structure, Functioning," *The Wall Street Journal* Nov 5, 2004, http://psyphz.psych.wisc.edu/web/News/Meditation_Alters_Brain_WSJ_11-04.htm (accessed Oct 19th 2010).

Does meditation promote generation of these types of brain waves?

Results of research seem to affirm that this is indeed true. Generation of theta waves has been recorded in more than 15 studies.[338] There also appears to be extensive evidence to support the claim that there is emission of alpha waves during meditation. This appears to occur from different types of meditation, and in different group sizes and experience level of meditators (ibid).

In an experiment done by J.P. Banquet in Massachusetts General Hospital and Harvard Medical School, Boston, the electroencephalograph (EEG) readings of 12 practitioners of TM were observed while they were meditating. In addition to the generation of alpha and theta waves, beta waves were also observed being emitted from the brains of advanced meditators. Even more interesting, it was found that the waves generated from the different areas of the brain were synchronized in frequency and amplitude unlike the random pattern of brain waves that occur in the waking state.[339]

In the research done on meditating Buddhist monks mentioned previously it was discovered that there was a dramatic increase in gamma waves generated by these monks.

"...Most monks showed extremely large increases of a sort that has never been reported before in the neuroscience literature,"

---

[338] *Institute of Noetic Sciences*, http://www.noetic.org/research/medbiblio/ch2_2.htm (accessed April 19th 2010).

[339] J. P. Banquet, "Spectral analysis of the EEG in meditation," *Electroencephalogr. Clin. Neuro* 35, no. 2.

says neuroscientist Richard Davidson of the University of Wisconsin, Madison.[340]

Stimulation of right side of brain
Meditation also seemed to suppress the functioning of the left side of the brain that is associated with analysis, logic and intellectualization and activated more of the right side. This latter enables greater intuition, creativity, and perception.[341] The process of meditating on a *dhikr* formula, mantra or koan, engages the analytic left-brain and blocks it allowing the right brain to be more readily activated.

The expansion of the brain
In a discussion on Islamicity website: IslamiCity Forum – Discussion – Basics of Islam. Posted: 05 March 2006 at 7:31 pm, it is postulated that recitation of *dhikr* leads to the expansion of the brain activity. This is explained in the following manner:

The activities of the brain are bioelectrical in nature. Countless bioelectrical currents flow as a result of interaction amongst countless neurons that make up the brain.

When a *dhikr* is chanted repeatedly it engages and activates certain regions of the brain and a bioelectrical flow is generated in the neurons in those regions. As the *dhikr* continues to be recited this neural activity increases resulting in an increase in bioelectrical energy. The increase in neural activity triggers the activation of new sets of neurons in other parts of the brain. This results in an expansion of the brain activity. The utilization of the

---

[340] Sharon Begley, "Scans of Monks' Brains Show Meditation Alters Structure, Functioning" (accessed Oct 19th 2010).
[341] S. Abdullah & H. Schucman, "Cerebral lateralization, bimodal consciousness, and related developments in psychiatry" *Research Communications in Psychology, Psychiatry and Behavior* 1.

expanded regions of the brain enables new meanings, interpretations, perspectives, to be brought out on a particular topic or verse or even a conversation, an ability that was not available before practicing of the *dhikr*. This can be viewed as the brain being more able to fully grasp truth.

This conclusion on the repetition of *dhikr* causing an expansion of the brain activity is based on results of laboratory tests done at Washington University and reported in the journal 'Scientific American', in December 1993. A summary of these tests as pertaining to the subject is as follows:

Investigators provided volunteers with a list of nouns. The volunteers were then required to read each noun and propose a corresponding verb. For example, if the noun was "dog" the corresponding verb that might be proposed would be "bark." While they performed this activity their brains were PET scanned.

The following was observed:

> when the subjects first did this task, several distinct parts of the brain, including parts of the prefrontal and cingulate cortex, displayed increased neural activity. But if the volunteers repeated the task with the same list of words several times, the brain activity shifted to different regions. When a fresh list of nouns was given to them, the neural activity increased and shifted back to the first regions again.[342]

---

[342] John Horgan, "Fractured Functions. Does the brain have a supreme integrator?" *Scientific American* 1993, http://wenku.baidu.com/view/1fe3a1717fd5360cba1adb47.html (accessed April 19th 2010).

A Muslim practitioner of TM has stated that she has observed, that, when she studied the Qur'an after completing a session of TM, Qur'anic verses took on new meanings. Similarly it is stated by Maulana Muhammad Zakariya in his book *Faza'il-e-A'maal* that after a Sheik practiced the chanting of *dhikr* for some time, when he opened the Qur'an, every word and *Ayah* in the book took on new meanings and significance.[343]

The expansion of the brain activity induced by these meditative techniques can be the explanation for how this is possible.

The Sufis assert that the meanings denoted by the Names of Allah are manifested in the brain and also the degree of certainty of human consciousness in knowing Allah is dependent on the brain capacity.

By *dhikr*, they proclaim, raw brain cells not assigned to a specific duty can be programmed. This would result in a much more powerful working brain.[344]

We were brought into being with the beautiful Names of Allah, they remark, and so when one constantly repeats the Names of Allah in one's mind, the brain is enabled to reveal better the meanings corresponding to these names and the capabilities such names indicate. Qualities and potentialities bestowed by Allah and lying dormant are awakened and expressed.

Dhikr, they claim, is thus a system of practice to increase the activity of cellular groups in the brain. This activation manifests

---

[343] *Faza'il-E-A'maal*, "Virtues of Zikr," 108.
[344] "Why Zikr is so important," Naqshbandiya Mujaddidiya Aslamiya, http://www.naqshbandiya.com/messageboard/index.php?topic=1254.0;prev_next=prev#new (accessed April 19th 2010).

the meanings of the word(s) of *dhikr* with the degree of manifestation dependent on the strength of activation.[345]

---

[345] http://www.aulia-e-hind.com/*Dhikr*.htm (accessed April 19th 2010).

On the Effect of Dhikr

"IT WOULD NOT BE AN EXAGGERATION IF I SAY THAT YOU WILL BE
DOING THE GREATEST SERVICE TO MANKIND."
(SWAMI KRISHNANANDAJI MAHARAJ)

The effect of *dhikr* on the environment

Does *dhikr* have any effect on the environment? In other words, when we perform *dhikr* does this affect other humans, animals, and inanimate objects?

To answer this question let us first explore whether inanimate objects such as mountains, trees, rocks, and even food are really "dead."

What does the Qur'an and *hadith* mention about this?

In *Surah As-Saba* it is stated:

$$وَلَقَدْ آتَيْنَا دَاوُودَ مِنَّا فَضْلًا يَا جِبَالُ أَوِّبِي مَعَهُ وَالطَّيْرَ وَأَلَنَّا لَهُ الْحَدِيدَ$$

> And indeed We bestowed grace on Dawud (David) from Us (saying): 'O you mountains. Glorify (Allâh) with him! And you birds (also)! And We made the iron soft for him.'[346]

The author of *al-Wujuh al-musfira `an ittisa` al-maghfira* comments on this that, "It is more likely that they literally glorify, except that this phenomenon is hidden from the people and is not perceived except through the rupture of natural laws."[347]

---

[346] Qur'an, 34:10.
[347] "Dhikr is the greatest obligation and a perpetual divine order," *The As-Sunnah Foundation of America*, http://www.sunnah.org/ibadaat/dhikr.htm (accessed Oct 20th 2010).

So here we see that the birds and even an inanimate object like the mountain have the capability to praise God!

Bukhari records the following *hadith*:

> Jabir bin 'Abdullah (R) narrated that the Prophet (S.A.W) used to stand by a tree or a date palm on Friday. Then an Ansari woman or man said. "O Allah's Apostle! Shall we make a pulpit for you?" He replied, "If you wish." So they made a pulpit for him and when it was Friday, he proceeded towards the pulpit (for delivering the sermon). *The date palm cried like a child!* The Prophet (S.A.W) descended (the pulpit) *and embraced it while it continued moaning like a child being quieted.* The Prophet (S.A.W) said, *"It was crying for (missing) what it used to hear of religious knowledge given near to it."*[348] (Emphasis mine).

The date palm tree's behavior indicated two things: it could hear and it had emotion!

In a narration by 'Abdullah (R) he said:

> We used to consider miracles as Allah's Blessings, but you people consider them to be a warning. Once we were with Allah's Apostle on a journey, and we ran short of water. He said, "Bring the water remaining with you." The people brought a utensil containing a little water. He placed his hand in it and said, "Come to the blessed water, and the Blessing is from Allah." I saw the water flowing from among the fingers of Allah's Apostle, and

---

[348] Bukhari, vol. 4, book 56, no. 784.

no doubt, *we heard the meal glorifying Allah, when it was being eaten* (by him).[349] (Emphasis mine).

Here is another example of an inanimate object (food in this case) having the ability to praise Allah!

And it is narrated by Abu Hurairah (R) that Allah's Apostle (S.A.W) said:

> (The Prophet) Moses was a shy person and used to cover his body completely because of his extensive shyness. One of the children of Israel hurt him by saying, 'He covers his body in this way only because of some defect in his skin, either leprosy or scrotal hernia, or he has some other defect.' Allah wished to clear Moses of what they said about him, so one day while Moses was in seclusion, he took off his clothes and put them on a stone and started taking a bath. When he had finished the bath, he moved towards his clothes so as to take them, but *the stone took his clothes and fled*; Moses picked up his stick and ran after the stone saying, 'O stone! Give me my garment!' Till he reached a group of Bani Israel who saw him naked then, and found him the best of what Allah had created, and Allah cleared him of what they had accused him of...[350] (Emphasis mine).

The stone took his clothes and fled! Incredulous isn't it?

Let me add here one final statement from the Prophet (S.A.W) on this amazing phenomenon.

---

[349] Bukhari, vol. 4, book 56, no. 779.
[350] Bukhari, vol. 4, book 55, no. 616.

According to the following *hadith* everything that hears the Muslim call to prayer will testify on the Day of Judgment for the person who delivered that call:

> Abdullah ibn 'Abdurahman (R) related from his father that Abu Sa'eed al-Khudri (R) said to him, "I see that you love the sheep and the desert. If you are with your sheep or in the desert, then raise your voice while making the call to prayer, for *any jinn, human or any other creature within hearing distance of your voice will be a witness for you on the Day of Resurrection*...I heard the Messenger of Allah say that."[351] (Emphasis mine).

Not only would *jinns* and humans who hear the *adhaan* testify for the giver on the Day of Judgement, rather any creature (i.e., creation of Allah (S)) that is within hearing range of the sound!

What can we make from the above narrations?

It seems clear that things we deem to be inanimate have the ability to display receptivity and responsiveness. They also possess some degree of consciousness. We can affect them. We have an impact on them. They can also display qualities that we thought would be exclusive to living things!

Maharishi Mahesh Yogi asserts, "through every thought, word, and action, we are producing an influence to affect all our surroundings." "The quality of that influence depends upon the quality of the vibrations emitted from us. Everything in the universe is constantly influencing every other thing."[352]

---

[351] Bukhari, vol. 1, book 11, no. 583; Ahmad, Nasa'i and Ibn Majah.
[352] *Transcendental Meditation*, 70.

This effect of vibrations also means that we can influence others either negatively or positively even by our mere thoughts and feelings.

Inayat Khan states:

> When a person speaks, thinks or feels either harshly or kindly of another, it reaches the spirit of that one, either consciously or unconsciously, by the power of vibration. If we happen to be offended with someone and do not show it in speech or action, yet it still cannot be hidden, for the vibrations of our feeling will reach directly to the person in question, and he will begin to feel our displeasure, however far away he may be. The same is the case with our love and pleasure: however we may try to conceal it in speech or action, it cannot be hidden. This explains the old adage that even walls have ears, which really means that even the wall is not impervious to vibrations of thought.[353]

He explains the effect of our actions on our environment and us in the following manner: "Life being like a dome, its nature is also dome-like. Disturbance of the slightest part of life disturbs the whole and returns as a curse upon the person who caused it; any peace produced on the surface comforts the whole, and hence returns as peace to the producer" (ibid).

Beneficially impacting the environment
It appears that it is an accepted fact by Sufis and practitioners of other spiritual traditions that man can beneficially affect the

---

[353] Inayat Khan, *The Sufi Message of Hazrat Inayat Khan/The Mysticism of Sound/Vibrations,* http://www.sufimessage.com/mysticism-of-sound/vibrations.html (accessed Oct 20th 2010).

environment. Inayat Khan states: "The saints and sages spread their peace not only in the place where they sit, but even in the neighborhood where they dwell; the town or the country where they live is at peace, in accordance with the power of the vibrations they send out from their soul" (ibid).

An interesting story is recorded of Buddha and a wild elephant. Once, a wild elephant was deliberately set loose on the path on which Buddha was walking to harm him. As the elephant came rushing at him Buddha remained unperturbed and continued to walk with composure and dignity. On approaching Buddha, the ferocious elephant suddenly became calm and meekly bowed before him out of respect.

This dramatic change in the animal's behavior has been explained to be due to the strong vibrations of loving-kindness that were emanating from the Buddha. These vibrations were felt by the raging elephant and transformed its disposition.

It has also been recorded that when a Zen Buddhist was practicing sitting in silence in one room, a mentally-ill person in another room was observed to display signs of calm.

It is also documented that when the healer Kathryn Kuhlmann was performing healing, persons in the congregation were healed even though there were no bodily contact with her. Even more amazing, pedestrians and motorists outside the building were also healed![354]

Weston mentions in his book *How Prayer Heals* an interesting case where a doctor was recording the brain waves of a patient in his office while, unknown to her, members of her church

---

[354] *How Prayer Heals*, 149.

prayer group were praying for her. It is stated that her "brain waves dramatically changed...in the process, the symptoms of the medical condition, for which she was seeing the doctor, disappeared" (ibid., 75).

What this is showing is that humans have the ability to beneficially affect the environment whether it be humans or other creations of God.

Is this effect of humans on the environment measurable?

An experiment investigating the quantifiable impact of Transcendental Meditation on crime rate was performed in Washington, D.C. in the summer of 1993.

Four thousand practitioners of TM from 81 countries assembled in that city to perform TM over an 8-week period from June 7th to July 30th. While they meditated the crime rate of the city was recorded to examine any impact this may have. A 27-member Project Review Board comprising of independent scientists and leading citizens who monitored the research process approved the research protocol. Civic leaders including members of the district city council and police force were also involved.

The abstract of the report on the experiment states:

> Weekly crime data was derived from database records provided by the District of Columbia Metropolitan Police Department (DCMPD), which are used in the FBI Uniform Crime Reports. Statistical analysis considered the effect of weather variables, daylight, historical crime trends and annual patterns in the District of Columbia, as well as trends in neighboring cities. Consistent with previous research, levels of homicides, rapes and assaults

(HRA crimes) correlated with average weekly temperature. Robberies approximately followed an annually recurring cycle. *Time series analysis of 1993 data, controlling for temperature, showed that HRA crimes dropped significantly during the Demonstration Project, corresponding with increases in the size of the group; the maximum decrease was 23.3%.*[355] (Emphasis mine).

Effect of *dhikr*/mantra

How about mantra and *dhikr*, can reciting them produce beneficial effects on the environment?

The answer appears to be firmly in the affirmative.

Robert Gass states, "when we chant, we are consciously sending out positive tones of peace and healing into the world all too often resounding with the echoes of fear, pain and violence."[356]

With specific reference to mantras it is said that the chanting of them produces vibrations that are not only soothing to the human mind but also to all plant and animal life. The emitted vibrations spread specific energy waves in the surrounding atmosphere.[357]

---

[355] John S. Hagelin et al., "Effects of Group Practice of the Transcendental Meditation Program on Preventing Violent Crime in Washington, D.C.: Results of the National Demonstration Project, June-July 1993," *Social Indicators Research* 47, no 2, 153- 201, http://www.springerlink.com/content/k2hg216724k21411/ (accessed Oct 20th 2010).

[356] *Chanting:Discovering Spirit in Sound*, 29.

[357] Bhattathiri, "Scientific Aspects of Yagna Environmental Effects," http://www.arizonaenergy.org/FireEnergy/Scientific%20Aspects%20of%20Yagna%20Environmental%20Effects.htm (accessed Dec 15th 2010).

Swami Krishnanandaji Maharaj asserts that mantra *produces a profound effect on the society*. According to him, *an aura is produced around the sincere practitioner that causes the surrounding atmosphere to become purified*. This will cause things to take shape and the atmosphere to slowly change. He even goes so far at to state that, with intense devotion to doing this practice (of *dhikr* or mantra), one "will see wonders, miracles manifesting themselves."[358]

The Sufis declare that when a Name of Allah is chanted it opens-up and unlocks the angelic power it possesses. The power, grace and virtues of that Name are released into the consciousness, soul and heart. This also protects the surrounding area from troubles and afflictions.[359]

It has been mentioned (and Allah knows best) that when a person was performing *dhikr* he noticed (with his inner eye) that as the *dhikr* wave spread everything that was in its path began to join in the *dhikr*. Eventually, he described, the wave had spread over the entire earth and everything was participating.

In summing up let us look at how the environment benefits from chanting of *dhikr*.

Recitation of *dhikr* produces coherent waveforms of energy. The more it is recited, the stronger are the amplitudes of these waveforms. These waveforms resonate outwards. In the process other vibrations regardless of whether they are emitted from humans or by inanimate objects that are in the path become transformed and resonate with them. This resonance creates harmony, tranquility, and peace.

---

[358] *Fruits From the Garden of Wisdom*, chap. 7.
[359] "Sufi Introduction to the 99 attributes of the Names of Allah and especially that of Ya Latif," (accessed Oct 20th 2010).

For instance if one begins reciting *Ya Salaamu*, the quality of this Name of Allah, peace, which lies dormant in the brain is activated. The recitor then begins to experience some level of peace. As he/she continues to recite that name greater and greater levels of peace are experienced where the degree of peace is dependent on the intensity of the recitation. These waves of peace are then generated outward affecting everything in the path.

A closer look at the Energy Field
How is it possible to affect the environment when we perform *dhikr* or other spiritual practices? It is because of the interconnectedness of all things, both animate and inanimate. This interconnectedness has long been held to be true in eastern traditions. The west, however, has mostly maintained until very recent times that reality must be perceived by the five senses and so there is nothing more beyond that.

Today the existence of a universal energy field that envelops and permeates all things is now gaining greater consideration. Quantum physics has yielded that matter is not solid but consists of particles and waves. Densification of the universal energy creates forms that are visible which includes the human body. Subtler forms of that energy exist. Examples of these are thoughts and consciousness.

This interrelatedness of all things can be summed up by the following statement by Belleruth Napersteck, a social worker in the field of guided imagery:

> We are nothing but vibration in a sea of living, intelligent energy – that although we are disguised as separate, solid matter, this appearance of solidity is only how we appear in the overt, concrete order of manifest reality; at

a deeper, truer level we are all nothing but interconnecting, interpenetrating energy fields, transcending time and space, each vibration containing everything in the universe, each subatomic bit of us a hologram of all that is. That is why we can experience instantaneous, direct knowing.[360]

Since all things are interconnected the vibrations that are generated from us when certain spiritual practices are indulged in appear to emanate outwards from the center and permeate the environment. These vibrations apparently are uplifting and healing. Due to the strength of these waves they influence other weaker ones to fall in line producing a resonant effect. This is known as entrainment.

This phenomenon is further explained as follows:

> ...Thought-forms and vibrations that have high frequency, coherent waveforms of energy are able to transform thought-forms and vibrations that have low frequency and incoherent waveforms of energy through a process of induction and entrainment. Moreover, the more that a certain thought-form or pattern of energy is produced, maintained, and given attention, the stronger that its presence and resonant effect becomes, making it more likely that other people and things will attune to it. A simple analogy is of a note that sounds louder and louder until all surrounding objects that can vibrate at that note do, helping that note to sound even louder.[361]

---

[360] *Your Sixth Sense*, 71.
[361] http://www.islamtheabsolutetruth.com/exec.html (accessed Feb 8th 2010).

Hagelin, an eminent physicist and a leading author of the study on the effect of TM on crime rate mentioned earlier, presents another perspective on this phenomenon. He states:

> It's analogous to the way that a magnet creates an invisible field that causes iron filings to organize themselves into an orderly pattern. Similarly, these meditation techniques have been shown to create high levels of coherence in EEG brain wave patterns of individual practitioners. This increased coherence and orderliness in individual consciousness appears to spill over into society and can be measured indirectly via changes in social indices, such as reductions in the rate of violent crime. We call this phenomenon a field effect of consciousness. [362]

The degree to which the environment is affected by these practices is likely dependent on the strength of activation of the energy field.

The religious view on universal energy

Walter Weston in *How Prayer Heals* feels that this energy that pervades the universe is nothing else but the Spirit if God. God, the giver of life, provides the life force that enables all things to function at their optimum. It is his Spirit, working in an intelligent way, which brings about healing to the body, mind, and soul. He states:

> As one who has personally experienced God's transforming presence and power, I cannot read the

---

[362] "Transcendental Meditation Experiment Arrests Crime Study Shows Dramatic Drop in Violent Crime During D.C. Project," *AllTM.org – Transcendental Meditation*, http://www.alltm.org/pages/crime- arrested.html (accessed Oct 20th 2010).

scientific data without recognizing that it is describing God and God's work among humanity. God created and continues to create and make all things new through the healing encounter. God is the Source of health and happiness.

...As the scientific data graphically portrays, when the healing energy flows into a human being, the energy fields become significantly larger and become white, like the mystic presence of God..."[363]

Elsewhere he states: "God is spirit. God can be described scientifically as an energy field. When people have strong experiences of God, God's presence or energy continue to linger..." and "God's presence has formed a sacred, information-laden energy field..." (Ibid., 150-151).

The act of healing, he indicates, "imparts an energy into the human energy field. This energy is the power of God, but for research purposes it is known as life energy or subtle energy. It is measurable at a specific electromagnetic frequency" (ibid., 66).

"Humans," Weston states, "are biophysical with a spiritual nature that is rooted in the human energy field" (ibid., 60).

The Sufis acknowledge that this universal energy field exists and that it is indeed spiritual in nature. By acquiring an ability termed High Sense Perception (HSP), Sufi healers are able to observe this energy. (HSP appears to be similar to clairvoyance). They state: "HSP reveals the dynamic world of the fluid, interacting spiritual energy fields which surround and permeate all living things. This energy supports us, nourishes us, and

---

[363] *How Prayer Heals*, 126-127.

gives us life. We sense each other with this energy as we are a part of it and it is a part of us."[364]

Now let us take a second reading of Swami Krishnanandaji Maharaj's statement mentioned previously. Asserting that the chanting of mantra produces a profound effect on the society he declares, "it would not be an exaggeration if I say that you will be doing the greatest service to mankind" with that practice. With intense devotion to it "you will see wonders, miracles manifesting themselves."

This effect that chanting a mantra has on society, according to the Swami, is not due to the individual's personal strength or thought but rather by that which the mantra is able to "rouse into activity and which is omniscient."

He says the invocations of God's Names "are converted into an impersonal force, which is the power of God, and the miracle is worked by God Himself" so that the action appears not to be done by oneself but rather by God himself.[365]

In scientific terminology, this entity that the mantra is able to "rouse into activity," this impersonal force or the power of God is referred to as the energy field, according the Walter Weston.

"Energy medicine," says Weston, "is based on the spiritual nature of man. In Eastern cultures, this spiritual nature is clarified by the presence of human energy field which contains our spiritual essence."[366] According to him, the reason why some

---

[364] Hisham Muhammad Kabbani, "Spiritual Healing in the Sufi Tradition," http://nurmuhammad.com/Meditation/EnergyHealing/harvardhealinglecture.htm (accessed Dec 21st 2010).
[365] *Fruits From the Garden of Wisdom*, chap. 7.
[366] *How Prayer Heals*, 41.

cultures speak only of the energy field and do not make reference to God is because of a lack of vocabulary or thought pattern to make the connection (ibid., 65).

Group energy fields
The human energy field that surrounds a person bears information on the mental, emotional, religious, and moral activity of the person. The energy field of a person radiates and intermingles with those of other persons. Walter Weston states that when the energy fields of a group merge, they become "one enormous, information-bearing, group energy field whose power is the square of the coherent number of persons gathered." This group energy field becomes an entity of its own, subduing individual will when it acts on the information it carries (ibid., 166).

This is the reason, he explains, why ordinarily well-behaved persons become irrational and aggressive in a crowd. This may also be the reason why wide-scale massacres have occurred in various parts of the world like in Rwanda and Bosnia. When the fear, anger, and prejudice contained in the energy field of each person merge with energy fields having the same type of information, this produces coherence and the angry information-bearing group energy field of a mob.

On the other hand, when there is caring and compassion, the group energy field "becomes filled with God, love, and peace." Anyone subjected to this field becomes transformed by its healing power (ibid., 170).

Walter Weston cites the peaceful break-up of the former Soviet Union as one case of this. According to him this event, which was "one of the most rapid peaceful and economic revolutions in human history" was a result of the effect of the pent-up feelings of the oppressed people on the group energy field. In his thinking, this coherent field containing the needs of the people at some critical juncture acted intelligently to achieve its goals (ibid., 171).

The beneficial effect of a group energy field that produces healing, he argues, has tremendous implications. Group energy fields can be designed to therapeutically help senior citizens and those with mental diseases, lower crime rate, and improve the quality of life not only in depressed neighborhoods but in society in general (ibid., 170).

He further elaborates that because this group energy field acts intelligently to enable the optimum functioning of all life, it can also be used to restore the ecological balance of the earth by its effect on water and air pollution. Since water and air do possess energy fields, these fields can be transformed enabling cleaning up of pollutants in the process. The same can also be true for toxic waste, he argues (ibid., 173).

Weston feels that beneficial utilization of the group energy field can result in a world changed for the better. Since the power of this energy field increases by the square of the number of persons involved, if enough people pray the amount of energy generated would be enough to avert natural disasters such as earthquakes and hurricanes and even reduce the temperature of the warming water of oceans. He goes so far as to suggest that, if a comet were heading towards the earth, the prayers of four billion people would be sufficient to cause the comet to veer away. The energy of the group energy field produced would exceed that of a nuclear bomb!

Group energy field and matter
It also appears that this group energy field has the ability to affect what we may call "matter".

Researchers have quietly been performing experiments to investigate the effect of consciousness on the numbers a machine called a random-event generator (REG), produces. This machine takes samples of electronic noise from the environment and then generates either ones or zeros. Normally, because the electronic noise varies randomly, the numbers generated would be random. When plotted, the resultant chart would show random variation centered on the horizontal axis at zero as a function of time. However, if the plot displays a consistent sloping trend away from the horizontal, this would be indicative that the electronic signal is no longer random – in other words, something in the environment is producing some order.

Experimental data were gathered from a network of these random event generators positioned basically around the globe on all continents and in nearly all time zones.

The researchers found that when major "World Events" such as the terrorist attack on September 11th, the Chechen hostage crisis in 2002, and the plane crash of U.S Senator Paul Wellstone occurred in 2002, the plots displayed clear deviations from the horizontal. A distinct positive trend was observed when all data from 122 events taken over 4 years were plotted.

The chances that this result could have been from random fluctuations were 1 million to one.

This result, according to them, is highly significant and appears to be attributable to the coherence of thoughts and emotions these events produced among millions of humans.[367]

One interesting experiment performed by Dean Radin, director of Consciousness Research Laboratory at the University of Nevada, occurred around the time of the verdict of the O. J. Simpson trial.

On October 3, 1995, when the verdict of the O. J. Simpson trial was about to be announced, around half-a-billion people across the world were either watching or listening to the live event. This was quite an unusually large audience size. It exceeded the number of people tuned in to one of the highest-rated television events in the United States, the Superbowl, for some years.

Radin and his colleagues decided to take advantage of this to explore the effect of field consciousness. Data from random number generators at Princeton University and the University of Amsterdam were combined with that of three random generators in his laboratory. The resulting data set was analyzed to look for any trends related to the verdict.

A plot of the data showing odds against chance versus time was created. If the audience had no effect on the data, no peaks would be seen. Data would vary randomly around the horizontal axis. However, if the audience did really made an impact, deviations from the horizontal should be observed.

The plot showed clear peaks when the TV preshows began and during the time when the verdict was about to be announced.[368]

---

[367] "The Global Consciousness Project," http://noosphere.princeton.edu/fristwall2.html (accessed Jan 24th 2011).

Similar results were observed by Radin and his team during the Centennial Olympic Games in July 1996 where there were some three billion viewers worldwide. The data showed progressively more order as the Olympics continued while data after the Olympics ended showed the typical expected behavior of a random event (ibid).

The above findings indicate that the collective consciousness of human beings, when focused on a common event, have the ability to influence even machines!

The performance of collective *dhikr* then, may have far reaching effects we may not be aware of.

Healing of the sick

Spontaneous and miraculous healings have been recorded. For instance Walter Weston mentions in his book *How Prayer Heals* some remarkable recoveries. Two cases will be stated here.

In the first case, Weston, for some unknown reason, rushed to the community hospital in the district in Ohio where he was a young pastor. There he learnt that Alex, one of the members of his parish, was dying.

The doctor told him: "Walt, I wouldn't give him more than half an hour to live."

Alex had developed an infection after having surgery for a ruptured appendix. He lay in bed with his abdomen enormously bloated and his complexion gray.

---

[368] Dean Radin, "Moving Mind, Moving Matter," *Noetic Sciences* Review no. 46 (Summer 1998): 20, http://psionslair.co.cc/pdf/movingmindmatter.pdf (accessed Jan 24th 2011).

Weston writes: "After some pastoral care I took his hand into mine and began offering a prayer for the dying. Almost immediately I became spontaneously filled with God, a peak state of consciousness involving holiness, love, joy, and peace. Then I felt energy descend upon my head and shoulders and flow down my arm into Alex's hand. I was sobbing in joy, tears freely flowing down my cheeks."

" I continued praying throughout this experience. When I finished the five-minute prayer, Alex's eyes were wide in awe as he said, "Pastor, I felt something flow from your hand into mine.""

Both surprised and shocked, Weston saw that Alex was now healthy, his abdomen was no longer bloated and his complexion was normal.

The doctor then entered. In amazement he saw that the wound from the surgery three days ago had been completely healed. He exclaimed: "Walt, this is impossible. This is impossible."[369]

In the second case, a car hit a four-year-old boy, Tim. On arrival at the hospital he appeared lifeless. The situation was critical. The doctor remarked that every bone in his body seemed broken. There appeared to be damage to internal organs. There was internal bleeding. He skull appeared to be fractured and there was probable brain damage.

Even though the situation seemed hopeless, Weston, together with the grieving family members, silently prayed and, also every half hour, he would perform a prayer for healing.

---

[369] *How Prayer Heals*, 33.

Over a four-hour period they periodically received updates about Tim's condition. "Internal bleeding has stopped." "Has fewer fractures than original x-rays had shown." "Has no fractures." "His condition has stabilized and we've put him in bed to sleep."

Tim slept for 16 hours. When he woke up "he got out of bed, ran to the nursing station, and asked for something to eat. He was healthy. No broken bones; no internal injuries; no brain damage; no bruises; no abrasions; not a scratch remained" (ibid., 101).

Weston believes that these cases of recovery that defy all logical medical explanation happen due to accessing of the universal energy field. In accessing this field an abundance of energy is made available. He says, "when we unite with God for healing prayer, it inevitably results in an unlimited supply of healing energy moving through us to the person for whom we are praying" (ibid., 17).

This field is information-bearing. The intent of a person is conveyed by it. If a person is desirous of healing someone then the transmitted energy contains that intention and healing results. However, if the intention is to harm then that intention is also transmitted and the energy would contain information that would be harmful (ibid., 79).

Another feature of this field is that it is intelligent. It appears to know exactly which body part needs healing. Hence, it knows how to provide the optimum healing effects.

In his book *How Prayer Heals*, Weston quotes Bernard Grad, regarded as the father of research on healing, on the nature of this energy. He states: "The energy is informational! The energy itself is an information-bearer, self-regulating, programmed.

Where healing calls for the slowing down of cell growth...thyroid development is inhibited. Where healing requires speeding up of cell growth...the process is accelerated. Slow down or speed up for healing? The same agent does both. The energy itself knows" (ibid., 71).

This description of the nature of universal energy fits well with Weston's position that it really refers to the power of God.

The same mechanism probably explains the phenomenon of distant healing. Weston believes that remote prayer by groups in worshipping or praying together is "extremely effective" (ibid., 82). Praying to Allah for help for someone, or *du'a* in Islamic terminology, can be viewed as a transportation of energy utilizing this energy field. Reciting of Qur'anic verses raises the energy vibrations and in the process of imploring Allah the healing thoughts are projected to the sick person via activation of the energy field. This is similar to the Reiki technique of distant healing.[370]

According to Weston clairvoyants report that this message is conveyed to the recipient via an electromagnetic carrier beam that is sent out from the region of the heart. It appears as "a white laser-like beam of light."[371]

The Sufis indicate that through HSP it can be seen how most diseases are initiated in the (human) energy field. Time, bad habits, and unhealthy living can distort this energy field. This distortion is then transmitted to the body producing a serious

---

[370] Rookaya Vawda, "Ṣalah and dhikr as Holistic Healing," http://www.ima.org.za/multimedia/Salah%20&%20dhikr%20as%20holistic%20healing.pdf (accessed May 5th 2010).
[371] *How Prayer Heals*, 66.

illness. The initial source of the problem can be either psychological or physical.

HSP can also be used to reveal how the disease process can be reversed.[372]

Healing frequencies
For healing to occur, according to Weston, the correct healing frequencies need to be accessed and transmitted. He points out that even if the amount of transmitted energy filled the size of a sports stadium healing would not occur unless it was at the right healing frequency. "A properly attuned healing frequency is the first requirement of any transmitted energy that heals" (ibid., 82).

The effectiveness of spoken prayer for healing, according to Weston, is because of the vocal frequencies it uses.

The frequency range for healing appears to be from 7.8 to 8.0 Hz. Lower frequencies may produce detrimental effects. When a healer placed his hand in water, the water emitted a frequency of 8 Hz according to a study done by Dr. Andrija Puharich and seven physicists in the United States navy. When mice were subjected to 5 Hz radiation they developed cancer within 48 hours. When they were then subjected to radiation at 8 Hz they were cured within 48 hours (ibid., 70-71).

The healing frequencies appear to be related to the frequency of the electromagnetic field around the earth. This frequency, called the Shumann Effect, appears to be 7.83 Hz, which is similar to

---

[372] Hisham Muhammad Kabbani, "Spiritual Healing in the Sufi Tradition," http://www.nurmuhammad.com/Meditation/EnergyHealing/harvardhealinglecture.htm (accessed Dec 21st 2010).

the frequency of alpha waves generated from the brain. Some researchers also believe that 7.8 Hz is the resonant frequency of the human body. Dr. Robert Beck also suggests that this frequency may also be how information is conveyed across the universe. The abilities of psychics and healers may be as a result of they being able to access or become entrained by this frequency.[373]

In the Sufi healing technique there appears to be agreement that it is necessary to have the correct frequency of the healing energy for curing diseases. They, however, believe that the appropriate frequency is dependent on the particular type of disease. In their methodology they use specific *dhikr* to access cosmic energy of a particular frequency. Repetition of the *dhikr* results in the healer becoming the recipient of huge amounts of this cosmic energy.[374]

Energy field, early disease detection and cure
One of the potential benefits of the energy field is the ability to detect signs that disease would be likely to occur long before it actually occurs. Healing by *dhikr* or other techniques or by using conventional medical approaches can then be applied to remove the risk of the disease occurring.

In the 1980's an Indian physicist, Dr. Ramesh Singh Chouhan, undertook research investigating the first of the human energy fields. He measured the depth and density of this field by use of Kirlian photography where ionized energy pictures around the fingertips are obtained. Using this method, he screened twenty-

---

[373] Jonathan Goldman, "Sound entrainment" in *Music Phyician for times to come*, 226.
[374] Hisham Muhammad Kabbani, "Spiritual Healing in the Sufi Tradition," http://www.nurmuhammad.com/Meditation/EnergyHealing/harvardhealinglecture.htm (accessed Oct 13th 2010).

five thousand women and examined the resulting data for possible correlations between the energy pattern and disease.

He was able to identify a consistent linkage between the pattern or signature of the field and several medical conditions. This produced four medical breakthroughs. These are[375]:

1) The signatures of cancer could be observed on the human energy field before the cancer actually appeared in the physical body. This resulted in detection of cancer three to six months earlier than when it can be detected using any other medical technique or device.

    In employing this method for diagnosing for and treating cervical cancer surgeons would then use this information about the energy field to remove suspicious tissues in the cervix. Another picture of the glow from around the fingertips would then be taken. If the surgery had successfully removed all tissues that would have become cancerous the energy field would become normal. If the cancer signature still existed then more cervical tissues would be removed.

    One of the great benefits of this method is the fact that there is real-time feedback as to the success of the surgery. How often times do we not hear of someone having had surgery for cancer but then not too long afterwards the cancer reappears and spreads swiftly – a possible indication that all cancerous tissues had not been removed by the surgery?

---

[375] *How Prayer Heals*, 93-95.

2) The symptoms of arthritis can be obtained six to twelve months before they actually occur in a patient allowing for much earlier treatment of this condition.

3) Pregnancy can be diagnosed moments after conception. This is observed by the energy field undergoing a significant energy shift as noted by the picture of the glow from the fingertips.

4) It can be used to accurately determine the most optimum time for conception to occur.

Weston makes an important observation regarding Chouhan's findings. The fact that signs of cancer or arthritis are registered in the energy field three to twelve months before these conditions manifest in the human body indicate that "whatever caused the distortions in the energy fields acted slowly in causing illness." On the other hand, he points out, healing energy acts quickly in transforming the energy fields. Hence, Chouhan's method can be used to detect early signs of disease and then the distorted energy fields can be immediately treated by healing thereby producing rapid cure of the condition. Using this approach, he believes, as an example, that all symptoms of osteoarthritis can disappear within minutes to an hour of a ten-minute healing session (ibid., 95).

Weston visited India in 1989 to participate in clinical studies with Chouhan exploring the effect of healing on the energy field and thus on disease. During the healing sessions the effect of prayer on the energy field around the fingers was observed using a video camera.

Preliminary trials showed that the effect on the energy field was the same regardless of where he placed his hands on the subject.

Thus, for the remaining tests, Weston would place his hands on the person's neck and forehead while praying aloud.

One experiment dealt with attempting to cure the cold symptoms of a 21 year-old laboratory assistant. This person was displaying all the symptoms of a severe cold: fever, running nose, watery eyes, sneezing, and skin pallor.

Weston states that within two seconds after the session commenced, the image of the energy field "changed from its baseline blue with a white outer fringe to a pure white hue about as twice as large; and it remained constant." Around 89 seconds into the session the subject "vigorously" pulled herself from Weston's hands complaining of feeling extreme heat. She explained that the heat was too painful. After about one hour, all cold symptoms had disappeared (ibid., 97).

Another experiment dealt with treating the back pain of a woman who had travelled more than 100 miles in desperate search of relief. This back pain had been bothering her for more than 10 years. Weston states:

> Upon my touching her for the first time, her normal energy field of blue with a white tinge changed, at three seconds, into a pure white field about as twice as large. I maintained hand contact for ten minutes during each of three sessions. On the second and third days, she arrived with her fingertip bioelectrography image (her energy field) still glowing with the transmitted healing energy of the previous day. She reported no change of symptoms until the third day. In the midst of that healing encounter, she reported the complete alleviation of all symptoms (ibid., 97-98).

The third case of healing cited here has to do with pre-treating cancer. Placing his hands on the patient's forehead and neck, Weston performed healing prayer in total darkness. The first eight minutes in the session, however, appeared not to produce any effect. Nevertheless he continued to pray. Just around ten minutes Weston suddenly exclaimed: "She has begun receiving the healing flow." He continued to pray for an additional two minutes.

A week later, an examination of the energy field surrounding the fingertips revealed what had happened. For the first ten minutes, it was observed that the human energy field had remained unchanged by the prayer. Then, at about nine minutes and forty-five seconds the image "became instantly pure white and almost three times longer." A later image showed no characteristic signature of cancer. The patient had been cured of cancer before it manifested in the body (ibid., 99).

Personal experiences

Feelings of peace
Those whom I have spoken to on how *dhikr* affected them have only words of praise and appreciation. One Pakistani friend related that in a mosque in Pakistan that he used to attend, collective *dhikr* used to be performed every night after the *Eshaa* prayers. He said that the feelings he experienced were so peaceful that nothing else mattered at that time. A similar experience is related by another friend from Morocco where collective *dhikr* was and still is performed after the *'Asr* prayers in a certain mosque. According to him all the problems in the world seem to be removed from one's mind during the recitation of the *dhikr*.

I have personally several times experienced the strengthening force of *dhikr*. At the passing away of my father, being in a despondent mood I recall how, after completing *Maghrib Salah* at home I remained seated and recited *dhikr* in an audible tone. I felt the strength and reassurance it gave me. An aunt in an adjacent room also heard the recitation of the *dhikr*. After I had finished chanting of the *dhikr* and entered that room she requested for the *dhikr* to be continued. She had also felt the strengthening force of it.

At other times I have experienced the protection it gave in warding off evil thoughts and feelings and evil influences. I have noticed its effectivity in fighting the *nafs* (the ego).

What is noteworthy is that at all times of urgent need I find that the greatest benefit is derived when the *dhikr* is done in an audible tone. The volume, however, should not be vey loud. It seems that the vibration of the sound within the body has a healing effect.

Relief from pain
Br. Zaman Marwat, the Imam of the Islamic Association of the Finger Lakes in Upstate New York says that many have related to him how they obtained relief from excruciating pain through chanting the Names of Almighty Allah or by reciting verses from the Holy Qur'an. Personally, when he, himself, chanted *dhikr*, he felt significant relief from pain.

My sister relates how, when she was having labor pains, she chanted *dhikr* and was able to deliver without using any pain medicine.

Recovery from surgery

A major open-heart surgery had to be undertaken on my nephew who was born with a congenital heart problem. During the operation complications developed and the situation became life threatening. When we visited him the next day he was lying on his hospital bed, unconscious to the world.

We prayed *Maghrib Salah* at the hospital. Then, after the *Salah* we decided to perform *dhikr* together in a group. As we chanted, I could feel the reassurance it was giving us in a situation that looked desperate. The *dhikr* lasted for about 10 minutes. After it was finished we made a *du'a* asking for Allah's help.

My nephew started to show signs of improvement. *Alhamdu lilah* he is now fully recovered. I firmly believe that the prayers of everyone and perhaps also the *dhikr* and appeal to Allah contributed to his recovery.

Charging and recharging of one's energy

Ibn Qayyim has mentioned that Ibn Taymiyyah said, *"Dhikr for the heart is like water for the fish. What would the condition of the fish be when it leaves water?"*[376]

He also mentioned: "I was once in the presence of Ibn Taymiyyah. He performed the *Fajr* prayer and then sat in the *dhikr* of Allah Most High until close to midday. Then he turned to me and said, *'This is my breakfast; if I wasn't to take my breakfast then I would lose strength,'* or some words similar to this" (ibid).

---

[376] Ibn Qayyim al-Jawziyya, *Al-Waabil as-Saib*, 60 quoted at http://www.sunniforum.com/forum/showthread.php?18276-Dhikr!!!&p=160728&viewfull=1 (accessed April 27th 2011).

In his book *The Tibetan book of living and dying*, the Tibetan monk Sogyal Rinpoche describes how he was conducting a workshop and at the end of the day he became quite exhausted and drained by responding to the many questions posed by participants. He then decided to recite one of the Buddhist mantras. He relates the amazing effect it had – how gradually the whole environment became transformed and how he felt energized again. [377]

A classic example of the effect of chanting is that of the Benedictine monks living in a monastery in South France.

After Vatican II the monks had begun to display signs of fatigue, mild depression, and poor motivation. Dr. Alfred Tomatis, a researcher who had established the healing and curative powers of sound and music, was asked to look into the affair. Upon arrival at the monastery Tomatis found seventy of the monks slumped in their cells. The doctor diagnosed that the problem was not physiological but rather had to do with the theological reforms that had been introduced in the monastery. Previously, the monks used to perform the Gregorian chant several hours daily. When a new abbot took over the monastery, however, the monks were forbidden to perform the chanting. The abbot had thought at that time that the monks' time could be more productively spent.

With the consent of the abbot, Tomatis permitted the monks to resume their daily repetition of the Gregorian chant. The effect was amazing. Within six months the monks were back to their normal selves – full of vitality and energetically performing their tasks.[378]

---

[377] *The Tibetan book of living and dying*, 72.
[378] *The Mozart Effect*, 103-104.

The effect of *dhikr* on the aura

The human energy field known as the aura appears to affect or leave an imprint on anything that one interacts with. Thus the vibrations we generate, according to Inayat Khan, leave their effect on the chair that we sit in, on the bed that we sleep on, in the house that we live, and on the clothes that we wear.[379]

According to Catherine Loveless and Damian Smythe in "Something in the aura," objects and places are magnetized by the electromagnetic nature of the aura. The imprint becomes stronger if the interaction is longer or more intimate. They posit that this is the reason why someone may have trouble sleeping in a strange bed since its energy pattern is unfamiliar or why a child is upset when his or her favorite toy is washed since washing would remove the magnetic charge from the aura.[380]

They also state that the strength of the aura is also related to the well-being of the person. The healthier the person is, both physically and emotionally, the stronger is that person's aura. If the aura is strong, therefore, it not only indicates that the person is in good health but he/she would also have the ability to leave a greater imprint on the environment.

Catherine and Damian indicate that a person's aura can be strengthened by various means including sunlight, physical exercise and music. They point out, in particular, that chants (*dhikr*) are powerful for purifying or cleansing the aura of negative energies and energizing it. The auric field can be

---

[379] Inayat Khan, *The Sufi Message of Hazrat Inayat Khan/The Mysticism of Sound/Vibrations*, http://www.sufimessage.com/mysticism-of-sound/vibrations.html (accessed Oct 20th 2010).
[380] Catherine Loveless and Damian Smythe, "Something in the aura," http://www.korotkov.org/file/saa.pdf (accessed Oct 29th 2010).

changed to promote healing or to access higher levels of consciousness by means of chants, they state.

The result of experiments by Dr. Knut Pfeiffer mentioned earlier, appears to corroborate the above statement. Dr. Pfeiffer had shown that meditation of which chanting (*dhikr*) is considered to be a part of, produces a fully rounded and vibrant energy field as pictured from the emissions from the fingertips.

The Sufis' State of *Fanaa'*

The Sufis claim that when *dhikr* is abundantly recited the recitor can attain to a state where "one forgets oneself and all there is, save God..."[381] This state named "fanaa'" by the Sufis, denotes the annihilation or the non-existence of the self.

According to Imam Ghazali this state is when God overwhelms the heart. "When a person has forgotten these worlds which are the existence of creation, they have become his non-existence. And when he has forgotten his own egotism, he, too, has become non-existent with respect to his "self." When nothing else remains with him except God Most High, his existence is God and nothing else" declares Ghazali.

He further elaborates:

> That person sees nothing except God Most High and says: "He is everything; except for Him there is no self." At this point the separation between one and God departs and unity is achieved. That is the beginning of the world of Divine Unity and Oneness. That is, when the separateness departs, one is not aware of separation and

---

[381] Al-Ghazali in *Alchemy of Happiness*, 223.

distance for a person knows separation when he knows two things: himself and God. But this person is, in this state, unaware of his self and knows nothing other that the One...(Ibid).

Abdul Qadir Jilani speaks about this in the following manner:

There are different levels of remembrance and each has different ways. Some are expressed outwardly with audible voice, some felt inwardly, silently, from the centre of the heart. At the beginning one should declare in words what one remembers. Then stage by stage the remembrance spreads throughout one's being – descending to the heart, then rising to the soul; then still further it reaches the realm of the secrets; further to the hidden; to the most hidden of the hidden...Remembrance pronounced in words is but a declaration that the heart has not forgotten Allah. The inward silent remembrance is a movement of the emotions. The remembrance of the heart is through feeling in oneself the manifestation of Allah's might and beauty, while the remembrance of the soul is through the enlightenment of the divine light generated by Allah's might and beauty. The remembrance of the level of the secret realm is through the ecstasy received from beholding the divine secrets. The remembrance of the hidden realm brings one to: the place of truth in the presence of Sovereign Omnipotent. The remembrance of the final level that is called *khafi al-akhfa* – 'the most hidden of the hidden' – brings one to a state of annihilation of the self and unification with the truth. In reality only Allah knows the state of the one who has penetrated into that realm containing all knowledge, which is the end of all and everything."[382]

According to Ibn 'Ata'llah al-Iskandari, this state of annihilation in respect to the ego occurs "when the One invoked takes possession of the heart and the *dhikr* is obliterated and vanishes, and the invoker does not pay attention to the *dhikr* nor to the heart."[383]

Inayat Khan remarks that *this state is the pinnacle of the purpose of life*. He states: "when he invokes the Names of God, man forgets his limitations, and he impresses his soul with the thought of the Unlimited. This brings him to the ideal of Unlimitedness. *This is the secret of life's attainment.*"[384]

Further elaboration on this state is given in an article by Abu Sa`îd al-Kharrâz in Nuzhat Al-Majalis. He states:

> When God desires to befriend (*yuwâli*) a servant of His, He opens the door of *dhikr* for that servant. After the latter takes pleasure (*istaladhdha*) in *dhikr*, He opens the door of proximity (*al-qurb*) for him. After that, He raises him to the meetings of intimacy (*majâlis al-uns*) and after that he makes him sit on a throne of Oneness (*kursi min al-tawHîd*). Then He removes the veils (*al-Hujub*) from him and He makes him enter the abode of Singleness (*dâr al-fardâniyya*) and unveils Majesty (*al-jalâl*) and Sublimity

---

[382] Abdur Qadir Jilani, *The Secret of Secrets*, 3rd ed., 45-46.
[383] "Dhikr -from Miftah al-Falah (The Key to Success)," *ISRA*, http://www.israinternational.com/knowledge/166-dhikr-from-miftah-al-falah-the-key-to-success.html (accessed Oct 20th 2010).
[384] Inayat Khan, *The Sufi Message of Hazrat Inayat Khan/Religion The Effect of Prayer*, http://www.sufimessage.com/religion/effect-of-prayer.html (accessed Oct 20th 2010).

> (al-`aZama) to him. When the servant beholds Majesty and Sublimity, he remains without 'he' (baqiya bila hu). He becomes extinguished (fâni), immune (bâri') to the claims and pretensions of his ego (da`âwa nafsihi), and protected for God's sake (maHfûZan lillâh).³⁸⁵

If one is fortunate enough to attain this state, according to Ghazali, then "the appearance of the empyrean begins to be unveiled to him and the spirits of the angels and the Prophets start to disclose themselves to him in wondrous forms. That which is reserved to the Divine Presence starts to appear to him. Tremendous events reveal themselves which cannot be described in words."³⁸⁶

This statement by Ghazali is echoed by Ibn 'Ata'llah al-Iskandari. He states:

> If the invoker continues, it becomes a fixed habit and a permanent state by which he may ascend to the celestial world. Then the purest real Being emerges and he is imprinted with nature of the invisible world (malakut) and the holiness of Divinity (lahut) is manifested to him. The first thing manifested to him from that world are the essences of the angels and the spirits of the Prophets and saints in beautiful forms through which some of the realities overflow onto him. That is the beginning. This continues until his degree is higher than forms and he encounters the Truth in everything with clarity.³⁸⁷

---

[385] Quoted by G. F. Haddad in article "On Dhikr Remembrance of God," http://www.livingislam.org/n/dhkr_e.html (accessed April 27th 2011).
[386] Al-Ghazali in *Alchemy of Happiness*, 224.
[387] "Dhikr -from Miftah al-Falah (The Key to Success)," *ISRA*, http://www.israinternational.com/knowledge/166-dhikr-from-miftah-al-falah-the-key-to-success.html (accessed Oct 20th 2010).

Appendix A

Quotes on *Dhikr*

Quotes on *Dhikr*

"The basic aim of *dhikr* is to silence the thinking mind and to shift the awareness from the rational to the intuitive mode of consciousness...When the rational mind is silenced, the intuitive mode produces an extraordinary awareness; the environment is experienced in a direct way without the filter of conceptual thinking. The experience of oneness with the surrounding environment is the main characteristic of this meditative state. It is a state of consciousness where every form of fragmentation has ceased, fading away into undifferentiated unity."
[Ibrahim B. Syed in article Sufism and Quantum Physics][388]

"It is my firm conviction that the remedy for all evils is the *dhikr* of Allah..."
[Moulana Zakariya in a letter to Maulana Abul Hasan Ali Nadwi][389]

"Whoever remembers God Almighty, God will enliven his heart and enlighten his mind and intellect."

"Remembrance of God is the key to proximity (to Him)."

"O He whose Name is a Remedy, whose remembrance is cure."

---

[388] Ibrahim B. Syed, "Sufism and Quantum Physics," http://www.irfi.org/articles/articles_1_50/sufism_and_quantum_physics.htm (accessed April 27th 2011).

[389] Abd al-Hafiz Makki, "An analysis of the evidence supporting the permissibility of Majalis (gatherings) of zikr in the Masjid" transl. Zubair Bhayat, http://www.yanabi.com/forum/Topic8166-4-1.aspx (accessed Oct 11th 2010).

"Remembrance of God is the medicine for the soul's maladies."

"Remembrance of God drives the Satan away."

"Perpetually remembering God gives sustenance to the soul."

"Whoever remembers God abundantly, God will love him."
['Ali (R)][390]

"A heedless person is like a corpse, whereas truly alive is the one who is constantly engaged in remembering Allah (S). Through the abundant remembrance of Allah (S) the heedless heart of a person is transformed into a living one. Hence, this light of *nisbah* (spiritual connection) is such a blessing that it gives life to the heart that was once dead and devoid of the remembrance of Allah (S)."
[Shaykh Zulfiqar Ahmad in a talk titled Attaining fina-e-qalbi: Annihilation of the Heart][391]

"All illnesses go away by glorifying the Lord. Through your love for the Lord you will reach health, pleasure and happiness here and hereafter."
[Shaykh Nazim in talks titled From Dunya to Mawla][392]

---

[390] Quoted in *The Elixir of Love*, chapter 5: The Dhikr of the Friends of God, by Muhammad Rayshahri, http://www.al-islam.org/elixiroflove/17.htm#_ftnref1 (accessed April 27th 2011).

[391] Zulfiqar Ahmad, "Attaining fina-e-qalbi: Annihilation of the Heart," http://www.tasawwuf.org/basics/finae_qalbi.htm (accessed May 4th 2011).

[392] Quoted in article "Dhikr Allah, Allah" by G. F. Haddad, http://www.livingislam.org/naw/daa_e.html (accessed April 27th 2011).

"Do not say 'I am nothing'; neither say 'I am something.' Do not say: 'I need such and such a thing'; nor yet: 'I need nothing.' But say 'Allah' and you will see marvels."
[Mulay al-Arabi ad-Darqari in Letters of a Sufi Master][393]

"Soften it (the hardness of the heart) with *dhikr*. The more forgetful the heart is, the harder it becomes, but if a person remembers Allah, that hardness softens as copper melts in the fire. Nothing can soften the hardness of the heart like the remembrance of Allah, may He be glorified and exalted. *Dhikr* is healing and medicine for the heart. Forgetfulness is a disease, the cure for which is remembrance of Allah."
[Hasan al-Basri][394]

"When a person takes the name of Allah, time and time again, then a special bond is created. Then upon this bond special effects come into existence."
[Mufti Mahmood Hasan Sahib Gangohi][395]

"Even a mere repetition of the Name of God has the capacity to produce an effect of its own, though you may not be really meditating, though you may not be in a position to contemplate the actual meaning hidden behind it."

"It would not be an exaggeration if I say that you will be doing the greatest service to mankind (in chanting the Names of God)."

---

[393] Quoted in article "Dhikr - Remembrance of God," http://www.naqshbandi.org/topics/dhikr.htm (accessed April 28th 2011).
[394] Quoted at *GreatMuslimQuotes*. http://greatmuslimquotes.com/?p=1514 (accessed April 27th 2011).
[395] Quoted in article "An Introduction to the Science of Tasawwuf" section 1: Nisbat and Ihsaan, by Moosa Badat, http://www.islamrocks.com/Islamic-Books/nisbat-ihsan.shtml (accessed April 27th 2011).

"May I repeat the request once again, that you take to this Sadhana (*dhikr*) honestly, with intense faith, and you will see wonders, miracles manifesting themselves..."
[H. H. Swami Krishnanandaji Maharaj in Fruits From the Garden of Wisdom][396]

"Resonance of the sound of mantra (*dhikr*) operates as a total energy system that engages with all levels of an individual's being. Each syllable in a mantra is a set of tonal frequencies that resonate with, and activate, energy centers (chakras) in the body, connecting and unifying them into a single integrated system."
[Ian Prattis in Mantra and Consciousness Expansion in India][397]

"The ancient science of *dhikr* utilized the cosmic forces that yield reactions that comes from intoning the divine Names of Allah as a mantra. The ancient practice can increase the energy flow in the asiatic individual's garment of light and calibrate the individual's DNA and RNA within the nuclei of the cells to release or unfold greater levels of understanding and psycho-spiritual development. Hence, this science of intoning the divine Names of Allah not only musically resonates a calibrating source for the asiatic's emotional body, but also increases the production of infection-fighting cells by generating frequencies that directly destroy invading bacteria."
[From the article The-cosmic-code-in-man-the-genetic-vibrations-of-allah][398]

---

[396] *Fruits From the Garden of Wisdom*, chap. 7.
[397] "Mantra and Consciousness Expansion in India" 3.
[398] Zothyrius Ali El, "The Cosmic Code Of Man: The Genetic Vibrations of Allah," *Moors Gate*, http://www.moorsgate.com/2007/06/24/ (accessed Oct 18th 2010).

"For a sincere worker, it does not take more than six weeks to see its effect upon oneself. It is wonderful in giving power and realization."[399]

"Take the grossest person, make him do the *dhikr*, in six weeks' time his vibrations will change."[400]

"*Dhikr* has one great advantage over all other practices. That is, in the body and mind both, the re-echo of *dhikr* is produced, and both planes of the *Dhaakir's* being are set to rhythm. Music constitutes rhythm and tone; and if they are both produced by the means of *dhikr* in one's body and mind, the very being of the *Dhakir* becomes musical" (ibid).

"By *dhikr*, the expression of the countenance becomes harmonious, the voice becomes melodious, the presence becomes healing, and man spreads his magnetism in the atmosphere. There is nothing that by *dhikr* cannot be accomplished, either an earthly or a heavenly thing. Some by *dhikr* have liberated their souls from all bondages and attained ideal perfection" (ibid).

"All illnesses come owing to lack of rhythm. *Dhikr* is a rhythmic suggestion to the heart, which at once sets it to rhythm when the *Dhaakir* is repeating *dhikr*, and the circulation of the blood that runs throughout the body from this center runs in rhythm, the pulsation becomes rhythmic, and the development of every muscle becomes rhythmic. In

---

[399] From "The Teaching of Hazrat Inayat Khan," http://www.hazrat-inayat-khan.org/pl/search.cgi?s=&h1c=47&r=1&h2c=7 (accessed May 4th 2011).
[400] Inayat Khan, *The Sufi Message of Hazrat Inayat Khan/Music/The Manifestation of Sound on the Physical Sphere*, http://www.sufimessage.com/music/manifestation-of-sound.html (accessed Oct 12th 2010).

other words, the physical body becomes rhythmic in every way, which is the first necessary step towards spirituality" (ibid).

"There are adepts who repeat one single sound or a sacred word for years, and sometimes for all their life, without being tired of doing the same thing again and again. The result proves to them its value; every month and every year, by repeating the same word, the power becomes increased" (ibid).

"*Dhikr* has two aspects of its being, one its spirit and the other its body. The spirit is the breath, which is naturally prolonged through every repetition of *dhikr*. The body of *dhikr* is its words. The word produces the fire element, and the breath is life. When fire is produced, the heart naturally becomes warmer, and coldness, which is the common disease of every heart, begins to vanish. Then the word, voice, atmosphere, glance, and touch, all express warmth and the presence of the *Dhaakir* radiates warm vibrations. The *Dhaakir*, in time, begins to respond to everything and every being. This warmth in time makes the fire blaze up, and from it a flame springs forth that lights the path of the *Dhaakir*. *Dhikr* is of special importance in the course of a Sufi's spiritual advancement, and by this a Sufi attains everything on earth and in Heaven" (ibid).
[Inayat Khan]

"When the heart will experience the pleasure in taking the Name of Allah then the pleasure experienced in finite things will drop from one's sight. One's experiences from a worldly point of view proves that one who has lived in the bright sunlight cannot be fooled by the dim light of the stars. This is why the planet closest to the sun is called Mercury. Scientists have explained that Mercury has not been given a single moon because it remains brightened by the sun all the time. This is why no moon is required there. Even if it had a moon the light of such a moon would not be visible at all. Similarly one whose heart is brightened by the sun of the closeness of Allah, one who is the companion of the creator of the sun, has so much light in his heart that all combined lights of the universe compared to the light of Allah is totally insignificant in his sight."[401]

"One who has already experienced the enjoyment and pleasure of *dhikrullah* of taking Allah's name in this world, becomes independent of all the combined pleasures of both the worlds. From this we learn that the pleasure and enjoyment of Allah's name is totally incomparable, infinite without beginning and without end" (ibid., 9).
[Moulana Shah Hakeem Muhammad Akhtar in The Enjoyment of *Dhikr* And Pleasure In Giving Up Sin]

"It is man's soul and spirit that constitute his real nature...Upon death his state changes in two ways. Firstly he is now deprived of his eyes, ears and tongue, his hand, his feet and all his parts, just as he is deprived of family, children, relatives, and all the people he used to know, and of his horses and other riding-beasts, his servant-boys, his houses and property, and all that he used to own. There is no distinction to be drawn between his being taken from these things and these things being taken from him, for it is the separation itself that causes pain...

---

[401] Shah Hakeem Muhammad Akhtar, *The Enjoyment of Dhikr And Pleasure In Giving Up Sin*, 8. http://www.scribd.com/doc/24360397/The-Enjoyment-of-Zikr (accessed April 27th 2011).

If there was anything in the world in which he had found consolation and peace, then he will greatly lament for it after he dies, and feel the greatest sorrow over losing it. His heart will turn to thoughts of everything he owned, of his power and estates, even to a shirt he used to wear, for instance, and in which he took pleasure.

However, had he taken pleasure only in the remembrance of Allah, and consoled himself with Him alone, then his will be great bliss and perfect happiness. For the barriers, which lay between him and his Beloved, will now be removed, and he will be free of the obstacles and cares of the world, all of which had distracted him from the remembrance of Allah. This is one of the aspects of the difference between the states of life and death."
[Imam Ghazali in the fortieth book of his *Ihya'* entitled "The Remembrance of Death and The Afterlife"][402]

"It must be known to you that Allah unveiled all the veils of ignorance and brought people to the state of vision through their continuous *dhikr*. The first stage of *dhikr* is the *dhikr* of the tongue, then the *dhikr* of the heart, then the Appearance of the Divine Presence in the recitor of *dhikr*, making him no longer need to do *dhikr*."
[Imam Ghazali in Kitab al-Arba'in fil-Usul ad-Din][403]

"Dhikr is a fire which does not stay or spread – so if it enters a house saying, 'Me and nothing other than me,' which is one of the meanings of *'La ilaha illallah'* (There is no god but

---

[402] Ghazali, *The Remembrance of Death and The Afterlife*, 124.
[403] Ghazali, *Kitab al-Arba'in fil-Usul ad-Din*, 52-55 quoted in article "Dhikr in Islam" by Muhammad Hisham Kabbani.
http://www.naqshbandi.org/naqshbandi.net/www/haqqani/Islam/Haqqiqa/Dhikr.html (accessed April 27th 2011).

Allah), and...there is darkness in the house, it becomes light. If there is light in the house, it becomes 'light upon light.'"

"*Dhikr* expels from the body impure substances produced by excess in eating or from the consumption of unlawful food. As for food that is lawful, it does not touch it. So the harmful components are burned up and the good components remain."
[Ibn 'Ata'llah al-Iskandari in Miftah al-Falah][404]

"It is no doubt that the heart oxidizes, as copper and silver oxidize. Its polishing is the *dhikr*, which will make it like a white mirror. The oxidation of the heart is due to heedlessness and sin. Its polishing is through two: repentance and *dhikr*. If someone's heart is oxidized, the reflections of images will be upside-down, he will see falsehood as truth and truth in the image of falsehood (batil). Because when there is too much oxidization on the heart, the heart will be darkened, and in the darkness the images of the Truth and Reality never appear. The best way to polish it is through *dhikrullah*."[405]

"If a person wants to be guided, he must look for a person who is from the People of *Dhikr*. If he found one who is from the People of *Dhikr*, keeping *dhikr* continuously, and

---

[404] "Dhikr - from Miftah al-Falah (The Key to Success)," *ISRA*, http://www.israinternational.com/knowledge/166-dhikr-from-miftah-al-falah-the-key-to-success.html (accessed Oct 20th 2010).
[405] Ibn Qayyim al-Jawziyya, *Al-Waabil as-Saib*, 52 quoted at http://www.naqshbandi.org/naqshbandi.net/www/haqqani/Islam/Haqqiqa/Dhikr.html (accessed Oct 12th 2010).

following the Sunnah of the Prophet Muhammad (peace be upon him), he must stick to him."[406]
[Ibn Qayyim al-Jawziyya in his book Al-Waabil as-Saib]

"*Dhikr* is the means by which Stations yield their fruit, until the seeker reaches the Divine Presence. On the journey to the Divine Presence the seed of remembrance is planted in the heart and nourished with the water of praise and the food of glorification, until the tree of *dhikr* becomes deeply rooted and bears its fruit. It is the power of all journeying and the foundation of all success. It is the reviver from the sleep of heedlessness, the bridge to the One remembered."
[www. Naqshbandi.org][407]

"All scholars of Islam agreed on the acceptance and permissibility of *dhikr* by men and women, and for children, for the one who has ablution, and for the one without ablution; even for the lady in her period. Moreover, it is allowed by all scholars that *dhikr* be in the form of tasbih, tahmid, takbir and praising and praying on the Prophet Muhammad (peace be upon him)."
[Imam Nawawi in his book Futuhaat ar-Rabbani 'ala-al Adhkaar an-Nawawiyya][408]

---

[406] Quoted in article "Stages of Zikr," at Naqshbandiyya Mujaddiyya Aslamiyya. http://www.naqshbandi.org.uk/Articles/stages.html (accessed April 28th 2011).
[407] "Dhikr-remembrance of God," http://www.naqshbandi.org/topics/dhikr.htm (accessed April 3rd 2011).
[408] Nawawi, *Futuhaat ar-Rabbani 'ala-al Adhkaar an-Nawawiyya* vol. 1, 106-109, quoted in article "Dhikr in Islam," at http://www.naqshbandi.org/naqshbandi.net/www/haqqani/Islam/Haqqiqa/Dhikr.html (accessed April 3rd 2011).

"Whoever made *dhikr* with the all-encompassing Name 'Allah' is the one who left himself behind, connecting to His Lord, Existing in His presence, looking at Him through his heart, where the Light of Allah has burned away his physical body."
[Junaid][409]

"The music of *dhikr* is...the sound of the falling of the leaves in the Garden of Eden."
[Sheikh Muzaffereddin Halveti al-Jerrahi][410]

"Pray to God with a yearning heart that you may take delight in His Name. He will certainly fulfill your heart's desire." [411]

"One must always chant the Name and Glories of God and pray to Him. An old metal pot must be scrubbed every day. What is the use of cleaning it only once?" (Ibid., 7).

"Ecstatic devotion develops in taking the Name of the Lord, eyes overflow with tears of joy, words are choked in the mouth, and all the hairs of the body stand erect thrilled with joy" (ibid., 7).

"If one continues the repetition with concentration and devotion, one is sure to be blessed with Divine visions.

---

[409] Quoted in article "Stages of Zikr," at Naqshbandiyya Mujaddiyya Aslamiyya. http://www.naqshbandi.org.uk/Articles/stages.html (accessed April 28th 2011).
[410] Quoted in article "The Halveti-Jerrahi Dhikr – An Ancient Sufi Ritual of Remembrance 1980" at http://bolingo69.blogspot.com/2011_05_01_archive.html (accessed April 3rd 2011).
[411] Dayatmananda, "The Five Commandments of Sri Ramakrishna," 6, http://www.estudantedavedanta.net/The-Five-Commandments-of-Sri-Ramakrishna.pdf (accessed April 3rd 2011).

Ultimately one is sure to have God-realization. Suppose a big log of wood is immersed in the Ganges with one end attached to a chain, which is fixed on the bank. Following the chain, link by link, you can gradually dive into the water and trace your way to it. In the same manner, if you become absorbed in the repetition of His holy Name, you will eventually realize Him" (ibid., 7).

"Call with *Bhakti* (devotion) upon His hallowed Name and the mountain of your sins shall go out of sight just as a mountain of cotton will burn up and vanish if it but catches one spark of fire."[412]

"The Name of God, when uttered with faith by a sinner, shall bring salvation unto him. "What! Have I not chanted His holy Name, and must I be a sinner still? Must I still be in bondage?" are words of faith in the Lord" (ibid., 15).

"All the sins of the body fly away if one chants the Name of God and sings his Glories. The birds of sin dwell in the tree of the body. Singing the Name of God is like clapping your hands. As, at the clap of the hands, the birds in the tree fly away, so do our sins disappear at the chanting of God's Name and Glories."[413]

[Sri Ramakrishna]

"Chanting of the Lord's Name does not go in vain. It must bear its benign result. It is like the philosopher's stone

---

[412] From article "Ramakrishna Upanishad: I have seen God, and you shall see Him too," 12, http://www.vedantaiowa.org/teachings/Joseph_Upanishads/Ramakrishna_Upan.pdf (accessed April 3rd 2011).

[413] From article "Ramakrishna quotes on Sin," http://www.angelfire.com/ma/ramakrishna/sin.html, (accessed April 3rd 2011).

converting all baser metal into gold. It is like the magic wand of the magician performing unbelievable and unthought of miracles; it transforms man's life for ever."
[Swami Dayatmananda][414]

"Very powerful indeed is the Lord's Name. It may not bring about an immediate result, but it must one day bear fruit, just as we find that a seed left long ago on the cornice of a building at last reaches the ground, germinates, grows into a tree, and bears fruit, perhaps when the building cracks and is demolished. Knowingly or unknowingly, consciously or unconsciously, in whatever state of mind a man utters God's Name, he acquires the merit of such utterance."

"There is a great power in the seed of God's Name. It destroys ignorance. A seed is tender, and the sprout soft; still it pierces the hard ground. The ground breaks and makes way for the sprout."
[Sarada Devi – the wife of Sri Ramakrishna also known as the Holy Mother][415]

"It does not matter if you do not know Him (God). You know His Name. Just take His Name, and you will progress spiritually. What do they do in an office? Without having seen or known the officer, one sends an application addressed to his name. Similarly send your application to God, and you will receive His grace."
[Swami Adbhutananda - a disciple of Ramakrishna][416]

---

[414] From article "Ramakrishna Upanishad: I have seen God, and you shall see Him too," 2, http://www.vedantaiowa.org/teachings/Joseph_Upanishads/Ramakrishna_Upan.pdf (accessed April 3rd 2011).
[415] Ibid., 3.
[416] Ibid., 4.

Appendix B

Glossary of Arabic Terms and Titles

Glossary of Arabic Terms

Allah. Proper name for the Creator.

Anwaar. Plural of "noor" meaning light.

Arafah. One of the places of Hajj (Pilgrimage) whereunto one's presence is required.

'Asr. Literally it means "time." It also refers to a particular period of the day when Muslims perform their third daily prayers. A short chapter of the Qur'an also has this name.

Ayah. A verse in the Qur'an. It means also a "sign" as every verse of the Qur'an is a sign from Allah.

Ayat-ul-Qursi. Verse of the Throne. It is verse # 255 of *Surah* al-Baqara (2nd Chapter of the Qur'an).

Bayt al-Maqdis. The Masjid (Mosque) in Jerusalem.

Bukhari. A book of *Hadith* [sayings of the Prophet Muhammad (S.A.W)].

Dawud. Arabic name of the Prophet David.

Deen. Arabic word for religion. It also means "reward and/or judgment" as in *maliki yawmiddeen* (the day of judgment).

Dhaakir. The one who does *"dhikr"* (remembrance of Allah).

Dhikr. Remembrance. The contextual usage in the book refers to the remembrance of Allah.

Dhikrullah. Remembrance of Allah.

Dhul-Hijjah. The 12th month of the Islamic lunar calendar.

Du'a. Informal prayer (supplication).

'Eid. A special celebration (holiday) of the Muslims.

'Eid Al-Adha. One of the two major celebrations of the Muslims, celebrated on the 10th day of the 12th month of the Muslim lunar calendar (which is also the time of Pilgrimage).

'Eid Al-Fitr. One of the two major celebrations of the Muslims, celebrated at the end of Ramadan (fasting month) which is the 9th month of the Muslim lunar calendar.

Fajr. Literally means dawn. The contextual usage in the book refers to the name of the first of the 5 daily prayers, offered at dawn (before the sunrise).

Fatwa. A religious decree issued by qualified Muslim scholars which, generally speaking, has no legal binding.

Hadith. Literally means something new. The contextual usage in the book refers to the sayings of Prophet Muhammad (S.A.W).

Hadith Nabawi. Saying of the Prophet Muhammad (S.A.W).

Hadith Qudsi. Saying of the Prophet Muhammad (S.A.W), the text of which is in 1st person, attributed to God Almighty.

Hajj. Pilgrimage. Refers to pilgrimage to Mecca, Saudi Arabia.

Hajees. People who have performed *hajj*.

Hasan. Literally means beautiful. The contextual usage in the book describes the authenticity of a particular *Hadith* [sayings of the Prophet Muhammad (S.A.W)]. *Hadith* categorized as *hasan* are acceptable for use as religious evidence. However, they are generally not as established as *Sahih Hadith* which are regarded as the most authentic.

Hasan gharib. Literally means beautiful yet strange. The contextual usage in the book refers to a category of *Hadith*.

Ihsaan. Perfection or doing things in the best possible manner.

Ikhlaas. Sincerity and right motivation. It is also a name of one of the chapters of the Qur'an.

Imaan. Faith or belief.

Imam. The leader in Prayers. It also refers to a spiritual leader of a Muslim community.

Isra'. The night journey of the Prophet Muhammad (S.A.W) from Mecca to Jerusalem and then onward to Heaven.

Jama'ah. Congregational prayers.

Jannah. Heaven or Paradise.

Jibril. Arabic name for Arch-Angel Gabriel who brought messages from God Almighty to all the prophets.

Jinn. An invisible creature (other than Angels) who has free will and is accountable for its actions as for human beings. Satan is one of them.

Ka'bah. First house build by Prophet Ibrahim and his son Isma'il for the worship of one God. It still exists and is in Mecca, Saudi Arabia.

Kalimah. Literally means word. Refers to the words used to testify and proclaim one's faith as a Muslim.

Khanqah. The contextual usage refers to a building designed specifically for gatherings of a Sufi brotherhood and is a place for spiritual retreat and character reformation.

Kufaar. Plural of Kaafir, meaning "non-believers."

Kun. Literally means "Be." It is an expression used to indicate the power of Almighty Allah that He can get things done just by saying "Be" and it is.

Ma'rifat. Literally means recognition and understanding. The contextual usage refers to recognizing and knowing Almighty Allah.

Manasik. The rituals of the Pilgrimage.

Masaajid. Plural of Masjid, meaning Mosque (a place of worship for Muslims).

Masjid. Mosque. A place of worship for Muslims.

Masjid of Bayt al-Maqdis. A mosque in Jerusalem, Palestine.

Mi`raj. Another name for "isra,'" the night journey of Prophet Muhammad (S.A.W).

Mina. A name of a place near Mecca that is part of the rituals of the pilgrimage. It is known as the "tent-city."

Mu'adhdhin. The Caller to the five daily prayers.

Musalli. A person who prays his/her daily prayers.

Mushrikin. Polytheists. The believers in more than one god.

Noor. Light.

Qur'an. The holy book, the last Testament that was revealed to the last Prophet, Muhammad (S.A.W) in 610-633 CE.

Rakat. A unit of measurement in Muslim prayers.

Riya. Show-off; doing things without sincerity just to show-off.

Ruqya. Seeking a cure for any illness by reciting verses from the Qur'an and making *du'a* (supplication) to Allah.

Sahabah. Companions of the Prophet Muhammad (S.A.W).

Sahih. Literally means correct or authentic. The contextual usage in the book describes the authenticity of a particular *Hadith* [sayings of the Prophet Muhammad (S.A.W)]. *Hadith* categorized as *Sahih Hadith* are regarded as the most authentic.

Salah. Prayer. Term used for Muslim daily prayers.

Sayyid. Literally means leader or chief. It's a term used for people who claim to have a lineage with the family of the Prophet Muhammad (pbuh).

Shaitaan. Satan or the Devil.

Soor. Refers to the blowing of the trumpet for bringing this world to an end and then for bringing everyone back to life to be gathered for the judgment day.

Sufi. A mystic. Someone who uses *dhikr* (chanting) to gain closeness to the Creator, Almighty Allah.

Sulaiman. A Prophet and a king who had the kingship over humans, jinns, birds, and wind.

Sunnah. The way of the Prophet Muhammad (S.A.W).

Surah. A chapter in the Qur'an. There are a total of 114 chapters in the Qur'an.

Surah Ikhlas. *Surah* or chapter # 112 of the Qur'an comprising of only four short verses that captures the essence of the teachings of the Qur'an. The recitation of this *Surah* is believed to be equivalent to reciting one-third of the Qur'an.

Surah Yasin. *Surah* or chapter # 36 of the Qur'an. This *Surah* is called the "heart" of the Qur'an.

Tabi'in. Those Muslims who have seen and met a sahabi (companion) of the Prophet Muhammad (S.A.W).

Tafsir. Exegesis/interpretation of the Qur'an.

Tahajjud. Optional nightly prayers that are offered at the last third part of the night.

Tahlil. Saying/chanting *"la-ilaaha illallaah"* (there is none worthy of worship besides Almighty Allah).

Tahmid. Saying/chanting *"al-hamdu-lillaah"* (All praises are due to Almighty Allah).

Takbir. Saying/chanting *"Allaahu-Akbar"* (Allah is the Greatest).

Talbiya. Chanting that takes place during *hajj* (Pilgrimage) to Mecca.

Tasbih. Saying/chanting *"subhaanallaah"* (Almighty Allah is all Glorious).

Tauhid. Oneness of Almighty Allah.

Tilawah. Recitation of the Qur'an.

Ummah. Nation. The Muslim people together form an *Ummah*.

'Umrah. Smaller pilgrimage to Mecca that is performed any time of the year.

Witr. The last three or one Rakat of prayer after *Isha Salah* (the night prayer).

Zam Zam. The ancient water-well that was discovered by Isma'il (the son of Prophet Abraham & Hagar, known in Arabic as Ibrahim and Hajrah) in present day Mecca, Saudi Arabia.

Zikr. Remembrance (of Almighty Allah); spelling variation of *Dhikr*.

Zuhr. The second (the early afternoon) prayer of Muslims.

Glossary of Titles

Maulana. A title for a Muslim religious scholar. A portion of it (i.e., Mawla, meaning "master/protector/guardian") is also an attribute of Allah.

Mufti. A learned religious scholar who is qualified to issue religious verdicts (or *fatwa*).

PBUH. Means Peace be upon Him. See also S.A.W.

Qari. A recitor of the Qur'an. One who can recite Qur'an with all its rules and with a beautiful voice.

R. This title, when used after the name(s) of a companion (or companions) of the Prophet Muhammad (S.A.W) represents *Radiyallahu 'anhu* (or *'anha, 'anhum, 'inhuman* etc.). It means "may Almighty Allah be pleased with him, her, them," etc.

When this title is used after the name(s) of any great/righteous Muslim(s) it represents *Rahmatullahi 'alayhi* (or *'alayha, 'alayhum, 'alayhunna* etc.) which means "may Almighty Allah's Mercy and Blessings be upon him, her, them," etc.

Rasulullah. The Messenger of Allah.

S.A.W. It is used after the name of the Prophet Muhammad. It represents *Sallallaahu Alayhi wa-Sallam* and means May Peace and Blessings of Almighty Allah be upon him. Both "S.A.W" and "PBUH" are used for this purpose. Sometimes only "S" is used.

Sheikh. Elder leader, tribal chief, or a religious scholar. Also spelt as Shaykh.

Swami. An honorific title for either males or females in the Hindu tradition. It is derived from Sanskrit and means "He who knows and is the master of himself", "owner of oneself", or "free from the senses". It is a title added to one's name to emphasize learning and mastery of yoga, devotion to god, and devotion to the swami's spiritual master (a guru or another swami).

Bibliography

Abdullah, S. & H. Schucman. "Cerebral lateralization, bimodal consciousness, and related developments in psychiatry." *Research Communications in Psychology, Psychiatry and Behavior* 1 (1976): 671-679.

Abu Dawud. *Sunan Abu Dawud*. Translated by Ahmad Hasan. Lahore, Pakistan: Sh. Muhammad Ashraf Publishers, 1984.

Ahmad, Zulfiqar. "Attaining fina-e-qalbi: Annihilation of the Heart," http://www.tasawwuf.org/basics/finae_qalbi.htm (accessed May 4th 2011).

Akhtar, Shah Hakeem Muhammad. *The Enjoyment of Dhikr And Pleasure In Giving Up Sin*, 8. http://www.scribd.com/doc/24360397/The-Enjoyment-of-Zikr (accessed April 27th 2011).

Al-Bukhari, Muhammad. *Sahih Al-Bukhari*. Translated by Muhammad Muhsin Khan. Medina: Dar Ahya Us-Sunnah Al Nabawiya'a.

Al-Haddad, Ahmad Mashhur. Miftah al-Janna (Key to the Garden). Translated by Mostafa Badawi. London: Quilliam Press, 1990.

Al Ghazal, Sharif Kaf. "Reflections on the Medical Miracles of the Holy Quran," *Islamic Medicine On Line*, http://www.islamicmedicine.org/medmiraclesofquran/medmiracleseng.htm (accessed Oct 12th 2010).

Al-Ghazali, Muhammad. *Alchemy of Happiness*. Vol. 1. Translated by J. R. Crook. Great Books of the Islamic World, Inc.

Al-Ghazali, Muhammad. *"The Remembrance of Death and The Afterlife"* in *Ihya' 'Ulum Al-Din*. Translated by T. J. Winter. Cambridge: The Islamic Texts Society, 1989.

Ali, Muhammad Sajad. "Sufi Introduction to the 99 attributes of Names of Allah and especially that of Ya Latif," http://www.docstoc.com/docs/22976421/Beautiful-Names-of-Allah-as-mentioned-the-Qur%60an-and-Hadith (accessed Oct 13th 2010).

Al-Jawzi, Ibn. "al-Qussas wa al-mudhakkirin (The Story-tellers and the Admonishers)" in *Gatherings of Dhikr*, http://qa.sunnipath.com/issue_view.asp?HD=1&ID=784#gath (accessed Oct 11th 2010).

Al-Jawziyya, Ibn Qayyim. *Al-Waabil as-Saib*, quoted at http://www.naqshbandi.org/naqshbandi.net/www/haqqani/Islam/Haqqiqa/Dhikr.html (accessed Oct 12th 2010).

Badaa'i' al-Fawaa'id, quoted in "The Importance of Knowing Allah's Names," http://www.islamic-life.com/beautiful-names-allah/article-importance-knowing-allahs-names (accessed Oct 11th 2010).

Al-Sawaa'iq al-Mursalah `Ala al-Jahmyyah wa'l-Mu`attilah, quoted in "The Importance of Knowing Allah's Names," http://www.islamic-life.com/beautiful-names-allah/article-importance-knowing-allahs-names (accessed Oct 11th 2010).

Alkaheel, Abduldaem. *The Qur'an's Healing Horizon*, http://www.scribd.com/doc/6172917/Healing-by-Quran-Eng, 18 – 20 (accessed April 12th 2010).

Al-Malaki, Muhammad `Alawi. "Al-Anwar al-bahiyya min isra' wa mi`raj khayr al-bariyya (the resplendent lights of the rapture and ascension of the best of creation)," http://www.scribd.com/doc/15850625/Collated-Hadith-of-Isra-and-MiRaj (accessed Oct 11th 2010).

Al-Tirmidhi, Muhammad. *Jami Al-Tirmidhi* (a.k.a. *Sunan Al-Tirmidhi*). Pdf version available at http://islamtomorrow.com/downloads/uploads/Islamasoft_Solutions_page.htm (accessed June 27th 2011).

Al-Yaqoubi, Muhammad. *Remembering Allah* track 6. UK: Sacred Knowledge, 2009. CD-ROM.

American Psychological Association. "Overwhelmed by workplace stress? You're not alone," http://www.apa.org/helpcenter/work-stress.aspx.

Andrews, Donald Hatch. *The Symphony of Life* quoted at http://www.rosecroixjournal.org/issues/2005/articles/vol2_11_21_braun.pdf (accessed Oct 13th 2010).

An-Nawawi. *Futuhaat ar-Rabbani 'ala-al Adhkaar an-Nawawiyya* 1:106-109, quoted in "Dhikr in Islam," http://www.naqshbandi.org/naqshbandi.net/www/haqqani/Islam/Haqqiqa/Dhikr.html (accessed Oct 11th 2010).

Arias, A. J., Karen Steinberg, Alok Banga, Robert L. Trestman. "Systematic Review of the Efficacy of Meditation Techniques as Treatments for Medical Illness." *Journal of Alternative and Complementary Medicine* 12 no. 8 (2006): 817-832.

As-Suyuti. *Natijatul-Fikr* quoted in "Majalis-Zikr," http://www.direct.za.org/Pdfs/Loud_Zikr.pdf (accessed Jan 18th 2010).

Aulia-e-hind, http://aulia-e-hind.com/Zikr.htm (accessed April 1st 2010).

Aziz, Shawana A. "The Blessings of Al-Masjid Al-Haram in Makkah" Islamic Subjects, January 2004, http://www.aljazeerah.info/Islam/Islamic%20subjects/2004%20subjects/January/The%20Blessings%20of%20Al-Masjid%20Al-Haram%20in%20Makkah%20By%20Shawana%20A.%20Aziz.htm (accessed Dec 3rd 2010).

Bacon, M. H. *The quiet rebels*. New York: Basic Books, 1969.

Badat, Moosa. "An Introduction to the Science of Tasawwuf" Section 1: Nisbat and Ihsaan, http://www.islamrocks.com/Islamic-Books/nisbat-ihsan.shtml

Baerbel. "Russian DNA Discoveries Explain Human 'Paranormal' Events," Rense.com. Extracted from book *Vernetzte Intelligenz* by Grazyna Fosar and Franz Blunder, Rense.com. (accessed Jan 10th 2011).

Banquet, J. P. "Spectral analysis of the EEG in meditation." *Electroencephalogr. Clin. Neuro.* 35 no. 2 (1973): 143-151.

"BBC British Journalist in Saudi Arabia." YouTube video, http://www.youtube.com/watch?v=F_OtXNclB9I (accessed April 4th 2011).

Bechtold, Matthew L., Srinivas R. Puli, Mohamed O. Othman, Christopher R. Bartalos, John B. Marshall, Praveen K. Roy. "Effect of Music on Patients Undergoing Colonoscopy: A Meta-Analysis of Randomized Controlled Trials," Digestive Diseases and Sciences 54, no. 1: 19-24, http://www.springerlink.com/content/m678364870x0q108/ (accessed May 3rd 2011).

Benson, H. *The relaxation response.* New York: William Morrow and Company, 1975.

Bernardi, Luciano, Peter Sleight, Gabriele Bandinelli, Simone Cencetti, Lamberto Fattorini, Johanna Wdowczyc-Szulc, Alfonso Lagi. "Effect of rosary prayer and yoga mantras on autonomic cardiovascular rhythms: Comparative study." *British Medical Journal* 323 no. 7327 (2001): 1446-1449.

Bhattathiri. "Scientific Aspects of Yagna Environmental Effects," http://www.arizonaenergy.org/FireEnergy/Scientific%20Aspects%20of%20Yagna%20Environmental%20Effects.htm (accessed Dec 15th 2010).

Bloomfield, H. H., M. P. Cain & D. T. Jaffe. *TM: discovering inner energy and overcoming stress*. New York: Defacorte Press, 1975.

Bormann, Jill et al. "Effects of Spiritual Mantram Repetition on HIV Outcomes: A Randomized Controlled Trial." *Journal of Behavioral Medicine* 29, no. 5 (October 2006): 499-499.

Braun, Melanie. "Exploring the Efficacy of Vowel Intonations" *The Rose+Croix Journal*, 2, 2005, http://www.rosecroixjournal.org/issues/2005/articles/vol2_11_21_braun.pdf. (Accessed Oct 12th 2010).

Brennan, Barbara. *Hands of Light: A Guide to Healing Through the Human Energy Field*, New York: Bantam Books, 1988.

Campbell, Don. *The Mozart Effect*, New York: Avon Books, 1997.

Cetin, Bedri C. "Universal Energy – A Systematic and Scientific Investigation," http://sapphirereiki.com/Downloads/universalenergy.pdf (accessed March 31st 2011).

Cruise, Charles J., Frances Chung, Suntheralingham Yogendran, D'Arcy Little. "Music increases satisfaction in elderly outpatients undergoing cataract surgery," *Canadian Journal of Anesthesia* 44, no. 1: 43-48, http://www.springerlink.com/content/lx6226654587m221/ (accessed May 4th 2011).

Dayatmananda, "The Five Commandments of Sri Ramakrishna," http://www.estudantedavedanta.net/The-Five-Commandments-of-Sri-Ramakrishna.pdf (accessed April 3rd 2011).

"Dhikr - from Miftah al-Falah (The Key to Success)," *ISRA*, http://www.israinternational.com/knowledge/166-dhikr-from-miftah-al-falah-the-key-to-success.html (accessed Oct 20th 2010).

"Dhikr is the greatest obligation and a perpetual divine order," *The As-Sunnah Foundation of America*, http://www.sunnah.org/ibadaat/dhikr.htm (accessed Oct 20th 2010).

"Dhikr (recitation of God's Names),"
http://www.thewaytotruth.org/heart/zikir.html (accessed April 19th 2011).

"Dhikr - remembrance of God,"
http://www.naqshbandi.org/topics/dhikr.htm (accessed April 3rd 2011).

Dongre, Archana. "Hardwar Institute Tracks Power of Gayatri Yagna," *Hinduism Today*, Sept 1992, http://www.hinduismtoday.com/modules/smartsection/item.php?itemid=960 (accessed Jan 25th 2011).

Donovan S, Murphy M & Taylor E. *The Physical and Psychological Effects of Meditation*. Institute of Noetic Sciences, 1997.

El, Zothyrius Ali. "The Cosmic Code Of Man: The Genetic Vibrations of Allah," *Moors Gate*, http://www.moorsgate.com/2007/06/24/ (accessed Oct 14th 2010).

Emoto, Masaru et al. "Double-Blind Test of the Effects of Distant Intention on Water Crystal Formation," *Explore The Journal Of Science and Healing*, 2, no. 5, 408-411.

Feinstein, David and Donna Eden. "Six Pillars of Energy Medicine Clinical Strengths of a Complementary Paradigm," *Energy Medicine*, http://www.innersource.net/em/publishedarticlescat/283-sixpillarsofem.html?q=prayer (accessed Oct 20th 2010).

Fosar, Grazyna and Franz Bludorf. "The Biological Chip in our Cells Revolutionary results of modern genetic," http://www.fosar-bludorf.com/archiv/biochip_eng.htm (accessed Jan 10th 2011).

Gass, Robert. *Chanting: Discovering Spirit in Sound*. New York: Broadway Books, 1999.

Gaynor, Mitchel L. *Sounds of Healing: A Physician Reveals the Therapeutic Power of Sound, Voice, Music.* New York: Broadway Books, 1999.

Gilani, Mubarak Ali. "Pillar of Lies" http://www.iqou-moa.org/sheikh_jilani/pillar_of_lies1.htm (accessed Jan 4th 2011).

Goldman, Jonathan. "Sonic entrainment" in *Music Physician for times to come.* Don Campbell. IL: Quest Books, 1991.

Goleman, D. *The varieties of the meditative experience.* New York: E. P. Dutton, 1977.

Gowan, J. C. *Trance, art and creativity.* Buffalo, New York: Creative Education Foundation, 1975.

GreatMuslimQuotes. http://greatmuslimquotes.com/?p=1514 (accessed April 27th 2011).

Guirand, F. ed. "Greek mythology" in *The Larouse Encyclopedia of Mythology.* Hong Kong: Hamlyn Publishing Group Limited, 1959.

Haddad, G. F. "Dhikr Allah, Allah," http://www.livingislam.org/naw/daa_e.html (accessed April 27th 2011).

Hagelin, John S.; Maxwell V. Rainforth; Kenneth L. C. Cavanaugh; Charles N. Alexander; Susan F. Shatkin; John L. Davies; Ann O. Hughes; Emanuel Ross; David W. Orme-Johnson. "Effects of Group Practice of the Transcendental Meditation Program on Preventing Violent Crime in Washington, D.C.: Results of the National Demonstration Project, June--July 1993," *Social Indicators Research* 47, no 2, 153-201, http://www.springerlink.com/content/k2hg216724k21411/ (accessed Oct 20th 2010).

Harinath, K., A. S. Malhotra, K. Pal, R. Prasad, R. Kumar, T.C. Kain, L. Rai, R.C Sawhney. "Effects of Hatha yoga and Omkar meditation on cardiorespiratory performance, psychologic profile, and melatonin secretion." *Journal of Alternative and Complementary Medicine* 10 no. 2 (2004): 261-268.

Horgan, John. "Fractured Functions. Does the brain have a supreme integrator?" *Scientific American* 12 (1993): 24.

Ibn Taymiyya. *Majmu`at fatawa,* King Khalid ibn `Abd al-`Aziz edition. Quoted in "The celebration of Mawlid as understood by the scholars of the "Salafi" movement and those of the four schools of Ahl Al_Sunna," http://www.caribbeanmuslims.com/articles/180/5/Permissibility-of-Mawlid-An-Nabi/Page5.html (accessed April 20th 2011).

Indopedia contributors. "Om Mane Padme Hum," *Indopedia,* http://www.indopedia.org/Om_mani_padme_hum.html (accessed Oct 18th 2010).

"Invocation of La ilaha illa'llah." *Technology of the Heart,* http://www.mysticsaint.info/2011/01/invocation-of-la-ilaha-illallah.html.

Kaandhlawi, Muhammad Zakariya. *Faza'il-e-A'maal.* Vol. I. Translated by Shafiq Ahmad, Abdul Rashid Arshad, Aziz-ud-Din, Yousuf Abdullah Karaan, Mazhar Mahmood Qureshi, Khwaja Ihsanul Haq. New Delhi: Idara Ishaat-E-Diniyat (P) Ltd, 1994.

Kabbani, Muhammad Hisham. "Dhikr in Islam," http://www.naqshbandi.org/naqshbandi.net/www/haqqani/Islam/Haqqiqa/Dhikr.html (accessed Jan 14th 2010).

"Spiritual Healing in the Sufi Tradition," http://www.nurmuhammad.com/Meditation/EnergyHealing/harvardhealinglecture.htm (accessed Oct 13th 2010).

Khan, Inayat. *The Sufi Message of Hazrat Inayat Khan,* http://www.sufimessage.com (accessed Oct 12th 2010).

Kothari, L. K.; A. Bordia; and O.P. Gupta. "The Yogic Claim of Voluntary Control over the Heart Beat: An Unusual

Demonstration." *American Heart Journal* 86 (1973): 282-284.

Jaret, Peter. "Battling Cancer with Complementary Therapies and Treatments," *AARP Bulletin* April 1, 2010.

Jenny, Hans. *Cymatic: A Study of Wave Phenomena and Vibration.* Newmarket, NH: Macromedia Publishing, 2001.

Jilani, Abdul Qadir. *The Secret of Secrets*, 3rd ed., interpreted by Tosun Bayrak al-Jerrahi al-Halveti. Cambridge: The Islamic Text Society, 1997.

Jim, Oliver. Notes from CD *Harmonic Resonance.* New York: The Relaxation Company, 1995.

Lewis, H. Spencer. *Rosicrucian Manual* 8, AMORC, 1980.

Loveless, Catherine and Damian Smythe, "Something in the aura," http://www.korotkov.org/file/saa.pdf (accessed Oct 29th 2010).

Maharaj, H. H. Krishnanandaji. "Mantra Shakti," *Fruits From the Garden of Wisdom* chapter 7, http://www.swami-krishnananda.org/fruit/fruit_07.html. Ebook.

Makki, Abd al-Hafiz. "An analysis of the evidence supporting the permissibility of Majalis (gatherings) of zikr in the Masjid" translated by Zubair Bhayat, http://www.yanabi.com/forum/Topic8166-4-1.aspx (accessed Oct 11th 2010).

Malik, Anas ibn. *Al-Muwatta.* Translated by Muhammad Rahimuddin. Lahore, Pakistan: Sh. Muhammad Ashraf Publishers & Booksellers, 1985.

Maman, Fabien. *The Role of Music in the Twenty-First Century.* California: Tama-Do Press, 1997.

"Mantra Yoga," *YogaWorld*, http://www.yogaworld.org/mantra2.htm (accessed Dec 6th 2010).

Masaru Emoto's Website, 29 December 2007, Questions from readers 28, http://www.masaru-emoto.net/english/ediary200712.html#1229 (accessed Jan 11th 2011).

McTaggart, Lynne. "DNA double helix: Our body's recording studio and radio station," *The Healing Universe.* http://www.thehealinguniverse.com/library.html (accessed Jan 17th 2011).

Muslim, Abul Hussain. *Sahih Muslim.* Translated by Abdul Hamid Siddiqi. Riyadh, Saudi Arabia: International Islamic Publication House.

Murphy, M., S. Donovan, and E. Taylor. *The Physical and Psychological Effects of Meditation.* 2nd ed. California: Institute of Noetic Sciences, 1997.

Nalimov, V. V. *Realms of the unconscious: the enchanted frontier.* Philadelphia: 1SI Press, 1982.

Naparsteck, Belleruth. *Your Sixth Sense.* Harper San Francisco, 1997.

Nawawi, *Futuhaat ar-Rabbani 'ala-al Adhkaar an-Nawawiyya* vol. 1, 106-109, quoted in article "Dhikr in Islam," at http://www.naqshbandi.org/naqshbandi.net/www/haqqani/Islam/Haqqiqa/Dhikr.html (accessed April 3rd 2011).

Nur Ashki Jerrahi Community of New York City. "Tasbih: Personal Dhikr," 2008, http://www.nurashkijerrahi.org/teachings/union_012.htm (accessed Oct 18th 2010).

Palakanis, Kerry C., John W. DeNobile, W. Brian Sweeney, Charles L. Blankenship. "Effect of music therapy on state anxiety in patients undergoing flexible sigmoidoscopy." *Diseases of the Colon & Rectum* 37 no. 5: 478-481, http://www.springerlink.com/content/g2ru65w235t4v230/ (accessed May 4th 2011).

Patel, C.H., and W.R. North. "Randomized Controlled Trial of Yoga and Biofeedback in Management of Hypertension." *Lancelot Journal* 2 (1975): 93-95.

Paul, Russill. "Why Sanskrit for Mantra? Why not English?" http://www.russillpaul.com/articles/article/1162814/14980.htm (accessed Oct 12th 2010).

Pfeiffer, Knut. "Islam's Zamzam water positive effect on human cells," YouTube video, http://internalmedicinebooks.net/dr-knut-pfeiffer-islams-zamzam-water-positive-effect-on-human-cells.html (accessed Dec 9th 2010).

"Physical Effects of Stress," *Stress mnt for Health*, 2009, http://www.stress-management-for-health.com/physical-effects-of-stress.html (accessed Oct 19th 2010).

Posen, David B. "Stress Management for Patient and Physician," *Internet Mental Health*, http://www.mentalhealth.com/mag1/p51-str.html (accessed Oct 19th 2010).

Prattis, Ian. "Mantra and Consciousness Expansion in India," http://www.ianprattis.com/pdf/mantraandconsciousness.pdf.

Qutb, Syed. *Fi Zhilal Al-Qur'an*, vol. XII, http://www.kalamullah.com/Books/Fi%20Dhilal/Volume_12_(*Surahs*_21-25).pdf (accessed Oct 11th 2010).

Rabbani, Faraz. "Effective Ta`wizes," SunniPath, July 05, 2005. http://qa.sunnipath.com/issue_view.asp?HD=1&ID=647&CATE=115 (accessed Dec 9th 2010).

Radin, Dean. "Moving Mind, Moving Matter," Noetic Sciences Review, 46, 20 Summer 1998, http://psionslair.co.cc/pdf/movingmindmatter.pdf (accessed Jan 24th, 2011).

"Ramakrishna quotes on Sin,"

http://www.angelfire.com/ma/ramakrishna/sin.html (accessed April 3rd 2011).

"Ramakrishna Upanishad: I have seen God, and you shall see Him too," http://www.vedantaiowa.org/teachings/Joseph_Upanishads/Ramakrishna_Upan.pdf (accessed April 3rd 2011).

Rayshahri, Muhammad. *The Elixir of Love*, chapter 5: The Dhikr of the Friends of God, http://www.al-islam.org/elixiroflove/17.htm#_ftnref1 (accessed April 27th 2011).

Remedies of the Quran. http://www.scribd.com/doc/17621/Remedies-From-the-Holy-QurAn (accessed April 13th 2010).

Rinpoche, Sogyal. *The Tibetan book of living and dying.* Revised and updated edition. New York: Harper San Francisco, 2002.

Robertson, Don. "Stories about the Effects of the Ragas of India," http://www.dovesong.com/positive_music/India.asp (accessed April 12th 2010).

Sabiq, As-Sayyid. *Fiqh us-Sunnah.* Vol. IV. Translated by Muhammad Sa'eed Dabas and Jamal al-Din M. Zarabozo. Jeddah, Saudi Arabia: Maktabat al-Khadamat-e Al-Hadithah, 1987.

Schwaller de Lubicz, R.A. *Sacred Science* quoted on the website: http://www.cymascope.com/cyma_research/egyptology.html (accessed Oct 14th 2010).

"Scientific Definition of Wazifa (Sacred Spells)." YouTube video, http://www.youtube.com/watch?v=5Ee-SYjq5Do (accessed Jan 18th 2011).

S. G. Asnani Foundation. "Sound Therapy" http://www.sgafsoundtherapy.org/sound/index.html, http://www.sgafsoundtherapy.org/sound/sound_diabetes.html (accessed Oct 12th 2010).

Shalhoub, Lulwa. "Water at the Nano Level," Arab News. April 2008, http://archive.arabnews.com/?page=21&section=0&article=108787&d=15&m=4&y=2008 (accessed Jan 11th 2011).

Shapiro, D. H. "Overview: clinical and physiological comparison of meditation and other self-centered strategies." *Amer. J. Psychiat.* 139 no. 3 (1982): 267-274.

"Spiritual Healing in Islam." Islamic Educational and Cultural Research Center. http://www.iecrcna.org/publications/Spiritual_Healing_Single.pdf (accessed Jan 18th 2011).

"Stages of Zikr," Naqshbandiyya Mujaddiyya Aslamiyya. http://www.naqshbandi.org.uk/Articles/stages.html (accessed April 28th 2011).

Stone, R., and J. DeLeo. "Psychotherapeutic Control of Hypertension."
New England Journal of Medicine 294 no. 2 (1976): 80-84.

Syed, Ibrahim. "Spiritual Medicine in the History of Islamic Medicine," http://www.scribd.com/doc/3321827/islamic-medicine (accessed Feb 16th 2010).

Syed, Ibrahim. "Sufism and Quantum Physics," http://www.irfi.org/articles/articles_1_50/sufism_and_quantum_physics.htm (accessed April 27th 2011).

Tafsir of Ibn Kathir (Abridged). 1st ed. Translated and abridged by Sheikh Safiur-Rahman Al-Mubarakpuri and others. Riyadh, Saudi Arabia: Darussalaam Publishers & Distributors, March 2000.

"The Effect of Mantra," http://www.tracysvision.com/effect_of_mantra.htm (accessed April 13th 2010).

"The First Korotkov Water Experiment – November 30, 2007,"

http://www.theintentionexperiment.com/korotkov1 (accessed Jan 11th 2011).

"The Second Korotkov Water Experiment, January 18, 2008," http://www.theintentionexperiment.com/the-second-korotkov-water-experiment-january-18-2008 (accessed Jan 11th 2011).

"The Global Consciousness Project," http://noosphere.princeton.edu/fristwall2.html (accessed Jan 24th 2011).

"The Halveti-Jerrahi Dhikr – An Ancient Sufi Ritual of Remembrance 1980," http://bolingo69.blogspot.com/2011_05_01_archive.html (accessed April 3rd 2011).

"The Teaching of Hazrat Inayat Khan," http://www.hazrat-inayat-khan.org/pl/search.cgi?s=&h1c=47&r=1&h2c=7 (accessed May 4th 2011).

"Transcendental Meditation Experiment Arrests Crime Study Shows Dramatic Drop in Violent Crime During D.C. Project," *AllTM.org – Transcendental Meditation*, http://www.alltm.org/pages/crime-arrested.html (accessed Oct 20th 2010).

Vawda, Rookaya. "Salah and dhikr as Holistic Healing," http://www.ima.org.za/multimedia/Salah%20&%20dhikr%20as%20holistic%20healing.pdf (accessed May 5th 2010).

Waite, A.E. *The Holy Kabbalah*. New York: Citadel Press.

Wallace, R. K., H. Benson, & A. F. Wilson. "A wakeful hypometabolic physiologic state." *Amer. J, Physiol.* 221 no. 3 (1971): 795-799.

Walsh, R. "Meditation practice and research." *Journal of Humanistic Psychology* 23 no. 1 (1983): 18-50.

Wasi, Jemille. "Dr. Jemille's Introduction to Qur'anic Psychiatry : The El Gilani Methodology" *The Islamic Post*, Aug 18th 2008, http://islamicpost.wordpress.com/tag/quranic-psychiatry (accessed Oct 12th 2010).

Weston, Walter. *How Prayer Heals: A Scientific Approach*. Charlottesville, VA: Hampton Roads Publications Co, 1998.

Whitehouse, David. "Listen to your DNA" BBC News, Sci/Tech, Nov 26, 1998, Thursday, http://news.bbc.co.uk/2/hi/science/nature/222591.stm (accessed Oct 13th 2010).

"Why Zikr is so important," Naqshbandiya Mujaddidiya Aslamiya, http://www.naqshbandiya.com/messageboard/index.php?topic=1254.0;prev_next=prev#new (accessed April 19th 2010).

Wikipedia contributors. "Aum," *Wikipedia, The Free Encyclopedia*, http://en.wikipedia.org/wiki/Aum (accessed Oct 7th 2010).

Wikipedia contributors. "Dhikr," *Wikipedia, The Free Encyclopedia*, http://en.wikipedia.org/wiki/Dhikr (accessed Jan 3rd 2011).

Wikipedia contributors. "Electroencephalography," *Wikipedia, The Free Encyclopedia*, http://en.wikipedia.org/wiki/Electroencephalography (accessed April 19th 2010).

Wikipedia contributors. " Gayatri Mantra," *Wikipedia, The Free Encyclopedia*, http://en.wikipedia.org/wiki/Gayatri_Mantra (accessed Oct 7th 2010).

Wikipedia contributors. "Names of God in Islam," *Wikipedia, The Free Encyclopedia*, http://en.wikipedia.org/wiki/99_names_of_God (accessed Oct 7th 2010).

Wikipedia contributors. "Sympathetic resonance," *Wikipedia, The Free Encyclopedia*, http://en.wikipedia.org/wiki/Sympathetic_resonance (accessed Oct 7th 2010).

World Health Organization, "The Global Burden of Disease 2004 Update," http://www.who.int/healthinfo/global_burden_disease/GBD_report_2004update_full.pdf (accessed Jan 4th 2011).

Yogi, Maharishi Mahesh. *Transcendental Meditation*. New York: The New American Library, Inc. 1968.

Zwemer, Samuel M. *A Moslem Seeker After God*. New York: Fleming H. Revell Company, 1920.

Index

AARP Bulletin, 222, 303
Abbas, Abdullah bin, 14, 57
Abdullah, Jabir bin, 234
Abdullah, S., 226, 295
Abraham. *See* Ibrahim
Abu al-Darda', 38, 39, 54, 63, 64
Abu Dawud, 25, 105, 106, 295
Abu Dharr, 55, 102, 107
Abu Hurairah, 16, 24, 26, 31, 33, 36, 37, 58, 61, 65, 71, 72, 80, 97, 98, 100, 101, 107, 108, 113, 114, 116, 235
Abu Ma'bad, 25
Abu Musa, 57, 106
Abu Sa`id, 55, 106
Abu Sa`îd al-Kharrâz, 267
Abu Talib, 114, 207
Adbhutananda, 283
Ad-Darqari, Mulay al-Arabi, 273
Addiction Research Center, 134
adhaan, 40, 41, 93, 236
African Americans, 217
Ahmad, 3, 16, 23, 25, 28, 34, 36-39, 49, 51, 54, 55, 57, 62, 63, 65, 69, 72, 100, 107, 109, 111-114, 116-118, 126, 180, 181, 236, 272, 295
Ahmad, Zulfiqar, 51, 57, 272
A'isha, 70
Akandanda, Swami, 188
Akbar, 23, 24, 32, 33, 37, 46, 56, 66, 71, 97-99, 103, 106, 108-111, 122, 291
Akhtar, Shah Hakeem Muhammad, 277, 295
Al-Ansari, Abu Ayyub, 101

Al-Ash'ari, Abu Malik, 98
Al-Ayed, Muhammad Abdullah, 161
Al-Baida, 40
Al-Basri, Hasan, 273
Alchemy of Happiness, 60, 265, 268, 295
Al-Daraqutni, 24
Alexjander, Susan, 197, 198
Al Ghazal, Sharif Kaf, 161, 295
Alḥamdu-lillah, 67, 91, 92, 97, 106
Ali, 44, 66, 70, 98, 112, 147, 175, 177, 179, 180, 185, 199, 200, 203, 271, 272, 274, 296, 300, 301
Ali, Muhammad Sajad, 175, 296
Al-Jawzi, Ibn, 39, 64, 296
Al-Jawziyya, Ibn Qayyim, 49, 52, 77, 262, 279, 280, 296
Alkaheel, Abduldaem, 129, 130, 139, 158, 296
Allahu Akbar, 24, 32, 46, 56, 66, 71, 97-99, 103, 106, 108-111
Al-Miqdad, 116
Al-Muwatta, 54, 303
alpha waves, 216, 224, 225, 256
Al-Waabil as-Saib, 52, 262, 279, 280, 296
American Psychological Association, 212, 297
Amr, 'Abdullah bin, 16
Anas, 17, 36, 39, 56, 62, 69, 110, 115, 303
Andrews, Donald Hatch, 198, 297
angels, 2, 3, 14, 32-35, 37-39, 57, 63, 64, 69, 268, 289

APA, 212, 297. *See also* American Psychological Association
Arabia, Saudi, 41, 51, 161, 178-180, 288, 289, 291, 298, 304, 306, 307
Arab News, 145, 161
Arias, Albert J, 215, 297
arthritis, 133, 135, 215, 258
Asr, 39, 40, 260, 287
As-Suyuti, Jalaluddin, 4, 14, 27, 25, 29, 58, 112, 205, 297. *See also* Suyuti
atom bomb, 168
Attaining fina-e-qalbi, 51, 57, 272, 295
aura, 140, 142-144, 169, 198, 241, 264, 303
Ayah, 26, 50, 67, 228, 287
Ayat-ul-Qursi, 77, 287
Bacon, M. H., 214, 298
Bangla-Wali Masjid, 29
Banquet, J.P., 225, 298
Bayhaqi, 4, 37, 54, 55, 72, 116-118
Bayt al-Maqdis, 38, 63, 287, 289
Beck, Robert, 256
Begley, Sharon, 186, 224, 226
Benson, H, 211, 215, 216, 221, 298, 308
Bernardi, Luciano, 222, 298
Bethesda Naval Medical Center, 162
Bible, 121, 122
bij, 193, 194
bioelectrical currents, 226
Blommfield, H. H., 224
blood pressure, 134, 159, 171, 215, 217, 218, 221

Bludorf, Franz, 200, 201, 300, 301
brahmashtra, 167
Brahmavarchas Research Institute, 46, 204
brain, 133-135, 143, 171, 175, 176, 186, 192, 194, 216, 224-228, 238, 239, 242, 244, 252, 253, 256, 302
brain waves, 133, 135, 225, 238, 239
Braun, Melanie, 172, 188, 198, 299
Buddha, 238
Buddhism, 166, 214, 221
Bukhari, 22-27, 33, 36, 37, 39, 40, 50, 57, 61, 63, 66, 71, 80, 98, 100-103, 106, 107, 113-115, 117, 126, 157, 234-236, 287, 295
Cain, M. P., 224, 299
California College of Medicine, 213
California Institute for Human Science, 132
California State University, 213
Campbell, Don, 122, 125, 135, 299, 301
cancer, 122, 125, 131, 132, 138, 139, 159, 161-163, 170, 202, 215, 218, 222, 255, 257, 258, 260
Capra, Fritjof, 136
Center for Natural Medicine and Prevention, 217
Center for Neuro-Acoustic Research, 132
Central Minnesota Heart Center, 171
Cetin, Badri, 141, 142, 299

chakras, 142-144, 183, 274
chapter of Qur'an. *See* Surah
charged water, 150
Chechen hostage crisis, 249
Chladni, Ernst, 126
Chouhan, Ramesh Singh, 256, 258
clairvoyant, 254
coherence, 244, 247, 250
companions, 16, 21, 22, 25, 33, 37, 39, 54, 71, 72, 101, 112, 115, 156, 157, 290, 292. *See also* Sahabah
congregation. *See* Jama'ah
consciousness, 61, 143, 163, 165, 167, 172, 183, 187, 192-194, 196, 198, 207, 208, 213, 223, 224, 226, 228, 236, 241, 242, 244, 249-252, 265, 271, 274, 295, 305, 308
Consciousness Research Laboratory, 250
cosmic forces, 200, 274
creativity, 200, 213, 215, 219, 224, 226, 301
Crohn's disease, 149
crystals, 145
cymatics, 127, 136, 162, 187, 199
Dagestani, 79
David. *See* Dawud
Davidson, Richard, 208
Dawud, 21, 25, 30, 31, 105, 106, 233, 287, 295
Dayatmananda, 281, 283, 299
Deamer, David, 197
deen, 4, 287
DeLeo, J., 222, 307
depression, 122, 135, 159, 178-182, 186, 187, 215, 217, 263
Devi, 283

Dhikr.
  effect on aura
    cleansing of, 264
    higher levels of consciousness, 265
    objects magnetized, 264
    strength, 264
  effect on environment
    afflictions, 192, 2158, 241
    aura, 140, 142-144, 169, 198, 241, 264, 303
    Buddha and the wild elephant, 238
    chakras, 142-144, 183, 169, 274
    coherent waveforms, 241, 243
    date palm tree crying, 234
    du'a, 147, 254, 262, 287
    effect on atmosphere, 169, 195, 240, 241, 275, 276
    effect on crime rate, 220, 239, 240, 248, 301, 308
    effect on society, 169, 220, 241, 244, 246, 248
    effect of Zen on mentally ill person, 238
    entrainment, 133, 243, 256, 301
    everything influences every other thing, 236
    feelings of peace, 260
    fighting the nafs, 261
    human energy field, 143, 245-247, 256, 257, 260, 264, 299
    increased coherence in individual consciousness, 244

interrelatedness of all things, 243
life force, 195, 196, 244. *See also* prana
magnetic charge, 264
meal glorifying Allah, 22, 235
miracles happening, 158, 169, 241, 246, 274, 283
mountain, 16, 71, 72, 123, 234, 282
prana, 195
quantum physics, 242, 271
Reiki technique of distant healing, 254
spread of dhikr over earth, 241
stone taking Moses clothes, 235
testification for caller to prayer, 125, 126, 236
universal energy field, 242, 245, 253
unlocking of angelic powers, 192, 241
gatherings
  adhaan, 40, 41
  assembly, viii, 30, 33-36, 50
  at Bangla-Wali masjid, 29
  gardens of paradise, 39, 69
  lifting dense veils, 40
  in the markets, 23-25, 40
  mountains and birds praising, 20, 21, 31
  sweetness of, 27, 59
  ten days of Dhul-Hijjah, 23-26
loud

  after congregational prayers, 25
  at Bangla-Wali masjid, 29
  in an assembly, viii, 30, 33-36, 50
  in the markets, 23-25, 40
  ten days of Dhul-Hijjah, 23-26
  washer men doing, 28
personal experiences
  feelings of peace, 260
  fighting the nafs, 261
  recharging of energy, 262
  relief from pain, 261
  strengthening, 5, 261
pertaining to
  a hundred good deeds, 65, 101
  Allah splits open the heaven, 102
  Balance, 98, 112, 118, 205
  emancipating ten slaves, 65, 101
  foam of the ocean, 66, 99, 107
  heavens and earth, 112, 205
  heavy in the Scales, 100
  idolater, 116
  intercession, 113
  Jannah has a vast plain, 66
  shortest way to Allah's Presence, 112
  the most beloved words to Allah, 109
  treasures of Jannah, 106
  wealthy people, 97
types of

in heart, 8, 15, 35, 50, 67, 78, 79, 102, 266, 267, 273, 275, 276, 278-280
loud, 24-29, 35, 112, 124, 261, 297
silent, 27, 35, 266
soft, 27
value of
  Allah remembers him, 62
  angels, 2, 3, 14, 32-35, 37-39, 57, 63, 64, 69, 268
  awe of Allah, 40, 59
  awareness, 62, 67, 166, 194, 197, 207, 213, 271
  being alive versus being dead, 57
  blessings, 14, 15, 57, 58, 207
  brightens face, 61
  brings noor, 51, 68
  cleansing heart of rust, 52
  closeness to Allah, 68, 277
  contentment, 68
  day of resurrection, 17, 55, 107, 109, 113, 115
  diseases, 68, 158, 174, 176-179, 181, 185
  divine assistance, 70
  earning Allah's pleasure, 50, 115
  effect on DNA, 199, 200, 203, 274
  effect on drinking alcohol, 148, 159
  effect on drug addiction, 193
  effect on heart, 15, 27, 29, 40, 49, 51, 52, 57, 60-62, 67, 68, 70, 79, 176-178, 182, 184, 185, 192, 193, 207, 223, 241, 262, 265-267, 271-273, 275-281
  effect on mind, 29, 50, 51, 61, 70, 78, 132, 144, 165, 168, 172, 182-184, 192, 194-196, 205, 214, 228, 244, 260, 271
  effect on smoking, 193
  evil converted to virtue, 37, 62
  faith, 5, 66, 114, 116, 182, 207, 274, 282
  food, 220, 282
  forgiveness, 3, 13, 34
  gardens of paradise, 37, 39, 69
  gateway to Allah's treasures, 68
  good deeds, 39, 56, 63, 65, 69, 101, 106, 109
  greater levels of understanding, 199, 200, 274
  happiness, 15, 52-54, 272, 278
  healing of the sick, 148, 157, 158, 251, 254
  heart and soul nourished, 61, 280
  Ihsaan, 56
  intention, 42, 43, 67, 115, 170
  is charity, 55
  keeps away Satan, 49, 64, 101, 272
  light, 57, 58, 79, 177, 185, 191, 200, 206, 207, 254, 266, 272, 274, 276, 277, 279

love, 15, 59, 69, 207, 272
maniac, 16
mentioning in the Court of Allah, 50
mercy, 37-39, 43, 63, 73, 78, 191
multiplicative rewards, 56
on psycho-spiritual growth, 199
paradise, 2, 4, 32, 34, 37, 39, 63, 66, 69, 71, 80, 113
piety, 54, 68
protection, 34, 43, 46, 73, 109, 189, 204, 261
protection against pitfalls, 62
protection from backbiting, 64
protection from punishment, 62, 64, 65
protection of territory, 43
rank is raised, 36, 55, 73, 102
relief from worries, 50, 51, 182
remedy, 44, 52, 271
removal of fear, 49, 70, 182
removal of lethargy, 44
removal of sins, 13, 37, 51, 62, 63, 65, 66, 71, 99, 101, 107, 109, 110, 282
reward greater than jihad, 54
reward of 'Umrah and Hajj, 17, 56
solution to difficulties, 50, 52
stone's praise, 20
supplication, 64, 114
sustenance, 61, 272
sweetness, 27, 28, 59

the key of happiness, joy, and divine love, 15
the polishing of the heart, 52, 279
the single-hearted, 16
throne of Allah, 62, 64
tongue, 8, 15, 72, 78, 79, 100, 102, 271, 278
tranquility, 37, 161, 182, 241
unlocking of angelic powers, 192, 241
Dhul Hulaifa, 39, 40
disease, 68, 125, 132, 135, 137-140, 142, 144, 149, 158-160, 162, 165, 172-181, 185, 202, 212, 215, 217, 218, 248, 254-258, 273, 276, 298, 304, 310
DNA, 197-203, 274, 298, 304, 309
Donovan, S., 215, 300, 304
drug, 178, 180, 193, 219
du'a, 147, 254, 262, 287
Dukhshum, Malik ibn, 115
Eastern Virginia School of Medicine, 128
Eden, Donna, 300
EEG, 134, 161, 225, 244, 298
ego, 194, 195, 261, 267, 268
Egyptians, 44
Eid Al-Adha, 24, 287
Eid Al-Fitr, 24, 287
EKG, 221
electromagnetism, 42, 130, 145, 201, 245, 254, 255, 264
emotions, 132, 143, 144, 186, 194, 195, 214, 219, 250, 266
Emoto, Masaru, 144-146, 152, 300, 304
Energy.

aura, 140, 142-144, 169, 198, 241, 264, 303
energy centers, 142, 183, 274
fields, 42, 143, 144, 170, 243, 245, 247, 248, 256, 258
group energy fields, 247, 248
power of coherent group, 42
entrainment, 133, 243, 256, 301
environment, 220, 233, 237-244, 249, 263, 264, 271, 298, 299
epilepsy, 135, 159, 179, 215
expansion of brain activity, 183, 226-228
Fajr, 17, 29, 102, 262, 288
fanaa', 60, 265
Farinelli, 122
Farsi, Salman, 38
Fatima, 70, 98
Faza'il-e-A'maal, 22, 28, 49, 51, 58, 61, 64, 67, 69, 71, 182, 228, 302
Feinstein, David, 300
formulas of dhikr, 95
forefathers, 26
Fosar, Grazyna, 200, 201, 298, 300, 301
frequencies, 131, 133, 136, 138, 139, 141, 142, 144, 150, 162, 165, 177, 183, 197-199, 201-203, 255, 274
Gabriel. *See* Jibril or Jibrael
galvanic skin response, 216
Gangohi, Hasan, 28, 273
Gas Discharge Visualization, 146
Gass, Robert, 29, 130, 171, 182, 194, 240, 301
Gayatri mantra, 46, 167, 204, 300, 309

Gaynor, Mitchel L., 126, 128, 132-133, 170, 301
genetics, 197, 200
Ghazali, Al, 14, 40, 53, 54, 58-60, 78, 265, 268, 278, 295
Gilani, Mubarik, 179, 180, 184, 185, 301, 309
glorification, 2, 8, 18-22, 26, 31, 55, 108, 280. *See also* tasbih
Goldman, Jonathan, 133, 256, 301
Goleman, Daniel, 213, 214, 301
Gowan, John C., 213, 301
Grad, Bernard, 253
Green, Michael, 140
Gregorian chant, 263
Grimal, Helene, 131
Haddad, Ahmad Mashhur al-, 34, 36, 295
Haddad, Habib al-, 54
Hadith Qudsi.
   Allah mentioning assembly of dhikr, 26, 35, 36, 50, 61
   angels seeking people doing dhikr, 32
   glorifying, 31-33
   forgiveness, 33, 34
   hellfire, 32, 34
   paradise, 32, 34
   praising, 32, 33
   servant remembers me in his heart, 35, 50
Hagelin, John S. 240, 244, 301
Hajees, 43, 288
Hajj, 17, 23, 26, 29, 56, 69, 97, 110, 287, 291
Hakim, al-, 16, 37, 38, 54, 62, 63, 65, 80, 106, 109, 110, 113, 118
Halimu, 192
Harinath, K., 222, 302

harmonics, 128
harmonic resonance, 131, 303
hasan, 4, 16, 38, 69, 114, 118, 288
Harvard Medical School, 225
Hawshab, Shahr ibn, 38, 63
healing, 127, 128, 132, 135, 140, 149-155, 159, 160, 161, 165, 170-173, 176-179, 181, 184, 187, 203, 246, 248, 251-263, 265, 273, 275, 302, 304, 308
heart disease, 215, 217, 218
hell, 32, 34, 71, 109, 115
Hermeticum, Corpus, 187
High Sense Perception, 245. *See also* HSP
Hindus, 46
Horgan, John, 227, 302
Hospital, Shahar, 178
HSP, 245, 254
Ibn `Abidin, 40
ibn 'Abdurahman, Abdullah, 125, 236
ibn 'Asim, Ya'qub, 101
Ibn 'Ata'llah al-Iskandari, 267, 268, 279
Ibn al-Jawzi, 39, 64
Ibn al-Qayyim, 77
Ibn Hibban, 16
ibn Jundab, Samurah, 108
Ibn Kathir, 3, 14, 16, 17, 27, 31, 58, 62, 72, 307
Ibn Majah, 3, 16, 25, 27, 36, 37, 50, 54, 61, 62, 65, 72, 100, 107, 111, 114, 116, 126, 236
Ibn Mas`ud, 66, 108
ibn Muslim, al-Walid, 81
Ibn Umar, 23, 24, 26
ibn Zayd, Usama, 116
Ibn Qutaibah, 151

Ibn Taymiyya, 41, 148, 262, 302
Ibrahim, 66, 108, 289, 291
Ihya ul Uloom, 14, 58
illness, 139, 150, 151, 158, 159, 164, 165, 173, 178, 181-186, 196, 215, 256, 258, 272, 275, 290, 297
Ilyas, 29
Institute for Natural Medicine and Prevention, 217
Institute of Noetic Sciences, 225, 300, 304
insomnia, 135, 179, 181, 219
intensity, 42, 146, 147, 242
intention, 42, 43, 67, 115, 145-147, 169, 170, 184, 185, 253, 300, 308
intuition, 226
Irvine Medical School, 213
Ishaq, 23, 25
Islam, 4, 15, 16, 37, 52, 81, 147, 151, 152, 160, 166, 178, 226, 272, 278-280, 296, 297, 302-309, 321
Islamic Association of the Finger Lakes, 261
IslamiCity Forum, 226
Islamic Medicine On Line, 161, 295
Isma'il, 101, 110, 289, 291
IQ, 219
Jaffe, D. T., 224, 299
Jama'ah, 43, 288
Jaret, Peter, 222, 303
Jenny, Hans, 126-129, 136, 137, 139, 187, 303
Jibril, 288
Jilani, Abdul Qadir, 51, 179, 185, 266, 267, 301, 303

jinn, 126, 236, 289, 290
Joshua, 122
Journal of Behavioral Medicine, 181, 182, 299
Jumal, Sulaimaan, 27
Junaid, 281
Ka'bah, 26, 29, 289
Kabbalah, 121, 214, 308
Kabbani, Hisham, 15, 176, 246, 255, 256, 278, 302
Key to the Garden, 54, 295
Khaliq, Jamal Abdul, 161
Khan, Inayat, 126, 157, 166, 174, 237, 264, 267, 275
Khanqah, 28, 44, 289
Khazin, 27
Khudri, Abu Sa'id al-, 37, 125, 156, 236
Kirlian photography, 129, 256
koan, 226
Koestler, Arthur, 167
Korotkov, 146, 147, 264, 303, 308
Kufaar, 289
Kuhlmann, Kathryn, 238
Kun, 121, 289
La ilaha illallah, 33, 56, 65, 66, 67, 99, 101-103, 106, 108-117, 205-208, 278
La ḥawla wa la quwwata illa billah, 106
language, 187, 188, 201-203, 219
lata'if, 162, 163
lateefa, 176
Latifu, 193
Lewis, H. Spencer, 140, 303
Levin, Jeffrey, 128
Loveless, Catherine, 264, 303
Lubicz, R.A. Schwaller de, 306

Massachusetts General Hospital, 225
Maalik, Anas ibn, 36, 39, 62, 69, 110
Maharaj, H. H. Krishnanandaji, 165, 167, 241, 246, 274, 303
Maharishi Mahesh Yogi, 223, 236
Maharishi University, 217
Makki, Abd al-Hafiz, 28, 44, 271, 303
Malaki, Muhammad 'Alawi al-, 16, 296
Maman, Fabien, 129, 131, 198, 303
Manners, Peter, 137, 138, 162, 199
mantra, 46, 124, 166-174, 181-184, 187, 193-197, 200, 203, 204, 214, 222, 223, 226, 240, 241, 246, 263, 274, 298, 299, 303-305, 307, 309, 317
masjid, 23, 25, 28, 29, 38, 41, 44, 63, 151, 271, 287, 289, 297, 303
Massachusetts General Hospital, 225
Marwat, Zaman, 261
McTaggart, Lynne, 146, 203, 304
Mecca, 16, 71, 152, 288, 289, 291
Medical College of Wisconsin, 217
Medina, 39, 295
Meditation.
  benefits of
    alcohol abuse, 219
    alpha waves, 216, 224, 225, 256
    arthritis, 215
    beta waves, 224, 225

biological age, 219
blood lactate, 216
blood pressure, 215, 217, 218, 221
brain stimulation, 225
brain synchronization, 224
cancer, 218, 222
conflicts, 220
crime, 220, 239, 240, 244, 301, 308
criminal behavior, 217
concentration, 219
creativity, 213, 215, 219, 226
depression, 215, 217
drug, 219
ecological, 220, 223
emotions, 186, 214, 219
environment, 220
epilepsy, 215
galvanic skin response, 216
gamma waves, 224, 225
heart disease, 215, 217, 218
insomnia, 219
intelligence, 219
international relations, 220
IQ, 219
language, 219
life expectancy, 219
loss of sleep, 215
mathematics, 219
maturity, 219
menopause, 215
mental illnesses, 186, 215
moral reasoning, 219
neoplastic, 215
neural networks, 225
oxygen consumption, 215
post-traumatic stress, 217, 218
premenstrual syndrome, 215
reading, 219
respiratory rates, 216
self-actualization, 217
self development, 219
smoking, 219
strokes, 217, 218
study skills, 219
theta waves, 224, 225
traffic accidents, 220
  definition of, 213
  forms of
    Vipassana, 214
    Zen Buddhism, 214, 221, 238
    Yogic techniques, 214
    Hatha Yoga, 222, 302
    Omkar, 222, 302
    Kundalini, 214
    Dhikr, 214
    Transcendental Meditation, 214, 218-220, 236, 239, 240, 244, 301, 308, 310. *See also* TM
    TM, 214-225, 228, 239, 244, 299
    teachings of the Kabbalah, 214
    silent contemplation of Quakers, 214
  stress, 215-217, 219, 224
Memorial Sloan-Kettering Cancer Center, 222
mental illness, 178, 181-186, 215
Mina, 23-26, 40, 289
Mobius Society, 139
mountains and birds praising, 20, 21, 30, 31, 233, 234
Moore, Abd al-Hayy, 29

Moors Gate, 177, 200, 274, 300
monks, 186, 224-226, 263
Monroe, Robert, 133
Moscow State University, 213
mosque. *See* masjid
Muhammad, Prophet, 2, 4, 15, 20, 22, 24, 25, 30, 33, 66, 77, 93, 107, 108, 112, 113, 115, 118, 125, 159, 166, 191, 205, 207, 280, 287-292
Mujahid, 31, 178
Mullah Jeewan, 14, 58
music, 113-115, 117-125, 128, 130, 134, 145, 149, 150, 153, 157, 160, 181-183, 236, 242, 244, 255, 260, 276-278, 281-283
music thanatology, 162, 163
muslim, 2, 3, 23, 41, 125, 163, 185, 214, 225, 236, 287-292, 301
muslim community. *See* Ummah
Murphy, M., 215, 300, 304
Munich, 151, 152
Musnad, 16
Nada Brahma, 121
Nadwi, Abul Hasan Ali, 44, 271
Nalimov, V. V., 213, 304
Names of Allah, 75-83, 90, 93, 145, 175, 177, 192, 193, 199, 200, 228, 241, 274, 296
Names of God in Islam, 81, 166, 309
Napersteck, Belleruth, 242
Nasa'i, 25, 37, 38, 102, 106, 107, 109, 113, 114, 116
Nawawi, 14, 7, 280, 297, 304
Nazim, 272
neural activity, 226, 227

neurons, 226
New Delhi, 29, 302
Night of Ascension, 66, 108
Nizamuddin, 29
North, W. R., 305
nouns, 227
O. J. Simpson trial, 250
Olympic Games, 251
oxidation, 52, 279
pain, 53, 73, 122, 124, 125, 135, 149, 159-163, 171, 173, 176, 179, 240, 259, 261, 277
Pakistan, 179, 260, 295, 303
Pandya, Pranav, 46, 204
paradise, 2, 4, 32, 34, 37, 39, 63, 66, 69, 65, 71, 80, 106, 113, 288
Patel, C. H., 221, 305
Paul, Rusill, 184, 305
PET, 227
Pfeiffer, Knut, 151, 152, 265, 305
Philip V, 122
Pilgrimage. *See* Hajj
Pilgrims. *See* Hajees
Popp, Fritz Albert, 200
Posen, David B., 212, 305
praises of Allah, 2
praising, 8, 15, 20, 22, 34, 280. *See also* tahmid
Prattis, Ian, 183, 274, 305
Puharich, Andrija, 255
prayer, 2, 10, 12, 18-20, 243, 25, 39-42, 55, 56, 97, 99, 102-105, 125, 126, 145, 149, 194, 207, 222, 236, 238, 239, 244, 248, 251-255, 258, 260, 262, 287-291, 298, 300, 309. *See also* Salah
prefrontal cortex, 186

Princeton University, 250
Psalms, 20
psychics, 256
Pythagoras, 128
Quakers, 214
quantum physics, 242, 271, 301
Qur'an, mentioning of dhikr.
   calling upon Allah, 9, 11
   constant remembrance of Allah, 2, 11, 15, 266, 271, 272
   glorification of Allah in nature, 21
   mountains and birds praising Allah, 20, 21, 30, 31, 233
   Names of Allah, 82-93
   remember Allah as you remember your forefathers, 26
   ten days of Dhul-Hijjah, 23
Qutb, Sayyid, 19, 305
radiation, 143, 144, 160, 201, 203, 255
Radin, Dean, 250, 251, 305
raga, 122, 306
Rahman, 80, 83, 191, 307
Ramakrishna, 282, 283, 299, 305, 306
random event generator, 249
random number generator, 250
Rasulullah, 16, 37, 115, 206, 292
relaxation response, 171, 221, 298
remembrance, circles of, 39
resonance, 129, 131, 132, 135-138, 183, 193, 194, 199, 207, 241, 274, 303, 309, 310
Rider, Mark, 132
Rinpoche, Sogyal, 166, 167, 183, 263, 306
riya, 27, 290

Robertson, Don, 122, 306
Rosicrucians, 140, 172
Ruqya, 156, 157, 160, 290
Sabiq, Sayyed As, 8, 306
Sahabah, 38, 39, 69, 290
Sahih, 16, 37, 38, 54, 62, 63, 106, 109, 288, 290, 295, 304
Sahih Muslim, 16, 27, 33-38, 50, 56, 61, 63, 66, 71, 80, 97-109, 114-17, 304
Salah, 2, 17, 29, 40-43, 93, 102, 103, 106, 261, 262, 290, 291, 308
Samit, Ibada bin, 103, 113, 114
Sanskrit, 165, 184, 187, 188, 195, 293, 305
Satan, 49, 64, 101, 272, 289, 290. *See also* Shaitaan
Scholem, G. G., 214
Schucman, H., 226, 295
Schneider, Robert, 217
Schwartz, John, 140
September 11th, 249
S.G. Asnani Foundation, 137, 138, 142, 144, 162, 306
Shapiro, Deanne H., 213, 307
Sharp Cabrillo Hospital, 132
show. *See* riya
Shumann Effect, 255
Simon, David, 132
Simpson, O. J. 250
Smith, Rebecca, 218
smoking, 151, 152, 193, 219
Smythe, Damian, 264, 203
snake, 156, 157, 180
Soor, 121, 290
Sound.
   creation of earth
      Bible, 121

Kun, 121, 289
Nada Brahma, 121
The Word, 121
Vedanta, 121
doomsday
  Soor, 121, 290
sound in history
  dipak, 122
  fire, 122
  Indian music, 122
  mahlar, 122
  myth of Orpheus, 121
  raga, 122
  song deflected rocks, 121
  symptoms of depression and chronic pain, 122
  wild animals listen, 121
  walls of the city of Jericho crumbled, 122
destructive effect of
  demons destroying themselves, 124
genetics
  BBC article, 197
  DNA of a 17-year-old boy, 199
  musical nature of atoms, 198
  sound of DNA, 198, 199
  strange, beautiful music, 197
Impression of
  cymatics, 127, 136, 162, 187, 199
  different sounds create different form, 127
  Muslim call to prayer, 117, 236
  sound affects physical matter, 126
skin and bone conduction, 130

healing with
  bells, 127
  body could be healed through, 129
  bone conduction, 130
  cell's energy field, 129
  cells response to sound, 129
  Chinese meditation gongs, 127
  drums, 127
  electromagnetic field, 130
  'Hela' cancer cell, 131
  Kirlian photography, 129
  music for healing, 128
  music as medicine, 128
  resonance, 129, 131, 132, 135-138, 162, 183, 193, 194, 199, 207, 241, 274, 303, 309, 310
  tamboura, 127
mantra
  air, 174, 175
  atom bombs, 168
  atmosphere purified, 169, 241
  Aum, 203, 204, 309
  Aum Mani Padme Hum, 204
  Bij, 193
  brain activity, 226-228
  cold and dry element, 175
  cold and moist element, 175
  compared to dhikr, 165-169
  curing of illnesses, 159-172, 179
  definition, 165
  effect on the society, 220, 239
  energy generated by, 183
  fire, 174, 175, 273, 276, 278

Gayatri, 46, 167, 204, 300, 309
Grand Canyon, 194
Gregorian chant, 263
heavy elements, 175
HIV patients, 181
hot and dry element, 174
hot and moist element, 174
International Academy for Traditional Tibetan Medicine, 165, 173
light elements, 175
mantra shakti, 165, 303
miracles, 169, 241, 246, 274, 283
nervous system, 184
prana, 195
sound as manifest energy, 168
spiritual pharmaceuticals. 184
superconsciousness, 194-196
relieving of subconsciousness, 196
Tibetan medicine, 165, 172, 173
the consciousness of cells, 172
transformation of oneself, 168
vital energies of the human body, 173
water, 145-152, 174, 175, 194, 262, 280, 282
words are forces, 168
potency of, 167
mental disorders, 178
sacred language
   Corpus Hermeticum, 187
   effect of Quranic verses, 139, 150, 154, 156, 158-160, 178, 254
   Egyptian words and object spoken about, 188
   Hermetic writings, 188
   sounds filled with power, 187
sound therapies
   AIDS, 135, 162, 181, 184, 202
   Alzheimer's, 135, 162
   arthritis, 133, 135
   bioresonance, 162
   bone fracture, 133, 159
   chanting and resonances, 132
   cymatic therapy, 133, 137
   diabetes, 135, 137, 138, 150, 162, 306
   entrainment of brain waves, 133
   greater immunity from disease and enhancing tissue regeneration, 132
   healing agents, 132
   muscle strain, 133
   music for healing, 128
   music thanatology, 162, 163
   painkillers, 133, 134, 170
   paralysis, 133, 151
   rheumatism, 133
   Snoezelen, 162
   synchronizing of the left and right hemispheres, 133
   treatments for various physical disorders and learning disabilities, 133
   the effect of music betaendorphine, 134

boost of endorphins, 134
cortisol, 134
EEG, 134, 161
heart rate, 134, 171, 221
human growth hormones, 134
increased immune cell messenger molecules, 134
lower blood pressure, 134
on pregnancy and childbirth, 134
on terminally ill, 134
reduction in heart and respiratory rates, 133
reduced cardiac complications, 133
reduced levels of stress hormones, 134
salivation, 134
resonance
  applicable to the human body, 137
  cell's natural sound, 138
  chemical and homeostatic balance, 138
  cymatic therapy, 133
  harmony, 128, 136, 139, 140, 176, 241
  ill health, 138
  periodicity and rhythm, 136
  rhythmic patterns appear throughout the universe, 136
  tuning forks, 137
  viruses and diseases, 138
re-programming of damaged cells, 139
the occurrence of disease

aura, 140, 142-144, 169, 198, 241, 264
chakra, 142-144, 183, 274
Universal Energy Field, 140-143, 242, 245, 253
effect of on water
  geometric crystals, 145
  water crystals, 145
Qur'an and healing
  black magic, 161
  bone fracture, 159
  cancer, 161
  depressive states, 179
  El Gilani Methodology, 179, 308
  every syllable has a certain effect, 157
  evil, 158, 185
  envy, 158, 161
  epilepsy, 159, 179
  headaches, 159
  infertility, 159, 161
  inflammation, 159
  insomnia, 179
  joint pain, 179
  Khawass al-Quran, 158
  kidney, 159
  leprosy, 148, 159
  magic, 158, 161
  mental diseases, 178, 179, 185
  migraine, 159
  miscarriage, 161
  miraculous properties of the Qur'an, 158
  neurosis, 179
  paralysis, 151, 159
  poor eyesight, 159
  psychosis, 179, 185

remedies of the Quran, 148, 151, 159, 306
ruqya, 156, 157, 160, 290
schizophrenia, 159, 178, 179, 185
snake bite, 156
spleen, 159
Zam Zam water, 150
Southern Methodist University, 132
Spring, Ralph, 134
spurs, 149
Stanley, Ruth, 171
Stone, R., 222, 307
stress, 124, 125, 134, 142, 144, 171, 181, 182, 211, 212, 215-219, 224, 297, 299, 305, 312, 328
St. Petersburg State Technical University, 146
Subḥan Allah, 32, 33, 65, 66, 97, 98, 100, 103-111
Subḥan Allahi wa biḥamdihi, 65, 100, 105
Subḥan Allahil 'Azim, 100
sufi, 123, 126, 157, 166, 170, 174-177, 179, 193, 237, 241, 246, 255, 256, 264, 267, 273, 275, 276, 281, 289, 308
sufism view of disease, 172, 173, 177
sunnah, 8, 20, 22, 28, 233, 280, 290, 295, 299, 306
Superbowl, 250
Superstring Theory, 140
Surah of Qur'an.
   Ahzab, 13
   Anbiya, 20, 30
   Anfal, 52, 189

Ankabut, 55
Baqarah, 49
Dukhan, 190
Fatiha, 156, 157
Fussilat, 155
Hajj, 23
Hashr, 8, 151
Ikhlas, 77, 290
'Imraan, 11
Isra, 10, 18, 122, 154
Kahf, 189
Muzzamil, 190
Nisa, 12
Noor, 18
Saad, 158
Saba, 21, 30, 233
Shu'ara, 12
Ta-Ha, 8, 188
R'ad, 50
Yasin, 163, 164, 290
Yunus, 154
Suyuti, 4, 14, 27, 29, 58, 112, 205, 297, 312, 326
Syed, Ibrahim, 158, 271, 305, 307
sympathetic resonance, 136-138, 309
Tabarani, 4, 37, 63, 65, 72, 112-114, 205
Tabligh Jamaat, 29
tafsir of Ibn Kathir, 3, 14, 17, 31, 58, 307
Tahajjud, 28, 29, 290
Tahlil, 8, 23, 106, 111, 291
Tahmid, 8, 15, 23, 71, 111, 280, 291
Tahrir Square, 44
Taif, 178, 180
Takbir, 8, 15, 23-26, 40, 71, 106, 111, 280, 291

Talbiya, 25, 39, 40, 291
Tansen, 122
Tasbih, 8, 15, 20, 71, 106, 111, 206, 280, 291, 304
Taylor, E., 215, 300, 304
Tayyib, 28
terrorist attack, 249
testification, 8. *See also* tahlil
the cosmic code of man, 177, 200, 274, 300
the importance of knowing Allah's Names, 77, 296
The Islamic Post, 179, 181, 184
Thompson, Jeffrey, 132
Tiller, William, 42, 43
Tirmidhi, 16, 17, 25, 34-39, 49, 50, 54, 55, 57, 61, 65, 66, 69, 72, 80, 81, 98, 100-110, 114, 116, 118, 296
Titles of works.
   Alchemy of Happiness, 60, 265, 268, 295
   Al-Qussas wa al-mudhakkirin, 39, 64, 296
   Al-Sawaa'iq al-Mursalah `Ala al-Jahmyyah wa'l-Mu`attilah, 72, 296
   Al-Waabil as-Saib, 52, 280, 296
   A Moslem Seeker After God, 79, 310
   A wakeful hypometabolic physiologic state, 216, 308
   Badaa'i' al-Fawaa'id, 77, 296
   Battling Cancer with Complementary Therapies and Treatments, 222, 303
   Cerebral lateralization, bimodal consciousness, and related developments in psychiatry, 226, 295
   Chanting: Discovering Spirit in Sound, 29, 123-125, 130, 171, 195, 300
   Cymatics: A Study of Wave Phenomena and Vibration, 127
   Cymatics and The New Age of Miracles, 199
   Durre Mansoor, 14, 58
   Effects of Hatha yoga and Omkar meditation on cardiorespiratory performance, 222, 301
   Effect of rosary prayer and yoga mantras on autonomic cardiovascular rhythms: Comparative study, 222, 298
   Electroencephalography, 224, 309
   Exploring the Efficacy of Vowel Intonations, 172, 188, 299
   Faza'il-e-A'maal, 22, 28, 49, 51, 58, 59, 61, 62, 64, 67, 71, 182, 228, 302
   Fi Zhilal Al-Qur'an, 20, 305
   Fiqh-Us-Sunnah, 8
   Fractured Functions. Does the brain have a supreme integrator, 227, 302
   Fruits From the Garden of Wisdom, 165, 167, 168, 241, 246, 274, 303
   Futuhaat ar-Rabbani 'ala-al Adhkaar an-Nawawiyya, 15, 280, 297, 304
Greek mythology, 121, 301

Harmonic Resonance, 131, 303
How Prayer Heals: A scientific Approach, 42, 143, 149, 238, 244-246, 251-254, 257, 309
Ihya ul Uloom, 14, 58
Jami` al-saghir, 4
Key to the Garden, 54, 295
Khawass al-Quran, 158
Listen to your DNA, 198, 309
Majmu`at fatawa, 41, 302
Meditation 'cuts risk of heart attack by half', 218
Meditation practice and research, 213, 308
Messages from Water, 145
Miftah al-janna, 34, 36, 295
Natijatul-Fikr, 27, 297
Neuroplasticity, Dhikr and Recovery, 186
Overview: clinical and physiological comparison of meditation and other self-centered strategies, 213, 307
Overwhelmed by workplace stress? You're not alone, 212, 297
Physical Effects of Stress, 212, 305
psychologic profile and melatonin secretion, 222
Psychotherapeutic Control of Hypertension, 222
Randomized Controlled Trial of Yoga and Biofeedback in Management of Hypertension, 221, 305
Realms of the Unconscious, 213, 304
Remedies of the Quran, 148, 151, 159, 306
Remembering Allah, 159, 188, 297
Rosicrucian Manual, 140, 303
Sacred Science, 188, 306
Scans of Monks' Brains Show Meditation Alters Structure, Functioning, 186, 224, 226
Sound entrainment, 133, 256
Sounds of Healing: A Physician Reveals the Therapeutic Power of Sound, Voice, Music, 126, 128, 132, 133, 138, 140, 170, 301
Spectral analysis of the EEG in meditation, 225, 298
Spiritual Medicine in the History of Islamic Medicine, 158, 307
Stress Management for Patient and Physician, 212, 305
Sufi Introduction to the 99 attributes of Names of Allah and especially that of Ya Latif, 175, 193, 296
Systematic Review of the Efficacy of Meditation Techniques as Treatments for Medical Illness, 215, 297
Tafseeraat-e-Ahmedia, 14, 58
Tasbih: Personal Dhikr, 206, 304
The Faces Made Radiant By the Vastness of Mercy, 20. *See also* al-Wujuh al-musfira `an ittisa` al-maghfira
The Holy Kabbalah, 121, 308

The Larouse Encyclopedia of Mythology, 121, 301
The Manifestation of Sound on the Physical Sphere, 126, 157, 166, 275
The Mozart Effect, 125, 135, 263, 299
The Physical and Psychological Effects of Meditation, 216, 221, 300, 304
The relaxation response, 211, 221, 298
The Remembrance of Death and The Afterlife, 53, 54, 278, 295
The Role of Music in the Twenty-First Century, 129, 131, 199, 303
The Qur'an's Healing Horizon, 130, 138, 139, 158, 296
The Secret of Secrets, 51, 267, 303
The Sufi Message of Hazrat Inayat Khan, 126, 157, 166, 174, 237, 264, 267, 275, 302
The Symphony of Life, 198, 297
The Tao of Physics, 136
The Tibetan book of living and dying, 165, 167, 183, 263, 306
The Yogic Claim of Voluntary Control over the Heart Beat: An Unusual Demonstration, 221, 303
TM: discovering inner energy and overcoming stress, 224, 299
Trance, Art and Creativity, 213, 301
Universal Energy – A Systematic and Scientific Investigation, 141
Varieties of the Meditative Experience, 213, 301
Virtues of Zikr, 22, 28, 182, 228. *See also* Faza'il-e-A'maal
Why Sanskrit for Mantra? Why not English? 184, 305
Why Zikr is so important, 228, 309
TM, 214-225, 228, 239, 244, 299
Transcendental Meditation, 214, 218-220, 236, 239, 240, 244, 301, 308, 310. *See also* TM
Ujrah, Ka'b bin, 97
Umar, 23-26, 40
Ummah, 2, 38, 66, 108, 117, 291
'Umrah, 17, 56, 97, 291
unbelievers. *See* Kufaar
verse. *See* Ayah
United States Navy, 255
Universal Energy, 140-144, 177, 242, 244, 245, 253, 254, 299
Universal Energy Field, 140-143, 242, 245, 253
University, Carleton, 183
University of Amsterdam, 250
University of Wisconsin, 226
Vawda, Rookaya, 254, 308
Vedanta, 121, 281-283, 299, 306
verb, 227
Virtues of Zikr, 22, 28, 182, 228
Vivekanand, 204
Waite, A.E., 121, 308

Wallace, Robert Keith, 215, 216, 308
Walsh, Roger, 213, 308
Washington Times, 171
Washington University, 227
Wasi, Jemille, 179, 308
water, 57, 66, 108, 141-159, 174-176, 194, 234, 248, 255, 259, 262, 280, 282, 291, 300, 305, 307, 308
wave, 42, 46, 127, 171, 204, 241, 244, 303
Wazifa, 169, 170, 306
Wellstone, Paul, 249
Weston, Walter, 42, 149, 150, 238, 244-248, 251-260, 309
Whitehouse, David, 198, 309
Wikipedia, 81, 137, 181, 203, 204, 224, 309
Wilson, Arhie F., 215, 308
Word, 121
Yahya, 28
Yaqoubi, Muhammad, 158, 159, 188, 189, 297
yoga, 188, 195, 197, 214, 221, 222, 293, 298, 301, 303, 305, 320
Yoga Foundation, 188
yogis, 165, 172, 193, 195, 196
Zakariya, Muhammad, 22, 27, 28, 43, 44, 49, 49, 51, 59, 67, 148, 182, 228, 271, 302
Zakir, 27
Zam Zam, 150-152, 291
Zen Buddhism, 214, 221
Zikr, 8, 22, 27, 28, 44, 79, 182, 192, 228, 271, 277, 280, 281, 291, 295, 297, 303, 309. *See also* dhikr
Zuhr, 39, 291